D0948214

Compelled To Appear In Print:
The Vicksburg Manuscript of
General John C. Pemberton

Edited by
David M. Smith

Ironclad Publishing
Cincinnati, Ohio

This text is printed on acid-free paper.

Copyright © 1999 by David M. Smith
Published by Ironclad Publishing

Maps and cover design by Michael Stretch
Interior design and layout by Michelle Frey, DOV Graphics

ISBN 0-9673770-0-5 (cloth)

Printed in the United States of America

For my wife, Kim, and best bud, Jennifer

Contents

Maps

Acknowledgments

It is strange, at times, how fate works in the plans of people. I have always known what I wanted to do with my life—write on the Civil War—but as an amateur, it also required putting myself in the position to have the time and money to do so. Of the projects, campaigns or personalities I might find myself involved in, Vicksburg and John C. Pemberton were among those I least expected to work with. I have learned, however, to never argue with fate.

How a manuscript written a Pennsylvania-born Confederate lieutenant general commanding a department in Louisiana and Mississippi for Jefferson Davis ends up in a flea market dealer in Cincinnati, Ohio is even stranger. But it did, and I am indeed fortunate to have the chance to work with it. Manuscripts written by Confederate generals are a rare find today.

First and foremost, I owe an incredible debt of gratitude to Alan Hoeweler of Glendale, Ohio. Not only did Alan find Pemberton's manuscript, but was generous enough to allow me the privilege of putting the words and explanation of the controversy to paper. What is more, it was Alan who provided the initial encouragement to step outside the comfortable limits of Round Table membership and begin writing on various topics on the war. Without his active and generous support, this work would not have been accomplished.

Transcribing the manuscript was easy; explaining and framing the controversy and story of the campaign and personalities was not. Without the help and support of a group of dedicated Civil War friends, I would still be struggling today. Brian Hampton of Ada, Oklahoma, a gifted writer and authority on Confederate general James Longstreet, helped more than he will ever know during the initial stages of my writing. His patient willingness to suffer through and comment perceptively on my attempts to begin this book are greatly appreciated. Kathie Fraser of Reston, Virginia helped clarify and craft my mundane writing into something passable. Her task was truly the thankless one—which she performed with unflagging cheerfulness. Jim Epperson of Huntsville, Alabama provided valuable suggestions and critique of my work. And finally, Chuck Ten Brink, of Chicago, Illinois has always been up front providing encouragement and support.

I would be very much remiss not to express appreciation to my traveling friend and fellow Round Table member Tom Breiner. Not only is Tom responsible for rekindling my interest in the Civil War back in 1986, but together we have tromped almost every battlefield east of the Mississippi River. Tom patiently read every word written, and provided invaluable corrections to my many factual errors.

Thanks also go to local Cincinnati graphic artist and Civil War buff Mike Stretch, who developed the dust jacket artwork as well as the maps associated with this book. Mike is a unique talent, and I was fortunate to avail myself of his interest and expertise.

I would like to express my appreciation and respect to several professional historians who have touched this work. Will Greene of Pamplin Park has been a good friend since his days at the APCWS. Alan Nolan has provided encouragement and support for the last eight years. Brooks D. Simpson of Arizona State University was kind enough to spend part of a Thursday afternoon discussing not only the Vicksburg campaign itself, but the pros and cons of various approaches to publishing this work. Brooks was also patient enough to review my work and provide valuable comments. And finally, Terry Winschel, historian at Vicksburg National Military Park, has been a constant source of encouragement, clarification and support. Terry is a gentleman in the true meaning of the word.

I cannot adequately express my gratitude and appreciation to Edwin C. Bearss, Historian Emeritus for the National Park Service. Not only did Ed read every word of my work, but made valuable corrections, and did me the extreme honor of writing a foreword for the book. That he wished he had access to the Pemberton manuscript while writing his definitive three-volume work on the Vicksburg Campaign says lots about the value of Pemberton's writings.

Last but certainly not least, my thanks go out to my wife, Kim, and daughter Jennifer. I know they think I am somewhat crazy with this "obsession" of mine, but they have encouraged me to live my dreams, and they will never know how much it is appreciated.

Foreword

My introduction to the serious differences in personality and military thought between Generals Joseph E. Johnston and John C. Pemberton and how they played out both during and in the decades after the Vicksburg Campaign commenced more than two generations ago. It began September 28, 1955, when I joined the National Park Service and entered on duty as historian at the Vicksburg National Military Park. My first task upon arrival in the Hill City was to familiarize myself with the park, the Vicksburg campaign and siege, and personalities. This involved extensive reading in the park library and traveling the back roads to tramp the landscape and campsites known to the men and boys of the 1860s.

My first months in Mississippi were a learning experience. Influenced by what until then was a Civil War in the east and Army of Northern Virginia bias, reinforced by the then current historiography, I sided with Johnston and his biographers in the Johnston—Pemberton acerbic controversy in assessing responsibility for Confederate disasters leading to the surrender of Vicksburg and its 29,500 defenders. One strike against Pemberton was the failure by his grandson John C. Pemberton III in his 1941 biography *Pemberton: Defender of Vicksburg* to marshal the evidence to make a compelling case in support of his grandfather *vis-a-vis* Johnston and his champions. Although the grandson used the *Official Records* and an "unfinished letter written in pencil," found by his family in 1931 among other papers, to defend the general against Johnston's aspersions, his arguments seem labored in view of Johnston's presumed reputation among the 1950s Civil War fraternity.

Until 1959 I could be found in Johnston's corner. But by 1960 I was shifting ground. With the Civil War Centennial at hand, Charles L. "Pie" Dufour—popular columnist, raconteur, and Civil War author—hosted a panel discussion broadcast over radio in New Orleans. Guests were Gilbert E. Govan coauthor with James W. Livingood of *A Different Valor: The Story of General Joseph E. Johnston C.S.A.*; Col. Ned Julian, executive director of the Atlanta Historical Society; and me. The subject was generalship and the significance of the Chickamauga-Chattanooga, Atlanta and Vicksburg campaigns. Of the major players, Johnston was center stage in two of these three campaigns. In the give-and-take, I turned on its head a statement attributed to Johnston in his post-war feud with Jefferson Davis, i.e., that the President sought to do what only God could do—"make a general of Braxton Bragg." In my version I substituted Johnston's name for Bragg's.

In March 1981, I again participated in a forum in which the Johnston—Pemberton impasse surfaced. The occasion was the annual meeting of the Mississippi Historical Society held in the state capital and the subject was the battle of Jackson and its significance. Dr. William K. Scarborough of the faculty of Southern Mississippi University and I debated the responsibility for the Confederate debacle that resulted in the loss of that city and subsequent defeats at Champion Hill and Big Black River. Dr. Scarborough defended Johnston and his actions, while not defending Pemberton's, I came down on Johnston hard, making a case that his actions and inactions following his May 13 arrival in Jackson and immediately thereafter doomed Vicksburg.

The early 1990s saw biographies of the antagonists published. In 1991 Michael B. Ballard authored *Pemberton: A Biography* and the following year Craig L. Symonds' *Joseph E. Johnston: A Civil War Biography* came off the press. Both biographers acknowledged the generals' Mississippi difficulties, including their interpersonal problems. But the bitter exchanges both then and later concerning responsibility for loss of Vicksburg were not centerstaged in these two excellent and readable books. Neither biographer, however, had access to Pemberton's "Compelled To Appear In Print." A similar situation insofar as the Pemberton's "Compelled" haunted me in the years of research leading up to publication by Robert and Mary Younger of Morningside in 1985-86 of my trilogy *The Vicksburg Campaign*.

History enthusiasts can understand the excitement that surged within when Alan E. Hoeweler, Civil War collector and preservationist extraordinaire, told me about a recent acquisition he had made at a Loveland, Ohio, flea market. A once in a lifetime gem: "Compelled To Appear In Print," a defense of his actions in the Vicksburg Campaign, prepared by Pemberton before his 1881 death had turned up in an estate sale. The sale included papers belonging to Brig. Gen. Marcus J. Wright. In 1878 Wright became an agent for the War Department charged with collecting Confederate records in conjunction with publication of *War of the Rebellion: Official Records of the Union and Confederate Armies*, a task he was employed on until his 1917 retirement from government service.

In early spring 1999, Alan telephoned me and said that the Pemberton manuscript was being prepared for publication and would I like to see it. Would I? Having spent more than 40 years campaigning and refighting the Civil War, the answer was a resounding yes.

On April 24 at the Richmond annual membership meeting of the Association for the Preservation of Civil War Sites the big day came. Alan introduced me to David M. Smith, who had undertaken the task of readying the manuscript for the printer. David, holding two degrees from Xavier University in Cincinnati, Ohio, spent nearly 19 years as an employee of Cincinnati Bell Telephone. His study of the Civil War became reenergized in 1986 when he first attended the Civil War Round Table of Cincinnati and listened to an address by James A. Ramage, professor of history at Northern Kentucky University, and author of the critically acclaimed *Rebel Raider: The Life of General John Hunt Morgan*.

Smith invited me to review and comment on the Pemberton manuscript and I embraced the opportunity. I spent the next six weeks with the manuscript and was pleased to discover that it was much more than Pemberton's apology.

The General's "Compelled To Appear In Print: The Vicksburg Manuscript of General John C. Pemberton," constitutes one of the five parts into which Smith divides his monograph. Parts One through Three provide a context in which the Pemberton-Johnston drama plays out. The first part sets the stage as the two generals battle with the pen and invective subsequent to the surrender of Vicksburg with a vigor that perhaps might have resulted differently for the Confederacy if they had cooperated and fought the Yankees with similar gusto. In Part Two Smith hones his historian's skills to provide a succinct overview of the 14-month Vicksburg Campaign beginning with Union Navy's 1862 efforts to capture the Hill City and ending with Pemberton's July 4, 1863 surrender. Part Three "The Controversy" introduces the principals soon to include President Davis and their expectations and concerns. The first bomb thrown by the Confederate president was his lengthy July 15, 1863 letter, which convinced Johnston that the chief executive had arrayed himself on Pemberton's side in what would become their increasingly strident exchanges. Johnston, in view of his ego and longstanding disdain for Davis, was not about to let such a challenge go unanswered, and a war of words ensued that led to Pemberton's detailed response to Johnston's savage critique of his generalship found in the Virginian's 1874 *Narrative of Military Operations*. Pemberton's heretofore unpublished reply "Compelled To Appear In Print" constitutes Part Four.

In Part Five, "Conclusions," the author reviews the military-political situation, the generalship and personalities of Pemberton and Johnston, the role of President Davis, the war of words and how it played out to the detriment of the Confederacy. David Smith's reasoning in sorting out responsibilities are sound, and few will quarrel with his statement that is herewith paraphrased: At Vicksburg, Jefferson Davis brought together Joseph E. Johnston and John C. Pemberton to battle the Union's best—U.S. Grant and "Uncle Billy" Sherman and David Dixon Porter. As happened, they did not measure up, and their pairing was disastrous for the Confederacy.

A bibliographic essay and appendices concludes a publication that will appeal to both the historian and buff concerned about command decisions and personalities that plagued and then doomed the Confederate response to U.S. Grant's masterpiece—the Vicksburg Campaign.

Edwin C. Bearss
Historian Emeritus
National Park Service

Part One

The Beginning

Part One — The Beginning

*General Johnston may have seemed to
have written orders enough, but unfortunately
did not cause them to be executed.*

— John C. Pemberton[1]

It was difficult not to react with anger. John C. Pemberton had spent four long years fighting against his family, and for a cause in which he and his country had lost everything. He had been disgraced and humbled. The years after the war had been spent attempting to regain his honor and dignity—both with his brothers, sisters, and family in Philadelphia, and the Southerners who blamed him for the loss of Vicksburg. All he wanted was for the record to be told fairly. And now, nearly ten years after Appomattox, General Johnston had reopened the old wounds of Vicksburg.

Papers covered his desk in the Warrenton, Virginia farmhouse. A copy of Johnston's book, *Narrative of Military Operations* sat in the corner. It read more like fiction, he thought to himself. Neat stacks of papers—correspondence from his time as army commander in Mississippi—occupied another corner. As he thumbed through them, the memories rushed back. Having just turned sixty, he knew he looked older than his years allowed. The siege of Vicksburg had so aged him, he knew. He recalled how his little girl had scarcely recognized her father upon their reunion after the campaign closed in 1863. He felt old and tired— nearly too tired to battle General Johnston yet again.

It had to be done, though, he thought with resignation. The story told in that book was so warped and twisted, that fairness to the noble soldiers who had served in his army, marched hard and endured scanty rations, and fought with such dedication had to be told.

The unanswered question that lingered was, quite simply, where to start. He had determined not to write a history of the campaign—that job he would leave to those General Johnston referred to as "the future historians." No, he would simply respond with dignity to the charges made by Johnston, and set the historical record right. Once written and published, the public would make up its own mind as to the story they would choose to believe.

---

1. Manuscript written by John C. Pemberton, in possession of author.

Starting at the beginning was best, he supposed—with the charges General Johnston made against him. Suppressing a deep sigh, and referring back to his scribbled notes, he began to write:

> I may sum up Genl Johnston's charges against me under the following headings:
>
> 1st: An exaggerated idea of the value of Vicksburg, which he says ceased to be of any importance after the passage of the gun boats.
>
> 2d: That notwithstanding, I determined to stand a siege, the inevitable result of which was surrender.
>
> 3d: That I failed to concentrate my troops—on the contrary, dispersed them.
>
> 4th: Disobedience of orders in not concentrating (for) Grant's crossing.
>
> 5th: Disobedience in not concentrating after his (Grant's) crossing and keeping him (Johnston) in ignorance.
>
> 6th: Disobedience in not attacking at Clinton; tardiness, refusing the orders of my superior, the advice of council of war, I executed a movement Johnston disapproved.
>
> 7th: Fighting at Baker's Creek [Champion Hill] without necessity and without all my forces.
>
> 8th: That after this defeat and siege I failed to cooperate in any movement, and fixed the number of the relieving column at 40,000, which exonerated Johnston from returning with a man under it (i.e., returning with any less than 40,000 men).[2]

What caused John Pemberton to react so strongly to Johnston's memoirs? Joseph E. Johnston was one of the first of Confederate generals to write of the Civil War years, and his resulting book was more a justification of his military career than a chronicle of war experiences. Johnston set the tone for his section on Vicksburg by summarizing his thoughts about Pemberton, and it was this passage that so infuriated Pemberton:

> Notwithstanding these advantages on his part, who, by his manner of using them, constituted himself my adversary, I should have made no comments on these publications, but should have limited my defense to the preceding narrative; because it is distasteful, even painful to me, although in self defense, to write unfavorably of a brother officer, who, no doubt, served to the best of his ability; the more so, because that officer was, at the time, severely judged by the Southern people, who, on the contrary, have always judged me with their hearts instead of their minds. But Lieutenant General Pemberton has recently revived the question, and published, or rather procured to be published, a longer, more candid attack upon me than those contained in his official report, and its two supplements.[3]

---

2. Ibid.
3. Joseph E. Johnston, *Narrative of Military Operations*, (1874, reprint; New York: Da Capo Press, Inc. 1990) 215-216.

Blame for the failures at Vicksburg were not be laid at the feet of Joseph E. Johnston.

Biographer Michael Ballard noted that Pemberton intended to write his accounts of the war, but had not finished the task. Although the work was not published, Pemberton made significant efforts to complete the work before he died in 1881. In 1883 his widow, Pattie, sent the bulk of her late husband's papers to General Marcus Wright, who was compiling the Confederate portion of the *Official Records* of the war. In those papers, we surmise, was a mostly complete manuscript. Running over 150 hand written, legal sized pages, it was unsuitable for inclusion in the records under compilation. It evidently languished in the Wright estate for more than 110 years.[4]

To fully understand the Confederate experience at Vicksburg, one must understand Joseph E. Johnston and his relationship with Jefferson Davis. Johnston never mentally accepted the assignment given him by the War Department in Richmond. Appointed to his position on November 24, 1862, he was uncomfortable in exercising command over the armies of Generals Braxton Bragg and Pemberton, as well as a small department in East Tennessee. His orders from the War Department were to "establish his headquarters at Chattanooga, or such other place as in his judgment will best secure communication and will repair in person to any part of said command, whenever his presence may for the time be necessary or desirable." Johnston continued a running battle of words with both Davis and Pemberton during and after the war. Pemberton's response to Johnston's memoirs is the culmination of those arguments.[5]

There are many things this book is not. It is *not* a definitive history of the Vicksburg Campaign. This book has been written to understand the controversies of Confederate command at Vicksburg and finish the work Pemberton started. It is *not* the definitive biography of either Joseph E. Johnston or John C. Pemberton. By design, it is clearly *not* non-partisan due to its bias towards the story of the campaign as told by Pemberton. And it will *not* change our fundamental understanding and knowledge of the facts of the Vicksburg campaign. What it is, however, is the story of a single general's response to the perceived bias and slanted placement of blame for the loss of Vicksburg.

A few words on the layout of this book are in order. Pemberton wrote his response between the time of the release of Johnston's *Narrative of Military Oper-*

---

4. Michael B. Ballard, *Pemberton: A Biography*, (Jackson: University of Mississippi Press, 1991) 195, 203.

5. United States War Department, *The War of the Rebellion: A Compilation of the Official Records of the Union and Confederate Armies* (hereinafter referred to as *OR*) ser. I, vol. XVII, pt. 2, (Washington, D.C.: 1880-1901) 757-758.

ations in 1874 and his death in 1881. In editing this work, it was clear that Pemberton intended this as a response to General Johnston, and that the release of this work would be at a point in time (the early 1880s) when Johnston's memoirs would be fresh in the minds of all interested parties.

In the late 1990s, however, more than 120 years have passed since Johnston's *Narrative* was released. The issues to which Pemberton felt Johnston held him personally accountable have been obscured with the passage of time. To the modern reader, the controversies so obvious to these two men, and to the majority of the readers of that time, are no longer quite as clear.

Within the text of his manuscript, Pemberton often refers to specific sections of the *Narrative*, often footnoting and quoting the appropriate section. In order to provide the reader with the full context of the sections to which Pemberton refers, appropriate paragraphs of Johnston's *Narrative* have been italicized and indented into the Pemberton manuscript. The reader should easily be able to distinguish between the appropriate words as written by the two generals.[6]

Pemberton asserts that Johnston found fault with him three major areas: 1) Pemberton allowed Grant to obtain a foot-hold on the east side of the Mississippi River in the segment of the campaign that resulted in the battle of Port Gibson; 2) Pemberton failed to take advantage of opportunities that finally resulted in the Battle of Baker's Creek [Champion Hill]; and 3) Pemberton retreated into the trenches of Vicksburg and endured a siege.

The papers associated with the manuscript also contained additional pages, some of which seemed to be earlier drafts. Pemberton agonized over the wording he would use to begin his response. One version came across as a highly incensed response to his commander, and another was more restrained in manner. His final version is reasonably professional in nature and neutral in its opening.

In editing the manuscript, it was interesting to follow the sections and words crossed out by Pemberton and to consider the replacement words. On occasion, bitter language was evidently reconsidered, as more reserved, professional wording replaced the original writing.

The format for this book is straightforward. After this short introductory chapter, single chapters on the Vicksburg campaign and the post-campaign controversies of the protagonists, Johnston and Pemberton, are presented. The focus of the book, Pemberton's response to Johnston, follows, and the presentation is concluded with some closing remarks and analysis. In the main, however, this book *is* Pemberton's response to Johnston. That he apologizes for his actions and attempts to shift blame back to Johnston and away from himself should

---

6. Johnston's *Narrative* covers the Vicksburg campaign and his involvement with it, from pages 147 to 252.

come as no surprise. The reader will have to be the judge as to the strength of Pemberton's arguments.

Joseph Eggleston Johnston was seven years Pemberton's senior, born in Farmville, Virginia in 1807. Graduating 13th out of 46 in the West Point class of 1829, Johnston served eight years in the Army before resigning his commission to entire private practice as a civil engineer. He shortly thereafter reentered the military service.

Johnston served in Mexico under Winfield Scott, and received promotion to captain. During the Mexican War he received three brevet promotions for gallantry. Johnston returned to the topographical engineers after the war, and was finally promoted to lieutenant colonel of the prestigious 1st Cavalry in 1855. His final U.S. Army promotion occurred in June of 1860 when he was named quartermaster general, which carried with it the staff rank of brigadier general.

Johnston resigned his commission and joined the Confederacy in April of 1861. Rapid advance led to promotion to General to rank from July 4, 1861. President Jefferson Davis ranked the full generals of the Confederacy by their prewar rank in the United States army, and placed Johnston fourth (using his line commission as lieutenant colonel, rather than the staff rank of brigadier general). Johnston believed the staff rank should have been used, argued vociferously with Davis, and never forgave the president for this perceived slight.

Johnston commanded forces in the Shenandoah Valley, and slipped past Federal forces to arrive at Manassas Junction just in time to influence the outcome of the Battle of Manassas (Bull Run) in favor of the Confederacy in July of 1861. Retaining command of Confederate forces in Virginia, he led them into the Peninsula Campaign of Union Major General George B. McClellan in mid-April 1862. Believing the War Department and press in Richmond could not keep military secrets, he earned the ire of Davis by withholding plans from his commander-in-chief. Johnston retreated from Yorktown to the gates of Richmond in May 1862, and was wounded severely during the Battle of Seven Pines on May 31, 1862. The wound gave Davis the opportunity to appoint Robert E. Lee to command of the army in Virginia. Johnston's first love of command was with the army in his native Virginia, and the desire for that command remained with him throughout the rest of the war.

Sufficiently recovered from his wounds in November 1862, he was assigned to a dual departmental command of the forces of Generals Braxton Bragg and John C. Pemberton. Ordered to Mississippi on May 9, 1863 by Richmond, he commanded an army of relief near Jackson, Mississippi. Johnston's army attempted little in the way of relieving the siege of Vicksburg; Johnston argued his forces were inadequate to the challenge.

Although blamed by President Davis for the loss of Vicksburg, the continuing failures and ultimate relief of command of Braxton Bragg left Davis with little choice other than to offer command of the Army of Tennessee to Johnston. Beginning in the spring of 1864, Johnston continually retreated before the forces of Major General William T. Sherman towards Atlanta. Again refusing to share plans with Davis, he was finally relieved of his command in mid-July of 1864 and replaced by General John Bell Hood.

Late in the war, Johnston received his final command, leading the remnants of the Army of Tennessee and other corps in the Battle of Bentonville in March 1865. He surrendered his army and command to Sherman on April 26, 1865. After the war, Johnston worked in the insurance business, served in Congress, and in 1874 published his memoirs, *Narrative of Military Operations*. In his memoirs, he continued his feud with Davis, and placed blame for the loss of Vicksburg on both Davis and Pemberton. He died in 1891 of pneumonia he contracted shortly after serving as a pallbearer at the funeral of Sherman.

John Clifford Pemberton was born on August 10, 1814 in Philadelphia, Pennsylvania. Graduating 27th of 50 in the West Point class of 1837, Pemberton served during the Second Seminole and Mexican wars. Like so many future generals of the Civil War, Pemberton was breveted for gallantry during the Mexican War, and later served on outpost duty in the west.

In spite of his Northern birth, Pemberton had close ties with many of the Southerners with whom he served. This affinity for positions associated with the South led to his marriage in 1848 to a lady from Norfolk, Virginia. At the outbreak of the Civil War Pemberton resigned his commission as captain and offered his services to the Confederacy. He had two brothers who served in the Union army.

Pemberton received his commission at lieutenant colonel in Confederate army in late April, 1861. Rapid promotion followed, and he was made a brigadier general of volunteers while serving in Virginia in June of 1861. He was named to head the Department of South Carolina, Georgia and Florida in January of 1862, and also received a promotion to major general. Pemberton proved to be a reasonably competent bureaucrat, but clashed with the governor of South Carolina over the best methods of protecting Charleston, South Carolina.

When Jefferson Davis decided to name a department commander to replace Major General Earl Van Dorn in Mississippi, he turned to Pemberton. Pemberton's transfer to Mississippi, as well as promotion to lieutenant general, occurred in October of 1862. He was placed in command of the Department of Mississippi and East Louisiana, and began the process of attempting to bring order to the confused military situation in Mississippi.

Pemberton commanded his department throughout the Vicksburg campaign, and he and Davis were of the same opinion regarding the need to hold Vicksburg at all costs. In this, he differed with his immediate superior, Joseph E. Johnston. As a result, Pemberton's army was besieged at Vicksburg, and the 30,000-man army was surrendered on July 4, 1863. Paroled with the army, he was exchanged in short order, but never again received a command commensurate with his rank as lieutenant general.

Pemberton resigned his commission as lieutenant general in May of 1864, and served the remainder of the war as a colonel of artillery in the Richmond area. He lived as a farmer in Virginia after the war, and became the scapegoat identified by Johnston in his memoirs for the failures at Vicksburg. Pemberton died in 1881 in Penllyn, Pennsylvania.

Bruce Catton put it well. John C. Pemberton, while trying to defend his department of Mississippi and Eastern Louisiana, faced four outstanding problems. First, he had the misfortune to face Major General Ulysses S. Grant. Second, President Jefferson Davis told Pemberton that Vicksburg must be held at all costs. The third problem was his immediate superior, Joe Johnston, who argued exactly the opposite of President Davis, and believed that fixed positions such as the trenches of Vicksburg should *not* be held, and that Pemberton's task was to maintain his army—not the city. And fourth, Pemberton faced the problem of meeting with a general who was willing to bring the military might of the Federal government to the forefront in their confrontation. "The Confederacy had few generals unluckier than John Pemberton," concluded Catton.[7]

Nothing Pemberton wrote in his manuscript, while written in righteous indignation, will change our fundamental understanding of the Vicksburg campaign. The record of the Confederacy and Civil War history, however, may be enhanced. The telling of his story of the campaign, the challenges, and the shortcomings with which he contended are finally told.

It is unfortunate that two men of the military capabilities of Pemberton and Johnston, with their inherent strengths and weaknesses, were brought together in the Confederate command hierarchy. That they faced as skilled an opponent as U.S. Grant is even more unfortunate. But it was the hand of cards the Confederacy was dealt, and the hand they chose to play. That it eventually led to the surrender and loss of an army is perhaps the most unfortunate aspect of the campaign.

---

7. Bruce Catton, *Grant Moves South* (Boston: Little, Brown and Co., 1960) 437.

Part Two

The Vicksburg Campaign

Part Two — The Vicksburg Campaign

"In my opinion, the opening of the Mississippi River
will be to us of more advantage than the capture
of forty Richmonds."

— *Henry W. Halleck[1]*

I t was a town of importance—an importance that went far beyond its popula-
tion of 4,500. Sitting as it did high above the mighty Mississippi River, it provided linkage between the Confederacy located on the western side of the river
and the state of Mississippi and points farther east. It was a relatively new town,
even as cities in the western wilderness went, dating its birth to 1814. Although
bridges across the Mississippi did not exist at that time, railroads ran to the city
from the east and came to the western bank of the Mississippi from the west. Ferries connected the two shores.

Vicksburg rapidly established itself as a commercial hub for the area. The
hub became even more important during the Civil War, for Vicksburg was of critical importance to the Confederate cause. It provided a vital linkage between
Texas, Arkansas and Louisiana in the west and the Confederate states east of the
Mississippi. Cattle as well as imperative blockade items, such as arms and med-
ical supplies, passed through Vicksburg. Abraham Lincoln called the city "the
nailhead that held the South's two halves together."[2]

Geography and the Mississippi River combined to place Vicksburg in a position of unusual importance to both the Union and the Confederacy by the latter
half of 1862. The seaport of New Orleans had fallen, and the Mississippi was
under Federal control as far south as Memphis. The opening of the Mississippi—
and the consequent severing of the eastern and western halves of the Confederacy, had become strategically important to the Union cause. But in order to reopen
the Mississippi, the batteries and city of Vicksburg had to come under Federal
control.

The problem facing Union Major General Ulysses S. Grant was how to get
an army in front of the city and its defenses. From Memphis south to Vicksburg,

---

1. *OR*, Ser. I, vol. XXIV, pt 1, 22.
2. Abraham Lincoln, quoted in Jim Miles, *A River Unvexed*, (Nashville: Rutledge Hill Press,
   1994) 190.

the land on the eastern side of the Mississippi was relatively flat, open, and subject to frequent floods. Good, dry land could be found, but it was as much as 50 miles inland. Even in dry weather, routes through the bogs and swamps were limited. An army could not be marched down the eastern bank of the Mississippi to confront the Confederates.

The high ground that Grant coveted returned to the Mississippi in the vicinity of Vicksburg, following the Yazoo River as it angled to the southwest, to empty itself into the "Father of Waters" just north of the city. High bluffs and strong defenses on the southern side of the Yazoo created difficulties to supply an invading army.[3]

What made Vicksburg an extremely difficult city to take was the way the Mississippi approached the town. Consistent with its habit of winding and twisting its way towards the Gulf of Mexico, the river bent back to the north before executing an almost 180 degree turn and starting south again. Just around that point on the eastern side, atop towering bluffs, sat Vicksburg. A fleet approaching from the north had to cautiously negotiate the bend in the river, and was subject to the unmerciful fire of the batteries. Heavily armored ships were hard pressed to run the gauntlet; for unarmed commercial boats, passage was not even an option. As long as Vicksburg was held in force, control of the river was denied to the Federals.

As Bruce Catton notes, things were not much better south of the city. The city's defenses were anchored at Warrenton on the southern side; immediately south, a strong position had been occupied at Grand Gulf. Although the ground was undoubtedly dry, the problem was getting an army in position to land south of Vicksburg. The land west of the Mississippi was much like that above Vicksburg—swampy, flooded and basically impassable for the movement of troops. Until the Federal Navy could somehow place transports south of Vicksburg, moving troops over to the eastern bank was out of the question.

The place Grant wished to be was east of the city, where he could establish a sustainable supply line with his base in Tennessee. It would take more than six months of backbreaking effort, marked by repeated attempts and failures before a solution was reached.

If Vicksburg was important because of its location on the Mississippi, it seems fitting to begin the history of the Vicksburg campaign with the Federal Navy's efforts to capture the city. After New Orleans fell to the fleet of Union Flag Officer David G. Farragut in the spring of 1862, Farragut was ordered to move his deep-water fleet up the Mississippi and capture Vicksburg.

---

3. A good description of the terrain near Vicksburg may be found in Catton, *Grant Moves South* 371-372.

The fall of New Orleans energized the Confederates. Heavy cannon were deployed on the bluffs commanding the river during the month of May, and they were placed none too soon. Farragut, a native of Tennessee who had remained loyal to the Union received 3,500 troops on May 1 (of which he was able to bring with him 1,500), and began his movements up the Mississippi.

While steaming up the Mississippi, Farragut forced the surrender of Baton Rouge. In terms of success, however, the capture of the Louisiana capital was the highlight of the opening efforts of the campaign. Upon reaching the river fortress of Vicksburg, the Union flag officer met with rebuff. The river defenses were not as substantial as they would become, but were strong enough. On May 18, 1862, one of Farragut's captains demanded the city's surrender. Not surprisingly, the demand was rejected.

Of greater concern to Farragut, however, was the unexpected realization that his guns would not elevate enough to reach the Confederate works. Soon to face a garrison of almost 10,000 men under the command of Major General Earl Van Dorn, Farragut concluded that his inadequate force could not carry the city. Most of the fleet and its infantry contingent returned to New Orleans.

While Federal efforts to take Vicksburg from the south were failing, a separate push was being made from the north. Flag Officer Charles H. Davis had recently assumed command of the Mississippi squadron of ironclads and gunboats operated against Fort Pillow. Plans called for Farragut to run the batteries at Vicksburg and link up with Davis and proceed to Vicksburg and take the city. While Farragut was steaming north, Davis was moving down the Mississippi River.

Davis faced significant opposition on the river. A Confederate ram flotilla checked the Federals on May 10 in a fleet action, and the Confederates continued to hold Ft. Pillow, located on the east bank of the river north of Memphis as late as early June. A fleet of Federal rams reinforced Davis, however, and on June 6 the fleet approached the city of Memphis.

The Confederate Navy's success on the river was not to be repeated. In a scene reminiscent of civilians streaming out of Washington to watch the battle of First Manassas (or Bull Run), spectators lined the eastern bank to witness the clash of arms. To their horror, the Confederate fleet was severely mauled, and only one Rebel boat escaped. Like its sister city New Orleans, Memphis fell quickly to the Union Navy. Without substantial opposition in his front, Davis leisurely moved down the Mississippi to within several miles of Vicksburg.

Not content with his initial failure to take Vicksburg Farragut again steamed north to try his hand at the city. On June 25 he stopped his fleet just to the south of the city. With him this time were more than 3,000 infantry under Brigadier General Thomas Williams, as well as a fleet of mortar schooners for use on the elevated Vicksburg defenses. Two days of bombardment preceded a June 28 naval attack on the city. While eight of his eleven ships managed to get past the defenses and join Davis, who arrived above Vicksburg on July 1, it was a hollow victory. The infantry forces at his disposal were entirely inadequate to contest for the city. Farragut had proven that the river and saltwater fleets could not subdue Vicksburg on their own.

The troops under General Williams were subsequently landed on the western bank and put to work digging a canal. The project, it was hoped, would divert the channel of the Mississippi and allow river traffic to bypass Vicksburg. Working in the heat of the summer, men dropped by the scores. Although this initial attempt at a canal failed, it would not be the last effort of its sort.

In the meantime, the Confederate Navy prepared a response. The ironclad ram *Arkansas* steamed out from the Yazoo on July 15 to confront Farragut's fleet. Twice Farragut challenged the *Arkansas*, and twice the ironclad thwarted the Union sailors. Farragut finally got a measure of revenge when the Confederates on August 6 blew the ironclad up after her engines failed. But after a month of futile effort against Vicksburg—and almost three months of effort in all—Farragut again had given up. Picking up Williams' infantry, and faced with a renewed Confederate threat to Baton Rouge, Farragut again sailed past Vicksburg and returned to the naval forces in the Gulf of Mexico.

Having failed twice in its attempts to take Vicksburg, the Federal Navy turned over primary responsibility for the capture of the city to the Army. The campaign to capture Vicksburg moved closer to the eventual climatic confrontation between U.S. Grant and John C. Pemberton, and to the dysfunctional relationship that would develop in the Confederate high command in Mississippi between Pemberton and Joseph E. Johnston.

The promotion of Major General Henry W. Halleck to the position of general-in-chief of the Federal forces on July 11, 1862, placed Major General U.S. Grant in charge of the forces in northern Mississippi and western Tennessee. Even at such an early date, Grant had his sights set on moving south and taking the river fortress of Vicksburg.

Grant had three major forces at his disposal in late July of 1862. Major General William T. Sherman was at Memphis, holding that city after its capture by the Union Navy. Major General Edward O.C. Ord was at Corinth with 8,000 men, while Major General William S. Rosecrans held the strategic railroad between Corinth and the resort town of Iuka with another 9,000 men. Grant found himself essentially in a defensive position.

Two significant Confederate forces opposed him. The first, under Major General Sterling Price, was at Tupelo, and consisted of 17,000 men. In addition, another 10,000 men under Major General Earl Van Dorn were en route to Holly

Springs. Van Dorn was in charge of the Vicksburg garrison and was free to maneuver his forces by late July following the withdrawal of Farragut's fleet back to New Orleans and the Gulf of Mexico.

After a month of relative inactivity, the Confederates took the offensive. On September 13, the Confederates occupied Iuka. Grant, headquartered in Corinth reacted by ordering Rosecrans and Ord to close on Iuka. By September 18, Ord had approached Iuka from the west, while Rosecrans watched the western approaches. It was hoped that this pincer-like movement would drive Price into the waiting Rosecrans and thus effect the destruction of Price's small army.

The converging Federal columns met with difficulties. Communications were disrupted by the combination of rain and the dense, thick woods. Although it had been originally planned that Ord would open the battle, Grant changed his mind and informed Rosecrans that Ord would attack after Rosecrans began due to the difficulties of continual communications. Price, meanwhile, had spotted the approach of Ord. Realizing he was in a tight spot, Price prepared to evacuate Iuka.

On September 19, Price stumbled into Rosecrans as he was confronting Grant. A nasty little fight ensued, but Grant and Ord sat outside Iuka, unaware that the engagement had been joined. A freak atmospheric condition conspired to block sound from the southeast, and while Price fought to extricate himself from Iuka, Grant and Ord sat and waited.

On September 20, Price made good his escape via a lightly guarded road. When the escape was discovered, Rosecrans mounted only a feeble pursuit. The battle of Iuka was a sharp little affair that settled nothing. Both sides lost a combined 1,500 men and set the stage for the battle of Corinth.

With Price's retreat from Iuka, the scene shifted west and focused on Corinth. Once again, the Confederates were on the offensive, this time under the leadership of Van Dorn. Price's forces had joined with Van Dorn to bring the Confederate striking force to 22,000 men. Opposing Van Dorn would be Rosecrans, with approximately 23,000 men.

Van Dorn moved northward from Ripley to Pocohontas in an unsuccessful attempt to deceive the Federals. On October 3, the Confederates under Van Dorn approached Corinth from the northwest and came up against the old earthworks in which Beauregard's army had confronted Halleck earlier in the year. The Confederates overran those fortifications, which had been built for an army of greater size. Extreme heat and lack of water (the October temperature was near 90 degrees) slowed Van Dorn's pursuit. The day ended with Rosecrans pulled back into a much tighter defensive perimeter around Corinth and awaiting the renewal of Van Dorn's attack the next day.

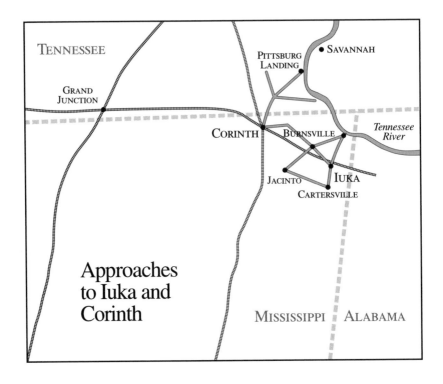

TENNESSEE

PITTSBURG LANDING • SAVANNAH

GRAND JUNCTION

CORINTH BURNSVILLE

Tennessee River

JACINTO IUKA
CARTERSVILLE

Approaches
to Iuka and
Corinth

MISSISSIPPI | ALABAMA

The battle flared again early on October 4. The Confederates were arrayed in a semicircle around Corinth, with divisions led by Brigadier Generals Louis Hébert and Dabney Maury and Major General Mansfield Lovell in place from left to right. Lovell was to demonstrate on his front, while Hébert and Maury attacked in earnest. Lovell was to engage once the Confederate attack had started to succeed. Hébert was sick, however, and time was lost on the left flank. In spite of the delays, the Confederate attack was nearly successful. The fighting, particularly desperate around Battery Robinett, was touch-and-go for a short time. But Lovell, on the right, never advanced, and Maury's attack was repulsed with great loss. By noon the fight was over, and there would be no future Confederate offensives in Mississippi for the rest of the campaign. Casualties on both sides were nearly equal, but captured Confederates pushed their total to more than 4,800 versus Federal losses of 2,800.

Although the battle of Corinth was over, the drama was not. Grant knew of the battle on October 3 and in typical fashion set forth to engineer the destruction of Van Dorn's army. Major General Stephen Hurlbut was dispatched to intercept the Confederates, but an anemic pursuit by Rosecrans left just enough room for Van Dorn to slip away. At the end of October, Rosecrans was promoted and transferred to Nashville to replace Major General Don Carlos Buell as commander of the Army of the Ohio, which was promptly redesignated the Army of the Cumberland. Grant wrote in his autobiography after the war that although he felt that Rosecrans would do well in independent command, he would have relieved him had he remained under his command.

On October 1, 1862 (two days before the start of the battle of Corinth) the War Department in Richmond issued Special Orders No. 73 placing Major General John C. Pemberton in charge of the Department of Mississippi and East Louisiana. Within the department was the vital river fortress of Vicksburg. A problem of rank (both Lovell and Van Dorn outranked Pemberton as major generals) was solved by promoting Pemberton to lieutenant general to rank as of October 13.[4]

A question often asked by those who study the Vicksburg campaign is whether Pemberton should have stood a siege in defending the river fortress. On September 30, 1862, Pemberton received a letter from Secretary of War George W. Randolph, in which the directives for command of his district were outlined. Pemberton was to "consider the successful defense of those states [Mississippi and East Louisiana] as the first and chief object of your command." In addition, "until further orders" Pemberton was to report directly to the War Department. Even after Pemberton began reporting to General Joseph E. Johnston, Pemberton and the War Department continued to communicate directly, often bypassing Johnston. Johnston himself never embraced the strategies for Pemberton's district command as outlined by Randolph.[5]

U.S. Grant was given the command of the Department of the Tennessee on October 25 and by early November took the initiative. While Pemberton was trying to bring order out of chaos in the Mississippi command, Grant had begun formulating the plan that would finally resolve the fate of Vicksburg.

Richmond's dissatisfaction with Van Dorn and the failure of the Corinth campaign contributed directly to the end of army command for Van Dorn and led to the appointment of Pemberton. Van Dorn's downfall began when charges were preferred against him by Brigadier General John S. Bowen. The embarrassment caused President Jefferson Davis was significant. Although a court of inquiry convened in early November acquitted Van Dorn of all charges, he found himself permanently removed from army command and relegated to command of cavalry.[6]

---

4. *OR*, Ser. I, vol. XXIV, pt 2, 727-728.

5. Ibid., 716-717.

6. Bowen was a brigadier in the division of Mansfield Lovell, a graduate of the West Point class of 1853 and an officer in the western armies. That Bowen of all officers would prefer charges is surprising. He would go on to fight with distinction with Pemberton in the Vicksburg campaign, achieve rank of major general, surrender with the garrison, and shortly thereafter die of disease in mid-July 1863. For more detail, see Robert G. Hartje, *Van Dorn: The Life and Times of a Confederate General*, (Nashville: Vanderbilt University Press, 1967) 239-246.

The Vicksburg campaign still awaited the arrival of another key Confederate. General Joseph E. Johnston, commander of the Confederate army in Virginia, had been wounded at the battle of Seven Pines on May 31, 1862. By late October he had recovered sufficiently from his wounds, and waited to be restored to command.

The now-healthy Johnston presented a significant problem for Davis. Not only did the he not like Johnston, who had a history of being secretive and aloof, but General Robert E. Lee had established a record of victories and battlefield dominance while leading the Army of Northern Virginia. Replacing Lee was out of the question; Davis would have to find another command for Johnston.

Davis chose to place Johnston in command of the departments headed up by Generals Braxton Bragg and Pemberton. On November 24, 1862, Special Orders No. 275 gave Johnston the "authority to establish his headquarters wherever, in his judgment, will best secure facilities for ready communication with the troops of his command." Furthermore, Johnston was given the latitude to go personally and take command if needed. Johnston established his headquarters with Bragg at Tullahoma, Tennessee.[7]

From the end of the battle of Corinth in October of 1862 until the conclusion of the campaign in July 1863, the initiative would primarily rest with the Federal forces under Grant. Since his ability to place a land force on the eastern shore of the Mississippi was hampered by the city's natural defenses, Grant chose an overland route that followed the railroad system into central Mississippi. Once he reached the Mississippi capital of Jackson, he would turn west and follow the east-west railroad to Vicksburg. The problem was and would continue to be one of supplying his army through enemy territory. Pemberton would use Grant's extended supply line to his advantage in foiling the remaining moves available to Grant in 1862.

Although Grant commanded in the west, another Union general had designs on Vicksburg. Major General John A. McClernand, a War Democrat from Illinois, visited and wrote President Lincoln during the summer and early autumn of 1862. What he proposed was of serious interest to Lincoln. McClernand would return to Illinois, raise an army of 60,000 men, load them aboard transports, and proceed to take Vicksburg. The very size of the force he would raise would overwhelm the tiny garrison of Confederates. As commander of the forces, a position McClernand felt entitled to for raising the forces, he would achieve personal military glory. By 1864, McClernand might well challenge for the presidency.

---

7. For the thoughts of Davis, see Jefferson F. Davis, *The Rise and Fall of the Confederate Government*, (1881; reprint, New York: Da Capo Press, 1990) Volume 2, 337-338.

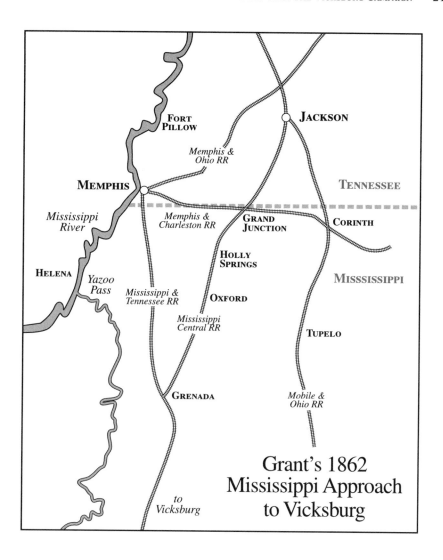

Grant's 1862
Mississippi Approach
to Vicksburg

During October and November, McClernand worked feverishly to forward troops to collection points at Columbus, Kentucky, and Memphis, Tennessee. Twenty regiments had been sent by November 10. Grant became more and more alarmed by this concentration of manpower, but received reassurances from Halleck that his command was secure. Halleck was quick to remind Grant that he outranked McClernand.

It had been a busy several weeks for Pemberton. Upon arriving in Jackson, Mississippi, in mid-October, he found a command in significant disarray. Van Dorn was heartily disliked by the residents of Mississippi for having imposed martial law, and the forces at Pemberton's command seemed woefully inadequate to defend the state against Grant. Paroled troops from the February surrender at Ft. Donelson had been exchanged, and Pemberton received permission to detain them for use in his theater of operations.

Pemberton's strengths as a military officer lay in his organizational skills, and he immediately set to work reorganizing the department that was now under his command. Capable officers were placed in staff positions, and gradually order was brought to the Department of Mississippi and East Louisiana.

Pemberton's previous assignment had been the command of the Department of South Carolina, Georgia and Florida, where local politicians did not appreciate his abilities at administration. The bureaucratic bent that had met with such displeasure in South Carolina, however, found a warm reception in Mississippi. Some of this may have had to do with the free-spirited nature of the previous commander, Van Dorn. But Pemberton set to work with a will, strengthening the defensive perimeters already established. The *Daily Citizen* was moved to note that "With the practised eye of a master—the science of an engineer—he [Pemberton] surveyed the ground at Vicksburg—at Port Hudson and at other points, and determined at a glance what was necessary, what was practicable, and what was possible."[8]

Grant moved the major portion of his forces south on November 20 from La Grange, Tennessee following the Mississippi Central Railroad. Sherman marched east from Memphis four days later, following the track of the Mississippi and Tennessee Railroad. These two rail lines came together at Grenada, Mississippi, at an intermediate point some eighty miles into the interior of Mississippi. Fully 50,000 men had started south towards Vicksburg.

The rivers in northern Mississippi run from east to west to eventually empty into the Mississippi River. Although defensive lines were available astride the Tallahatchie and Yocona Rivers, Pemberton retreated all the way to the defensive line behind the Yalobusha River at Grenada. Grenada was still some 110 miles from Jackson. The farther Grant moved into the state, however, the more tenuous his supply line became. Grant established a forward supply depot at Holly Springs, some twenty miles into Mississippi.

By December 5, Federal forces had reached Oxford, Mississippi. Grant had, meanwhile, become worried about his supply lines and decided upon a bold plan that would move his timetable forward. Sherman would return to Memphis, organize and take command of the troops McClernand had been forwarding south, load them aboard transports and steam south with Rear Admiral David D. Porter's fleet of gunboats. While Grant held Pemberton at the Yalobusha River line, Sherman would slip down river with his substantial force (although less than the envisioned 60,000 men McClernand wished to command) and take Vicksburg.

---

8. Quoted in Samuel Carter III, *The Final Fortress: The Campaign for Vicksburg, 1862-1863* (1980; reprint, Wilmington: Broadfoot Publishing Co., 1988) 84.

Although McClernand was still up river recruiting, he would lead the expedition if he were to arrive in Memphis in time. While Lincoln supported McClernand's right to command, Halleck politicked and used his office behind the scenes to keep command away from McClernand and in the hands of Sherman. Possibly motivated by the impending arrival of McClernand, or simply fearing such an event, Sherman left Memphis on December 20 in command of the river forces bound for Vicksburg.[9]

Grant's movement south signaled another time of crisis for the Confederates. Pemberton left his department command at Jackson and took the railroad to meet with Van Dorn and corps commanders Price and Lovell. He set in motion the retreat that would eventually end up at Grenada. Early December found the Confederate forces digging lines of defense behind both the Tallahatchie and the Yalobusha Rivers. During this time Pemberton was able to work out a cooperative relationship with Governor John J. Pettus of Mississippi. Supplies began to flow into the region, in spite of typical wrangling from Richmond as to where Pemberton's district could draw its supplies.

Johnston was summoned in early December to meet with President Davis in Chattanooga. The result of this meeting was the President's order (against Johnston's wishes) to dispatch a reinforced division led by Major General Carter Stevenson from Bragg's army to Pemberton. Johnston argued with Davis that reinforcements for Pemberton should come from the Arkansas forces under Lieutenant General Theophilus Holmes, not from Bragg. In addition, Davis planned to continue his trip west to visit Pemberton and wanted Johnston to accompany him. It took a personal invitation and a near order from Davis to get Johnston to visit his own operations in Mississippi.

Luckily for the Confederates, Grant's advance was slow (the result of an inadequate road network and a railroad in need of repair), plus a preoccupation with Sherman's impending push down the Mississippi, gave Pemberton time for a counter-strike. On December 19 with the President on hand in Jackson, Pemberton ordered Van Dorn to take the available cavalry, numbering approximately 3,500, and attack Grant's supply depot at Holly Springs. Brigadier General Nathan Bedford Forrest attacked elements of Grant's supply line further north in Tennessee while Van Dorn closed in on Holly Springs.

---

9. Kenneth P. Williams argues that Grant was not engaged in duplicity in desiring to move Sherman south from Memphis. See Kenneth P. Williams, *Grant Rises in the West* (1956; reprint, Lincoln: University of Nebraska Press, 1997) 187-189. What does seem clear from the record is that all parties involved, from Lincoln, Secretary of War Edwin Stanton, and Halleck to Grant, Sherman and McClernand, understood what was going on. There was enough duplicity on all parties to go around.

On December 20 Van Dorn forced the surrender of the garrison at Holly Springs, capturing 1,500 troops and destroying supplies estimated to be worth as much as $1.5 million. Grant termed the surrender of the garrison "a disgraceful one" and found his forward efforts to keep Pemberton pinned in place at Grenada compromised. Van Dorn returned to the Confederate lines on December 26, having eluded all attempts to capture or destroy his cavalry force.

With his supply base gone, Grant had no choice but to return to Memphis. Worse, Van Dorn's raid had severed telegraphic communications, and Grant was unable to inform Sherman that his important diversion had failed. As Grant scoured the countryside for provisions and forage (much to the dismay of the local inhabitants), Sherman steamed south for a rendezvous with Pemberton's forces at Chickasaw Bayou.

During that same period, Davis and Johnston took the railroad west to visit Pemberton's command. Leaving on December 15, they took all of four days to arrive in Jackson, Mississippi. On the evening of the December 19, they continued on to Vicksburg.

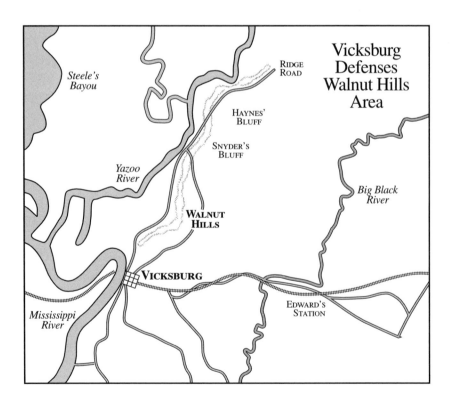

Vicksburg's two high-ranking visitors remained there until December 22. During their stay, Johnston had time to prepare a lengthy memorandum detailing all of the aspects of Vicksburg's defenses that he did not like, and the list was long. The defenses were a trap, he felt, and would require many more defenders than were in the district at the time. In short, the memorandum identified much that was wrong with the department but offered no useful suggestions as to how to solve the problems.[10]

Even though Grant had abandoned the inland diversion, Sherman's movement still had an excellent chance of success. On December 20, 1862, he left Memphis with slightly over 20,000 troops. When he reached Helena, Arkansas, additional forces were added to bring his army to approximately 30,000 men. Although General Halleck had wired as early as December 18 that Major General McClernand was to be in charge of Sherman's expedition, problems with communication allowed Sherman to leave without McClernand. McClernand himself would not leave Cairo, Illinois, until December 26, and would not play a part in the battle shaping up near Vicksburg.[11]

As Christmas Day 1862 drew closer, Sherman's army approached the vicinity of Vicksburg. The plan was working; initial Confederate forces under Major General Martin L. Smith and Brigadier General Stephen D. Lee totaled only 5,000, half of which were used to garrison the city defenses proper. Pemberton was not present and the city was open to capture.

In the meantime, Johnston and Davis had gone back to Jackson, and on December 23 departed for a visit with Pemberton at Grenada. Although by this time Pemberton was aware of the movement of Sherman's forces towards Vicksburg, it was not until Christmas Eve that he ended his conference and hurried to Vicksburg for the defense of the city. Neither President Davis nor General Johnston chose to accompany Pemberton.

On Christmas Day Sherman tied up at Milliken's Bend, on the western shore of the Mississippi River just above the mouth of the Yazoo River. His troops spent the day wrecking a section of the railroad to Monroe, Louisiana. In hindsight, the expenditure of effort was questionable and of little military value. The few miles of wrecked rail, plus the beef cattle captured by the Federal forces, did not compensate for the lost time the diversion afforded the Confederates. On Christmas Day, Smith wired Pemberton several times with accurate information regarding the buildup of Federal forces on the Mississippi. Pemberton had been entertaining President Davis as well as General Johnston, and the flurry of activ-

---

10. For Johnston's analysis, see *OR*, ser. I, vol. XVII, pt 2, 800-801.

11. While the historical record does not categorically clear either Grant nor Sherman from maneuvering McClernand out of the command of the naval expedition to Vicksburg, they certainly could not have been upset at not having him there.

ity sent Davis back to Richmond and Johnston to Jackson. Pemberton himself took the railroad to Vicksburg.

The arrival of Sherman's force caused Pemberton to concentrate his department's resources. With Grant falling back on Memphis, several brigades helping to man the Yalobusha line were rushed back to Vicksburg to counter Sherman's threat, where they were joined by the vanguard of Stevenson's troops then coming in from Middle Tennessee. Interior lines and the well-developed rail network facilitated Pemberton's concentration efforts.

Sherman proceeded up the Yazoo on December 26, finding a place to disembark his troops in the swampy lowlands that approached Walnut Hills, and maneuvered forces into position for the attack the next day. Pemberton feverishly rushed as many troops as possible into the city and into the defenses. The day the Confederates gained while Sherman destroyed the railroad at Milliken's Bend would provide Pemberton with just enough time.

On December 29, after probing for a good approach, Sherman was ready to attack. Word that Grant had not remained in his diversionary position on the Yalobusha River and that a much larger force was on hand than anticipated had not reached him. The swampy bayou and the lack of ground high enough over which to channel troops forced Sherman to attack positions of great strength. The attacks failed miserably. The day ended with the Confederates holding safe, dry ground while the Federals huddled around what little dry land that could be found.

Things became progressively worse on the next day. Dense fog hampered movement, and further attacks proved fruitless. Sherman was fixed in position with little room to maneuver, and Pemberton was growing stronger by the hour. Sherman was in a serious quandary. That same night he considered again the feasibility of an attack the next day. He eventually chose to look for a better location further up the Yazoo, but that attempt proved fruitless as well. Rain began falling in torrents, and soldiers looked with some trepidation at high water lines on trees some 10 feet above the ground upon which they were standing. Although it could not have been an easy decision, Sherman chose to pull back and abort the attempt to take Vicksburg. In perhaps the classic battle report of the Civil War, he summarized his efforts to Washington thusly: "I reached Vicksburg at the time appointed, landed, assaulted, and failed." For his efforts, Sherman lost nearly 1,800 men, compared with slightly less than 200 for the Confederates.[12]

As the New Year dawned, Federal efforts appeared doomed to disappointment. Grant's army was back in Tennessee, and Sherman was retreating to Milliken's Bend. Sherman had lost contact with Grant, and vice versa and to compound matters, John A. McClernand finally reached Sherman and took command.

---

12. *OR*, ser. I, vol. XVII, pt 2, 613.

Both Sherman and McClernand resolved to not allow their forces to rest. Their target was the Arkansas Post, which sat on the left bank of the Arkansas River and was believed to hold 8,000 Confederate troops. McClernand first came across Arkansas Post as a target on December 30, at a conference in Helena. To what extent Sherman actually decided the Arkansas Post as a target is unclear; his memoirs suggest the idea was completely his, although the official army records clearly document McClernand's participation in the December 30 conference. In any event, on January 5, 1863, Sherman informed Halleck "General McClernand agreed and Admiral Porter also cheerfully assented and we are at the moment *en route* for the Post of Arkansas, 50 miles up the Arkansas River."[13]

Early in the morning of January 4, McClernand left with two Federal corps for Arkansas Post. The move did not agree with Grant's strategic thinking, but there was little he could do about it owing to lags in communications. Believing the expedition to have been hatched by McClernand, he complained to Halleck that the Illinois politician "was on a wild-goose chase." Halleck responded, although again the communications were entirely out of date with events, that Grant was authorized to relieve McClernand should he feel such action appropriate.[14]

Grant's concerns were justified. Major General Nathaniel P. Banks was in command of a force moving up the Mississippi from New Orleans, intent on joining forces with Grant in order to open the Mississippi. A sister fortress to Vicksburg was in his way at Port Hudson, but Grant had no way of knowing the status or whereabouts of Banks. He needed, however, to be ready to reinforce Banks, and with McClernand at Arkansas Post, such support was not possible.

While Grant sorted things out in Memphis, McClernand enjoyed a measure of success. The troops left their transports on January 9. In advance of the troops was the naval support under Admiral David D. Porter. Ironclads *Louisville*, *De Kalb*, and *Cincinnati* pounded the fort on the January 10 as the infantry approached the defense perimeter. The next day the fleet again took on the defenses of the fort, and in the afternoon the infantry assaulted the Confederate works. Shortly after 4 p.m., a white flag appeared, and the garrison surrendered. At a time when Washington needed good news, McClernand presented the capture of Arkansas Post.

Grant remained unsatisfied, however. "…[U]nless there is some object not visible at this distance," Grant wrote McClernand on January 13, "your forces should return to Milliken's Bend, or some point convenient for operating on Vicksburg." That same day, he wrote his subordinate, Major General James B. McPherson, "It is my present intention to command the expedition down the river in person." Both Sherman and Porter encouraged Grant to come command

---

13. Ibid.
14. Quoted in Edwin C. Bearss, *Vicksburg is the Key*, (Dayton: Morningside House, Inc., 1985) 408-409.

in person. Since McClernand was second in rank in the department, Grant concluded to move to Milliken's Bend. This he did on January 29. It was a move that
did not meet with McClernand's approval.[15]

Although it might have seemed prudent to return to Memphis and go into
winter quarters, Grant refused to do so. In spite of the incessant rains, high water,
and ever-present mud, he was determined to keep pressure on Pemberton and his
Mississippi command.

One final tug-of-war with McClernand remained. With his forces stationed
at Milliken's Bend, he launched his final test of command with Grant. Referring
to orders issued from Grant's headquarters, he protested that they properly
should have come through him. "One thing is certain, two generals cannot command this army..." he wrote Grant on January 30.[16]

Grant reacted quickly. He issued General Orders No. 13 on the same day,
noting in a letter to Washington that "I do not have confidence in his [McCler-
nand's] ability as a soldier to conduct an expedition of this magnitude successfully." He immediately assigned McClernand command of the XIII Corps. McClernand protested twice to Grant, but to no avail. Eventually he capitulated,
requesting that his protest be forwarded to Halleck in Washington.[17]

Grant's main problem remained the same: how to get to the high, dry ground
in the rear (east) of Vicksburg. During the early months of 1863, he tried no less
than four "experiments," as he later called them, in an effort to gain that dry ground.

The first attempt involved finishing the canal started by Williams that previous summer. Sherman was given the task, but it was doomed from the start. The
channel of the Mississippi flowed on the eastern shore of the river, across from
the entrance of the canal. No matter how hard Sherman's troops worked, the
Mississippi was not going to change its course to flow through the canal.

In addition, those attempting to dig the canal were under occasional fire from
Confederate guns at Vicksburg. Sherman himself did not believe the project
would succeed. The rains continued, the Mississippi flooded, and nothing seemed
to work. In spite of President Lincoln's belief in the project, Grant finally gave up
on the canal project.

The second attempt to bypass Vicksburg involved an ambitious project to cut
a passage through several bayous on the Louisiana side of the Mississippi and
eventually join the Red River. With the Red emptying into the Mississippi at the
southwestern corner of the state, Grant would be better positioned to effect his
desired landfall on the eastern bank; he would also be in a position to cooperate
with and support Banks.

---

15. *OR*, ser. I, vol. XVII, pt 1, 559.
16. *OR*, ser. I, vol. XXIV, pt 3, 19.
17. *OR*, ser. I, vol. XXIV, pt 1, 11-13.

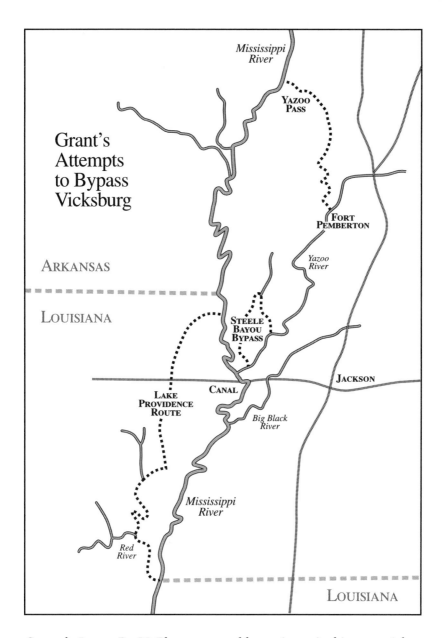

Grant's
Attempts
to Bypass
Vicksburg

General James B. McPherson, an able engineer in his own right, was assigned the project. A small steamer was hauled overland to Lake Providence, from which McPherson was to find his route to the Red River. The swampy lowland proved to be an insurmountable obstacle, however, as McPherson's troops were forced to cut their way through huge tree stumps in the bayous. After several weeks of backbreaking effort, this attempt was also called off.

While Grant was trying his various means of bypassing Vicksburg, the Federal Navy was mounting operations of its own. In early February, the ram *Queen of the West* passed the Vicksburg batteries and, after sparring with a Confederate steamer, sailed down the Mississippi. It then marauded Southern shipping on the Red River until she ran aground and had to be abandoned.

The Confederates moved quickly and claimed the prize. Admiral Porter sent the ironclad *Indianola* down the river, where much to his chagrin, she too was bested and was abandoned. Porter eventually won the battle, however, when he sent the ironclad version of the "Quaker gun," a barge outfitted to look like a massive ironclad, down the river. The Confederates aboard *Queen of the West* encountered this Quaker monster and fled. When news reached the salvage crew working on *Indianola*, they panicked and blew up the ironclad.

While Grant's efforts moved towards finding a way around the seemingly impregnable bluffs along the eastern shore of the Yazoo River, Pemberton continued to build up his forces in the Department of Mississippi and East Louisiana. In early March, he informed President Davis that he had 20,000 men available for Vicksburg, and 15,000 for Port Hudson. His most pressing need was for more heavy guns with which to defend the river. As noted previously, Davis had ordered Major General Carter Stevenson's reinforced division from Bragg's army in Tennessee for duty with Pemberton in Mississippi. But theater commander Johnston in turn ordered the majority of Pemberton's cavalry, under Van Dorn, to Tennessee in January 1863. As events unfolded in April and May of 1863, this lack of cavalry support would leave Pemberton without the "eyes" he needed to combat the aggressive raids that would be forthcoming.

Grant turned his attention to the eastern bank of the Mississippi. Pemberton's defense line north of the city prevented the movement of Federal transports up the Yazoo River to dry ground. If a route that would enable Grant to ferry troops down the Yazoo could be found, he would at last be in a viable position to threaten Vicksburg.

Lieutenant Colonel James H. Wilson, a young engineer destined to end the war a major general, found a way to reach the Yazoo. It involved blowing a gap in the levee across from a previous channel of the Mississippi in an area known as Yazoo Pass, entering Moon Lake, and gaining the Coldwater and Tallahatchie rivers to the Yazoo and down to Vicksburg. This route had a chance to work.

The levee was blown up on February 3. This time the Mississippi did scour out a channel some 200 feet wide; after some cleanup, reaching Vicksburg was possible.

The Confederates knew of this route. Naval Commander Isaac Brown had warned several weeks earlier that Yazoo Pass still remained unblocked and could allow the enemy to reach the Yazoo River. Davis and Pemberton exchanged messages regarding this exposed point, but they moved too late.

The Federals, on the other hand, moved quickly. On February 6, Grant began coordinating efforts between his army forces and the Navy. By February 12, five miles of Yazoo Pass had been cleared of felled trees. Nine days later, the route to the Coldwater River had been opened.

The Federal invasion force of 4,500 faced a tortuous 350-mile trip. Overhanging tree limbs battered the Federal ships. Felled trees had to be removed. Yet, by March 11, the force had reached a bend in the Tallahatchie River, a scant few miles from its goal, the Yazoo. Waiting for it, however, was a "fort" named Pemberton, situated on a strip of the only dry ground in the area and composed of cotton bales and sandbags. Its armament, while not overpowering, was enough to stop the effort in its tracks. Three times the flotilla tried to pass; three times it failed. With some difficulty, the Federal forces turned themselves around and returned to Yazoo Pass.

Major General William W. Loring was the defender Fort Pemberton. During the repulse, Loring had shouted to his men, "Give 'em blizzards, boys!" earning him the nom de guerre of "Old Blizzards". During the defense, however, Loring had also badgered Pemberton with requests for additional men and guns. Pemberton, realizing that the limited dry land near Greenwood (near where Fort Pemberton was located) precluded sending additional forces, had several sharp exchanges with his subordinate. Loring had a history of defying superior officers, having provoked Thomas J. "Stonewall" Jackson into submitting his resignation after problems with Loring in late January 1862. The difficulties at Fort Pemberton would augur future problems between Pemberton and Loring.

Coincidentally, as Grant was losing confidence in the Yazoo Pass expedition, his attention was being drawn to a fourth "experiment," this one much closer to Vicksburg. On the March 13, Grant complained to McPherson (trying to wind up his aborted operations on Lake Providence) that "The Yazoo expedition seems to move slowly." Rather than redirect McPherson's troops towards Yazoo Pass, he moved a division of Sherman's troops to Steele's Bayou in preparation for cutting a route to the Sunflower River, which also emptied into the Yazoo. To get 20 miles up the Yazoo behind the Confederate fortifications guarding the river, Grant's forces would have to travel more than 200 miles.[18]

The problems inherent with the Steele's Bayou expedition were very similar to those faced by the others. The channel, which started out wide and deep, quickly narrowed upon entering Deer Creek. Trees had to be cut down and cleared out of the channel, and Porter's fleet was bedeviled by a plague of swamp

---

18. *OR*, ser. I, vol. XXIV, pt 3, 105.

animals, snakes, lizards, and cockroaches. Chimneys were toppled by over-hanging limbs.

As the Rolling Fork, a connector to the Sunflower River came into sight, the fleet ran into an obstacle that would prove to be insurmountable. The channel was blocked by growth, and the Confederates were landing infantry to contest the passage. Sherman had to throw together a hastily prepared rescue force, which eventually staved off disaster for his friend Porter. Without room to maneuver, Porter's ironclads backed their way to water in which they could turn around. The effort lasted less than a week and had accomplished little other than putting part of Porter's fleet in significant danger.

In spite of the failures of Yazoo Pass and Steele's Bayou expeditions, they did have an impact on Pemberton's operations. As troops continued to be centered in Mississippi and Vicksburg in particular, Pemberton worked on building his supply lines. The passing of the batteries by the *Queen of the West*, and its impact on Red River traffic, cut into supplies flowing up the Mississippi to Vicksburg. With the rail system in northern Mississippi rapidly falling into disrepair, Pemberton had hoped to use the water system to float supplies down to the Vicksburg area. But with Porter pushing forces almost to Greenwood as well as the Big Sunflower River, the hauling of supplies by river was curtailed.

Grant's detractors argue that the four failed "experiments" reflect indecision and an inability to solve the problem of getting around Vicksburg's defenses. Grant himself saw the efforts as a logical progression inevitably leading to the final decision to run the batteries and cross the Mississippi below the city. Others argue that the failed efforts added to Pemberton's growing indecision. He had been slow to react to warnings of the Yazoo Pass expedition, and now had multiple possible actions to worry about.

By the end of March, Grant had seemingly exhausted his options. Pemberton remained secure and dry on the bluffs of Vicksburg, while Grant's forces were surrounded by water no matter which direction they looked. Unless something different could be found, Grant's only option, it seemed, was to mass his troops and assault the same seemingly impregnable positions that Sherman had failed against that previous December.

A reading of Grant's memoirs, written well after the war, leads to the conclusion that sometime during the winter, he contemplated running the batteries in order to land his infantry on the eastern bank of the Mississippi south of Vicksburg. He kept silent about the plan for two reasons. First, his distrust of the northern press, and their likelihood of leaking vital information, was well established by that time. Second, as long as there was a chance of success with any of his four "experiments," he would withhold the plan to pass the batteries.

As late as March 22, 1863, the specter of assaulting Pemberton's stronghold at Snyder's Bluff loomed in Grant's mind. Such an assault, he wrote to Banks, would "be attended with much loss, but I think it can be done." He even went so far as to offer Banks the use of one corps from his army for holding Confederates at Port Hudson. In any event, an attack on Snyder's Bluff could not "possibly take place under two weeks, if so soon." Historian Bruce Catton notes, "If Grant had a new plan it was time to try it. He had been on the river for two months, and Vicksburg was no nearer falling now than when he came."[19]

With the four expeditions to bypass Vicksburg ending in failure, Grant moved to consolidate his forces and bring them back to Milliken's Bend and Young's Point. Pemberton, by now, was clearly guessing what his opponent was doing. Diversionary raids near Greenville, Mississippi (100 miles north of Vicksburg), by forces sent upriver from Young's Point and cavalry operations in northern Mississippi further muddied the picture for Pemberton. Finally, simple river traffic heading back towards Memphis left Pemberton thinking that Grant was pulling out and heading north, either to consolidate at Memphis or to reinforce Rosecrans in Middle Tennessee.

Confederate correspondence between Pemberton, Johnston, and Davis in early April reinforce this point. On April 3, Johnston denied Pemberton's request for the return of Van Dorn's cavalry, claiming that Pemberton had what he most needed: infantry (in the form of Stevenson's division) from the army in Tennessee. On that same day, Pemberton informed Johnston that it appeared that Grant was moving to reinforce Rosecrans.[20]

Johnston was quick to pick up on this news, informing Pemberton on the April 5 that, should the reports be true, the very troops Pemberton "most needed" (Stevenson's division) should be returned to Tullahoma immediately. Pemberton further muddied the waters that day, noting that 17 carloads of troops supposedly moved through Memphis on April 2. On April 7, Davis wired Pemberton directly, inquiring as to available troops that could be moved to Tullahoma.[21]

Johnston spent a tumultuous March with Bragg's army in Tennessee. Dissension among his officers had led to the calls for Bragg's dismissal. Johnston was a logical replacement, and Secretary of War Seddon (who had become Secretary in November of 1862) and President Davis had done everything other than directly order Johnston to take the job. Johnston, however, would not order Bragg's removal. After spending ten days in Richmond, while Johnston filled in, Bragg returned to find his wife seriously ill. Johnston used the illness as a further excuse to keep Bragg in command. In spite of all this, however, Johnston was

---

19. *OR*, ser. I, vol. XXIV, pt 3, 126, Catton, *Grant Moves South*, 387.
20. *OR*, ser. I, vol. XXIV, pt 3, 712.
21. *OR*, ser. I, vol. XXIV, pt 3, 714, 719.

bored. "For more than three months," he wrote in March, "I have been doing next to nothing."[22]

The Confederate position at Hayne's Bluff would not be attacked. Instead, Grant determined to pass transports and supplies past the Vicksburg defenses, hook up with the base McClernand had established at New Carthage, and cross to the first available ground south of Vicksburg. His target was Grand Gulf.

Grant called for additional transports from up the river and informed Halleck in Washington, as well as Porter and the Navy, of his plans. Grant put his plans in place none too soon, for the Northern press was putting pressure on Washington to relieve him. Secretary of War Edwin Stanton sent newspaperman Charles A. Dana to the Mississippi to spy and report back on Grant. Grant, however, skillfully parried Stanton's thrust and turned Dana into an ally.

April 16 was set as the night for running the batteries. Porter put together a twelve-ship convoy and rigged to minimize possible damage. Cotton bales were placed on the decks for protection. Coal barges were lashed to the transports. The coal would be used for operations further down the river. The movement was timed to coincide with a gala ball to be held in Vicksburg. Grant hoped to catch the Confederates napping.

The Confederates, however, were not surprised. Great fires were lit on both sides of the Mississippi, making the passage look like a noontime event. The ball was closed with haste, and the batteries on the bluffs opened fire. As it was, the passage took two and a half hours to complete; only one transport and a number of barges were lost. Grant had his transports south of Vicksburg.

Grant created two major diversions to continue befuddling Pemberton once the transports had run the batteries. He kept Sherman in place in front of Hayne's Bluff; even though the Union general had now discounted a frontal assault, his counterpart, Pemberton, could not. More importantly, he sent an obscure cavalry colonel, Benjamin Grierson, on a raid that set up the entire forthcoming campaign.

Grierson's orders were to prey on the railroad system in Mississippi and disrupt Pemberton's communications. A successful raid would also tie up vital forces in the interior of the state. Pemberton would argue after the fact that Johnston's stripping his department of cavalry forced him to react to Grierson's raid by deploying infantry, which hampered his ability to concentrate forces once Grant crossed the Mississippi.

Grierson left La Grange, Tennessee, on April 17, the day after the transports ran the batteries at Vicksburg. He commanded 1,700 men in his attacking column. At best, 1,500 Confederate troopers were available to contest his advance.

---

22. Joseph E. Johnston to Louis T. Wigfall, March 8, 1863, quoted in Craig Symonds, *Joseph E. Johnston: A Civil War Biography*, (New York: W. W. Norton & Co., 1992) 196-201.

Four days into the raid and some 70 miles south of La Grange, Grierson used the 2nd Iowa Cavalry to create a diversion that would spring him deeper into the heart of Mississippi. The 2nd Iowa moved to the east, drew off pursuit, and worked its way north towards the Tennessee border.

The 2nd Iowa's efforts were a success, and the regiment retreated back to La Grange, arriving there on April 26. The chase to La Grange did the task intended, drawing off most of the Confederate cavalry in the area.

Grierson continued to ride south after the Iowa detachment left on April 21. The next day saw another flurry of activity from Pemberton, who was trying to manage the entire state of Mississippi, keep an eye on Grant, and deal with Grierson from his headquarters in Jackson. He dispatched Loring to Meridian and complained to Johnston that his lack of cavalry was hampering his ability to react to Grierson's raid. And, more ominously, a dispatch from Brigadier General John Bowen, commanding at Grand Gulf, warned that the Federal fleet had anchored at Judge Perkins'.

On April 24, Grierson struck the Southern Mississippi Railroad at Newton Station, some 40 miles east of Jackson. The Southern Mississippi was the east-west rail line connecting Vicksburg and Jackson with points east. Railroad track was ripped up, and several locomotives and supply trains destroyed; Grierson continued on. At one point, he swung within 30 miles of Grand Gulf before moving south in a desperate run for the Union lines at Baton Rouge, Louisiana. He arrived there safely on May 2, having kept Pemberton's attention focused on the interior of the state of Mississippi. Grierson later claimed to have kept as many as 20,000 troops tied up during his raid.

Grant intended to attack the Confederate forces at Grand Gulf and land forces there. Grand Gulf was a defensive bastion just south of where the Big Black River emptied into the Mississippi. It had been under construction for only six weeks and was commanded by Bowen. On April 29, Porter's fleet moved in and could not silence the Confederate batteries. Even though McClernand stood poised to land his troops, Grant had to call off the landing.

In the meantime, McPherson was marching his corps down the western bank of the Mississippi to join McClernand. Grant determined to move further down and land at Bruinsburg, which he did on April 30. After months of attempting to find a way to get at Vicksburg, Grant could finally state in his memoirs "I was on dry ground on the same side of the river with the enemy." Sherman, with one-third of the army, still threatened Vicksburg at Snyder's Bluff, doing such a good job of threatening attack that Major General Carter Stevenson was convinced the major Federal effort was going to take place there. Grierson was raiding through central Mississippi, and McClernand and McPherson were crossing the

Mississippi. At a time when Pemberton needed to concentrate to meet Grant's invading forces, his troops were instead spread over the state of Mississippi.

Even though he was across the Mississippi, Grant was still in some jeopardy. Bowen had already scouted the area near Port Gibson, looking for defensive positions, and began his preparations to resist Grant's invasion. Pemberton continued to run his command from Jackson, and although he tried to get an understanding of the overall situation, he remained confused. Infantry was still scattered over a good portion of Mississippi, and Loring had troops trapped on the wrong side of the railroad cut near Newton Station.

On May 1, McClernand's forces clashed with Bowen on the roads that led from the Mississippi to Port Gibson. Outnumbered three to one, Bowen made use of the deep ravines and tangled thickets that comprised the ground between Bruinsburg and Port Gibson to delay Grant's movements as long as possible. The inevitable occurred, however, and, by May 2, Bowen's forces had retreated back through Port Gibson and north of the Bayou Pierre. Although losses were approximately even, the fact that Grant's crossing could not be stopped set the tone for the remainder of the campaign. Pemberton had, in his theater of operations, more troops than Grant. At Port Gibson, however, as would be the case throughout the campaign, Grant managed to bring to the battlefield more troops than Pemberton.

Pemberton struggled to understand the magnitude of the situation. He maintained his behind-the-scenes style of command, directing troops to Port Gibson as quickly as possible. He professed himself pleased with Bowen's effort but then criticized his subordinate when he retreated on May 3 behind the Big Black. That he could have believed that Bowen's 8,000 men should have been able to further resist Grant's 24,000 shows how confusing the situation was to Pemberton. He asked for additional cavalry to protect his rail lines (and free up infantry performing garrison duty). He also kept Davis in Richmond, and Johnston in Tullahoma appraised of the situation. From Joseph Johnston came the following gratuitous advice: "If Grant's army lands on this side of the river, the safety of Mississippi depends on beating it. For that object you should unite your whole force."[23]

The loss at Port Gibson also necessitated the evacuation of Grand Gulf. Bowen and the remainder of the Confederate forces fell back behind the Big Black River and took up defensive positions there. Grant had an established beachhead and a safe base from which to mount his offensive.

It was at this point that Grant claimed to have made his famous decision to cut loose from his base of supplies and move inland. Although Grant main-

---

23. *OR,* ser. I, vol. XXIV, pt 3, 808.

tained a strong link with Grand Gulf throughout the campaign, detailing precious troops to guard the vital supply line, there is little doubt that his troops did obtain substantial quantities of food and forage from the surrounding countryside prior to establishing siege operations. Although Grant could find food and forage locally, ammunition supplies had to be moved inland from Grand Gulf.

Now more than ever, it was important for Grant to seize the initiative and maintain it. Thus he made one of his more bold strategic decisions. Rather than confront Pemberton's defense line along the Big Black River and force the fight for Vicksburg immediately, he chose to strike inland and break the Mississippi Central Railroad between Edward's and Clinton, threaten or capture the Mississippi capital of Jackson, and pivot his army 90 degrees and approach Vicksburg from the east.

Pemberton dispersed his army in defensive positions behind the Big Black River. He believed that the logical place for Grant to attempt to cross the river would be at Big Black Bridge at the Southern Mississippi Railroad crossing. His orders during the first week of May reflect a skillful handling of his divisions as he side-stepped his defensive line further to the east to counter the movements of Grant. Historian Edwin Bearss notes: "After evaluating these reports, some of which conflicted, Pemberton decided that his May 7 estimate of the situation was correct—Grant's immediate objectives were the railroad and Big Black Bridge. Pemberton's deductive powers cannot be faulted because, until the evening of May 12, Grant's army was striking toward these places."[24]

McPherson's Corps took the lead, and only a single brigade under Brigadier General John Gregg stood between Grant's army and Clinton. Pemberton moved his command back to Vicksburg once Grant had established himself south of the Big Black. The Confederate commander continued preparations for defensive positions astride the Big Black River, but the initiative clearly rested with Grant.

McPherson clashed with Gregg just outside of the town of Raymond on May 12. Gregg took a position behind Fourteen Mile Creek and fashioned an aggressive flanking attack. The Confederates enjoyed initial success until the overwhelming Federal numbers took their toll. By mid afternoon, the battle was over, Gregg's brigade was in retreat, and the roads to Clinton and Jackson lay open. Grant now turned his army toward Jackson. On May 13, McPherson marched from Raymond to Clinton, Sherman passed through Raymond and then pushed on to Mississippi Springs; McPherson bluffed an attack on Edward's and then closed on Raymond.

---

24. Edwin C. Bearss, *Grant Strikes A Fatal Blow*, (Dayton: Morningside House, Inc., 1985) 477.

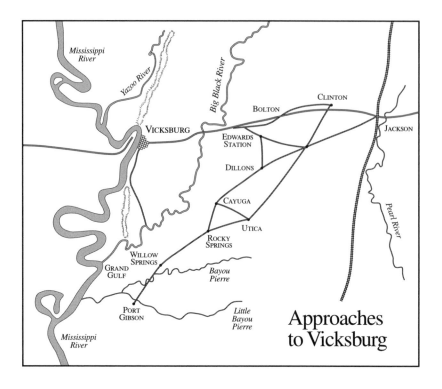

Approaches to Vicksburg

There was, however, a new Confederate commander in Jackson. On May 9 Secretary of War Seddon ordered Joseph E. Johnston to go to Mississippi and take command in person. He was also ordered to take 3,000 troops from Bragg's army with him. The manner in which Seddon's message is worded is curious (and one can only wonder as to the degree of sarcasm intended): "Proceed at once to Mississippi and take chief command of the forces, giving to those in the field, as far as practicable, the encouragement and benefit of your personal attention." Johnston replied, somewhat ominously, "I shall go at once, although unfit for field service."[25]

The first week in May also sowed the seeds of controversy concerning whether Pemberton should hold Vicksburg at all costs. On May 7, President Davis noted the importance of holding both Vicksburg and Port Hudson in order to maintain control of a segment of the Mississippi. Pemberton passed along to Major General Franklin Gardner, commanding at Port Hudson, "President says both places must be held."

Johnston very much disagreed with the sentiments of Davis and Pemberton. He believed in concentrating Confederate forces in Mississippi and avoiding the

25. *OR,* ser. I, vol. XXIV, pt 1, 215.

protection of too many "valuable locations." In a letter written to his brother Beverly, he spoke of Pemberton: "...our general (don't mention it) can't comprehend that by attempting to defend at all valuable points at once he exposes his troops to being beaten everywhere." He concluded with a rather odd statement, given his clearly defined command relationship with Pemberton: "I have urged him to concentrate to fight Grant, with no hope that he will regard a suggestion of mine, & at this distance can't give orders." It is strange that Johnston considered himself incapable of giving Pemberton orders.[26]

It was a long rail trip from Tullahoma to Jackson; Johnston arrived May 13. He telegraphed Richmond upon his arrival "I arrived this evening finding the enemy's force between this place and General Pemberton, cutting off communication. I am too late." [27]

In spite of his obvious dejection at the situation he faced, Johnston looked to Pemberton to generate a consolidation of forces. Late in the evening of May 13, he directed Pemberton:

> I have lately arrived, and learn that Major-General Sherman is between us, with four divisions, at Clinton. It is important to reestablish communications, that you may be re-enforced. If practicable, come up on his rear at once. To beat such a detachment, would be of immense value. The troops here could co-operate. All the strength you can quickly assemble should be brought. Time is all-important.

Pemberton received the message early on May 14.[28]

Johnston had approximately 7,500 men at Jackson, with more reinforcements expected to arrive daily. The morning of May 14 dawned with a pouring rain; in spite of his order to Pemberton to move to Clinton to attack Sherman and his promise that "troops here could co-operate," Johnston began the evacuation of Jackson and moved away from Clinton and northeast toward Canton. General Gregg was left in Jackson with two brigades to slow the advance of Sherman and McPherson. Given the disparity in troop numbers, the Confederate defense lasted but a short time. Jubilant Federal troops entered the capital, and manufacturing and industrial locations were put to the torch.

Johnston's dispatch to Pemberton on May 13 was sent in triplicate, and a spy delivered one of those copies to Grant, who immediately ordered his troops under McClernand, to move to the railroad and make sure he would be between Pemberton and Johnston. McPherson marched posthaste to Clinton; Sherman's corps remained in Jackson on May 15 destroying the railroads radiating out from

26. Gilbert Govan and James W. Livingood, *A Different Valor*, (1956; reprint, Westport: Greenwood Press, 1974) 195-196, Johnston to Beverly Johnston quoted from Ibid., 196, *OR*, ser. I, vol. XXIV, pt 3, 842.

27. *OR*, ser. I, vol. XXIV, pt 1, 215.

28. *OR*, ser. I, vol. XXIV, pt 3, 870.

the city. Johnston, however, retreated away from Vicksburg, Pemberton was placed in an extremely difficult position.

With Johnston effectively out of the way, Grant turned on Pemberton. Pemberton sent a reply to Johnston on May 14, noting he was moving forward to comply with his commander's orders to move on Clinton. He marched with 23,000 troops and left 10,000 men behind to defend Vicksburg. Pemberton remained uneasy about some of the lower fords on the Big Black. Still convinced that his primary role was to protect Vicksburg, Pemberton closed: "I do not think you fully comprehend the position that Vicksburg will be left in…"[29]

That same day, May 14, Johnston sent another message to his subordinate to inform him of the evacuation of Jackson and his retreat away from Vicksburg. It is indicative of the communication problems between the two Confederate forces that Pemberton did not receive the message until 5:45 p.m. on May 16 while retreating from Champion Hill to his Big Black position. In the note, Johnston encouraged concentration of forces. "I am anxious to see a force assembled that may be able to inflict a heavy blow upon the enemy," he wrote. But Johnston chose not to move toward Pemberton, leaving the initiative to his subordinate. Until the eventual surrender of Vicksburg, Johnston continually looked to Pemberton to set the strategies for the campaign.[30]

Pemberton had moved forward on May 14 from Edwards Depot with the intent of complying with Johnston's order. He evidently became concerned upon finding out that the "detachment" described by Johnston was Sherman's corps and chose to halt his command at noon that day and call a council of war.

There were three options available to Pemberton: proceed as planned to Clinton, remain at Edward's and await Grant's approach, or move on Grant's supply line towards Raymond at a place called Dillon's Plantation. The record is cloudy on exactly what was discussed or decided, a possible reflection on the futility of councils of war. Pemberton apparently argued for the continued defense of Vicksburg. He suggests in his report on the campaign that a majority favored continuing the move on Clinton. Stevenson and Loring favored the move to Dillon's. A staff officer in attendance, writing in July 1863, suggested that no officers present were in favor of the move to Clinton.

Why Pemberton chose to move on Dillon's may never be fully understood. Because his junior officers were in favor of an advance of any sort and because the Johnston move to Clinton was impractical in his eyes, he determined to move on the perceived opportunity at Dillon's. In the early evening of May 14, Pemberton wrote Johnston informing him of his decision.

---

29. Ibid., 877.
30. Ibid., 877-878.

Pemberton's response reached Johnston early on May 15. Historian Ed Bearss notes that Johnston "saw red" upon receiving the message. He realized that the decision would mean additional hours of delay and increase the difficulties joining their respective forces. Johnston's arguments, written in his memoirs, come across as somewhat self serving in light of the fact that, once ensconced on the road to Canton, he moved in a half-hearted manner only, and not until May 17.[31]

Johnston immediately countermanded Pemberton's decision in a dispatch written early on May 15. Like so many of their messages, this one took another day to reach Pemberton. "The only mode by which we can unite is by moving directly to Clinton," Johnston wrote. Even though he did not give his subordinate a direct order, the stage was still set for the decisive battle of Champion Hill.[32]

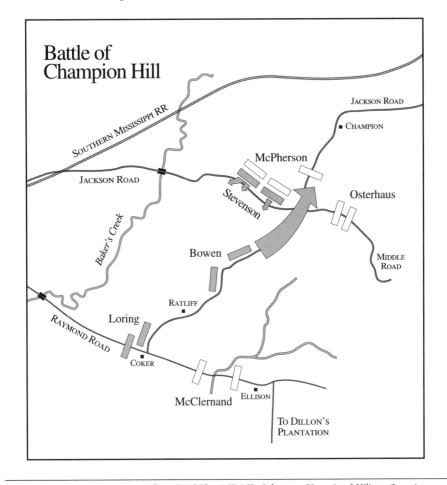

31. Edwin C. Bearss, *Grant Strikes a Fatal Blow*, 567-568, Johnston, *Narrative of Military Operations*, 179.
32. *OR*, ser. I, vol. XXIV, pt 3, 882.

Grant's forces spent the day of May 15 closing in on Pemberton. McPherson's and McClernand's corps took to the roads early in the morning. Half of Sherman's corps remained in Jackson to finish the destruction of Confederate property and to keep an eye on Johnston. One of McClernand's divisions occupied Clinton and then turned west and camped at Bolton. Two divisions took positions at Chapel Hill on the Middle Road, and one of McPherson's and one of Sherman's occupied the Raymond-Edwards Road. McPherson marched west on the Jackson-Vicksburg Road.

Whereas the Federal marches were orderly, quick, and timely, the same could not be said for Pemberton's effort. His orders for an early march failed almost immediately. Loring, Bowen, and Stevenson were to take the Raymond Road as far as Mrs. Ellison's home, at which point they would turn to the south and move to Dillon's Plantation. Provisions, which should have been available, were not, and the march did not start until 1:00 p.m. A bridge over Baker's Creek on the Raymond Road that had been assumed to be intact was in fact gone, and the army had to detour around Champion Hill in order to regain the Raymond Road.

McClernand's corps made first contact with Pemberton on May 16, encountering Confederate forces of Loring on the Raymond Road. It was obvious that the Confederates were not going to make their turnoff to move south without fighting a major battle. Worse, early that same day, Pemberton received Johnston's message from May 15, in which he was told to continue moving his army to Clinton. Rather than developing the Federal forces in his front or falling back to his defense line at Edward's Depot, the bewildered Pemberton attempted to turn his army around, march back to Edward's, take the road north to Brownsville and bypass Grant in order to join Johnston. Thus, the tail of the marching column became the head and the head the tail. The wagon train had to turn around and by midmorning reported itself on the Brownsville Road.

Grant was not about to let Pemberton get away. McClernand developed his sector on the Raymond Road cautiously, with Loring contesting his front. Strong skirmish lines were thrown forward, but little of any significant nature occurred. The same was true of McClernand's advance along the Middle Road.

It was left to McPherson's corps, along with a single division of McClernand's, moving forward along the Jackson Road to pin Pemberton's forces in position and bring on the engagement. Stevenson was in the process of trying to turn the left of the Confederate column around when three Federal divisions deployed in his front. Stephen D. Lee had extended the Confederate line to protect the left flank, but there were too many Federal troops in the sector and Lee was flanked. As the Confederates fell back, Pemberton's army found itself in severe danger.

The early contact on the Middle and Raymond Roads had led Pemberton to believe that the main battle would be fought on the right. He could not have been more wrong. As it was he almost delayed too long in forwarding troops to the left. He was not helped when his initial order to Bowen to move to the left was returned via courier with the request to make the order peremptory. The courier had to return to Pemberton's headquarters, receive the command to make the order peremptory, and return to Bowen. At this point, it was past 1:00 p.m. and Stevenson was in danger of destruction.

About an hour later, as Lee struggled to hold the Jackson Road, the two brigades in Bowen's division swept forward over Champion Hill and drove Federal forces within sight of the Champion House. A major hole had been punched in the Federal offensive, but there were no reserves to back it up. Meanwhile, Pemberton ordered Loring to begin moving to the left, leaving a skeletal force in place to hold against McClernand. Loring obstinately chose to remain in place, worried that an attack by McClernand would turn the Confederate right.

More Federals were arriving down the Jackson Road. A combination of Brigadier General Marcellus Crocker's division, 16 pieces of artillery, and the hot Mississippi sun stopped, then forced back Bowen's advance. Brigadier General Peter Osterhaus was finally permitted to move forward along the Middle Road, and his movement threatened Bowen even further. With that, the Confederate line collapsed. There were two crossings over Baker's Creek on which Pemberton's forces could retreat. The northern Jackson Road bridge, however, was under Federal control, leaving the Raymond Road crossing as the only means across Baker's Creek left to Pemberton.

Loring was ordered to hold the Raymond Road and protect the retreating Confederates. In the midst of the retreat, Loring decided he was unable to cross Baker's Creek and turned his division to the southwest. An enemy advance down the eastern side of Baker's Creek had, in Loring's estimation, made a crossing too dangerous. Loring moved away from Edwards and eventually swung back to the east, marched to Jackson, and joined the forces under Johnston.

The Battle of Champion Hill (called by Confederates the Battle of Baker's Creek) was Pemberton's first real test as a battlefield commander, and he did not perform well. Although Johnston's confusing and untimely communications put Pemberton at a disadvantage, Pemberton's own indecisiveness over how best to counter Grant was equally harmful, and his decision to turn his command around while in contact with Grant was his poorest decision.

Pemberton was poorly served by Loring. The friction that had manifested itself during the defense of Fort Pemberton, continued on to the Champion Hill battlefield. Whether the decision to move away from Pemberton's army and towards Johnston was made deliberately is not clear. That there was a decided lack of harmony between the two, however, is not in doubt.[33]

Champion Hill was the decisive battle of the Vicksburg campaign. Grant forced Pemberton to retreat back toward the Vicksburg defenses and away from Johnston. Confederate losses left few options for Pemberton. Grant lost 2,400 men killed, wounded, and missing. Pemberton lost 3,800, of which 2,400 alone were missing (most of which were probably captured). In addition, Loring's division of more than 7,000 men was lost to Pemberton. Finally, 27 cannon were left on the field.

Pemberton fell back to his next position, 10 miles closer to Vicksburg where the road and railroad crossed the Big Black River just east of Bovina. Defensive works had been thrown up on the eastern side of the river, and one brigade of fresh troops along with Bowen's veterans manned the works. Pemberton was uncertain about Loring's whereabouts and hoped to hold his May 17 position long enough for his division commander to rejoin the army.

The resulting Battle of Big Black Bridge was scarcely a battle. The fresh troops manning the defense line were exceedingly unreliable; the remainder were exhausted and dispirited. Federal troops under McClernand moved into position, and the Confederate works fell. This time, 1,750 irreplaceable troops were captured, along with another 18 cannon. In two days, Pemberton had lost more than 4,000 troops captured and 45 cannon lost, plus associated ammunition and small arms.

The Big Black River presented enough of an obstacle to the Federals to allow Pemberton to retreat to the defenses of Vicksburg. With the bridged in flames and alternate crossings too far away, Grant was unable to close quickly enough. As McClernand's troops trudged towards the city, Sherman's men crossed upstream at Bridgeport. Sherman, who had disagreed with Grant's strategies throughout the campaign, said to his commander on May 19 when they arrived in front of Vicksburg that what he had just witnessed since the landing at Bruinsburg was "one of the greatest campaigns in history" and "whether [Vicksburg was] captured or not, this was a complete and successful campaign." Grant could take justifiable pride in the accomplishments of his army.[34]

Delays in communication, as well as lack of focus and control, continued to plague the Confederate command. May 16, the day of the Battle of Champion Hill, saw Johnston remain quietly in camp on the Canton Road. An early morning dispatch to Richmond noted Pemberton's planned move to Dillon's, but Johnston neither censured Pemberton's choice nor made a move to effect a

---

33. For examples of the Champion Hill friction between the two, see Bearss, *Grant Strikes a Fatal Blow*, 583, 620.

34. U.S. Grant, *Personal Memoirs of U.S. Grant*, (1885; reprint, New York: Da Capo Press, 1985) 276.

consolidation of his forces and Pemberton's. President Davis, after receiving Johnston's message, could not "perceive why a junction was not attempted…[which] might have resulted in his [the enemy's] total defeat…" How much of this criticism is directed at Johnston, and how much at Pemberton is unclear.[35]

The same evening another courier arrived, bringing Pemberton's hastily written dispatch announcing his intent to turn his army around and move via the Brownsville Road to join Johnston. Although both officers had had a full day's march to Clinton, and Pemberton had the obvious early start, Johnston did not leave until the morning of May 17. Johnston's delays in moving his force would have left Pemberton facing the same risks regardless of his orders—the risk of his detachment facing most of Grant's army.

Johnston's march of May 17 (the day of the Battle of Big Black Bridge) left him some miles north of Clinton and without word from Pemberton. That evening, a courier dashed all hopes by bringing Pemberton's dispatch announcing the defeat at Champion Hill. To compound matters, local citizens brought word of the Big Black defeat as well. All of Johnston's worst fears were coming to pass.

For Joseph E. Johnston, there was only one logical course of action, and he wrote to Pemberton:

> If Haynes' [Snyder's] Bluff is untenable, Vicksburg is of no value, and cannot be held. If, therefore, you are invested in Vicksburg, you must ultimately surrender. Under such circumstances, instead of losing both troops and place, we must, if possible, save the troops. If it is not too late, evacuate Vicksburg and its dependencies, and march to the northeast.

Pemberton did not receive this message until May 18 while in Vicksburg.[36]

Pemberton called another council of war, and this time the results were much clearer. In his official report, written well after the campaign ended, he described his decision process:

> The evacuation of Vicksburg! It meant the loss of the valuable stores and munitions of war collected for its defense; the fall of Port Hudson; the surrender of the Mississippi River, and the severance of the Confederacy. These were mighty interests, which, had I deemed the evacuation practicable in the sense in which I interpreted General Johnston's instructions, might well have made me hesitate to execute them. I believed it to be in my power to hold Vicksburg. I knew and appreciated the earnest desire of the Government and of the people that it should be held. I knew, perhaps better than any other individual, under all the circumstances, its capacity for defense. As long ago as February 17 last, in a letter addressed to His Excellency the President, I had suggested the possibility of the

---

35. *OR*, ser. I, vol. XXIV, pt 1, 215-216.
36. *OR*, ser. I, vol. XXIV, pt 3, 888.

investment of Vicksburg by land and water, and for that reason the necessity of ample supplies of ammunition as well as of subsistence to stand a siege. My application met his favorable consideration, and additional ammunition was ordered. With proper economy of subsistence and ordnance stores, I knew that I could stand a siege. I had a firm reliance on the desire of the President and of General Johnston to do all that could be done to raise a siege. I felt that every effort would be made, and I believed it would be successful. With these convictions on my own mind, I immediately summoned a council of war composed of all my general officers. I laid before them General Johnston's communication, but desired them to confine the expression of their opinions to the question of practicability. Having obtained their views, the following communication was addressed to General Johnston: "The opinion was unanimously expressed that it was impossible to withdraw the army from this position with such morale and material as to be of further service to the Confederacy. While the council of war was assembled, the guns of the enemy opened on the works, and it was at the same time reported that they were crossing the Yazoo River at Brandon's Ferry, above Snyder's Mill. I have decided to hold Vicksburg as long as is possible, with the firm hope that the Government may yet be aide to assist me in keeping this obstruction to the enemy's free navigation of the Mississippi River. I still conceive it to be the most important point in the Confederacy."[37]

Setting aside the brilliance of the campaign conducted by Grant, which obviously had much to do with the resulting siege, the question remains as to whether Joseph Johnston was correct in his belief that Vicksburg should have been evacuated and Pemberton's army marched to Jackson? Assuming a concentration with Johnston had been effected, what then?

Johnston had strongly urged Pemberton to vacate Vicksburg; Pemberton chose to stay. Grant commanded three army corps totaling nearly 50,000 men. Pemberton had approximately 30,000 men inside the formidable defenses of Vicksburg.

The Federal army was in a jubilant mood. Since the landing at Bruinsburg, Grant's troops had enjoyed one success after another. The enemy manning the Vicksburg defenses had run from the battlefield on two consecutive days. One more push, it seemed, and Vicksburg would fall.

The Confederate works, however, were well laid out. Noted one Federal officer when he saw the Confederate trenches along the Jackson Road: "The approaches to this position were frightful—enough to appall the stoutest heart." Seven miles of earthworks remained to be carried by the Federal troops.[38]

Confederate forces were arrayed in a semi-circle with the flanks of the defense line anchored on the Mississippi. The left of the fortifications, held by the

---

37. *OR*, ser. I, vol. XXIV, pt 1, 272-273.
38. William E. Strong, quoted in Catton, *Grant Moves South*, 450.

fresh division of Major General Martin L. Smith, was enhanced by the dominance of Ft. Hill. Opposite of Smith was the Federal corps of Sherman. In the center, the division of Major General John Forney opposed the troops of McPherson. On the right, the area least worried about by Pemberton, were the dispirited troops of Major General Carter Stevenson. Opposite Stevenson was McClernand's corps. McClernand's forces extended a short distance south of where the Southern Mississippi Railroad entered the defense line. Major General John Bowen's crack division constituted Pemberton's reserve.

Engineer Samuel H. Lockett laid out the Confederate exterior works. As Pemberton's tired and beaten troops filed into Vicksburg after the defeat at Big Black Bridge, Lockett put the divisions of Smith and Forney to work enhancing the previously prepared defense line. Lockett placed his defenses along a series of deep ravines and steep slopes that characterized the area outside Vicksburg. The road network of the day followed the ridge lines, and he placed a series of lunettes, redans, redoubts, and other field works at these critical points. They would be the most likely avenues of approach for Federal troops. A network of rifle pits connected the field fortifications. A stout defense could be generated if Pemberton could muster enough troops to man the trenches.

Grant set May 19 as the day to end the campaign. At 2:00 p.m. the artillery signaled the start of the assault. Troops of all three Federal commands were to sweep forward simultaneously; the high morale of the Federal soldier, it was believed, would easily overcome that of the Confederates. The Federal army, however, had blundered in their estimation of the morale and fighting spirit of the Confederate soldier at Vicksburg.

The attack on May 19 was a failure. Sherman's attack against Smith's line made little headway other than the build up of Union casualties. McPherson and McClernand made minimal efforts, and the Federal command lost nearly one thousand men. Although disappointed with the outcome, Grant prepared to attack again.

The successful repulse steeled the Confederate defenders for the upcoming attack of May 22. Realizing the piece-meal attacks that were made in the first assault would not work if repeated, Grant decided to attack simultaneously along his three corps front. Artillery would soften the Confederate position prior to the attack. Grant had concern about Johnston's presence near Jackson, and was determined to bring to conclusion the campaign as quickly as possible. With Pemberton destroyed, he would turn on Johnston.

Synchronized watches signaled the attack on May 22. Sherman and McPherson pushed forward, reaching the works in several places but were unable to break through. On the Federal left, however, McClernand pushed Confederate troops out of a redoubt and reported success to Grant. Grant later claimed to have doubted McClernand's reports, but sent him a division and ordered Sherman and McPherson to renew their attacks. The Confederates, however, counterattacked and drove McClernand back.

It was now obvious that the garrison in Vicksburg was not going to fall quickly. The assault on May 22 cost Grant more than 3,000 casualties, with the Confederates losses perhaps 500. Grant chose to undertake a siege.

The decision to stand a siege did not come easily to Grant. The specter of Johnston, raising an army near Jackson, worried him. Writing later in his official report, he noted: "It was known that Johnston was at Canton with the force taken by him from Jackson, re-enforced by other troops from the east, and that more were daily reaching him. With the force I then had, a short time must have enabled him to attack me in the rear, and possibly succeeded in raising the siege."[39]

The Federal fleet remained a constant presence for the citizens of Vicksburg, who responded by digging caves in the backside of hills to protect themselves from incoming fire. Morale remained surprisingly good, in spite of the incessant shelling. It became common for citizens to head to Sky Parlor Hill to observe the shelling and the Federal fleet, and people brought telescopes with which to observe. Food was more abundant than it would be later in the campaign, and the citizens of Vicksburg managed to keep their sense of humor intact.

Pemberton was elated with his success, and he and the citizens of Vicksburg looked to Johnston for relief. Pemberton's messages to Johnston, sent repeatedly throughout the latter half of May as well as early June, continually held out the belief that Johnston would attempt to break Grant's lines in some way. Grant held a tenuous line of ridges circling Vicksburg, and while Pemberton had to deal with an enemy in his front, Grant had one in both his front and rear.

"Our men have considerably recovered their morale, but unless a large force is sent to relieve it, Vicksburg must before long fall. I have used every effort to prevent all this, but in vain," Pemberton wrote President Davis on May 19. He informed Johnston the next day of the first assault and requested additional musket caps. "An army will be necessary to relieve Vicksburg, and that quickly. Will it not be sent?" he queried of Johnston. Johnston, however, was falling back on Canton, approximately fifteen miles northeast of Jackson.[40]

Although the siege had just begun, it was taking considerable time to get messages from Pemberton to Johnston, and back again. Pemberton's message of May 19 was received and responded to by Johnston on May 24. In the response,

---

39. *OR*, ser. I, vol. XXIV, pt 1, 55.
40. *OR*, ser. I, vol. XXIV, pt 3, 891-892, 899.

he instructed Loring to forward the needed musket caps. He wrote, however, no news regarding the relief of Pemberton's beleaguered forces.[41]

Vicksburg held out hope for the arrival of Johnston. Local newspapers promised the impending relief of the city by the forces Johnston was collecting near Jackson. One newspaper noted "the undaunted Johnston is at hand."[42]

The recent reverses at Champion Hill and Big Black Bridge had eroded confidence in Pemberton. One of Johnston's generals recently arrived from South Carolina, writing to General P.G.T. Beauregard, noted "Pemberton, of course, is censured by everyone...It is said that the troops were badly handled by Pemberton, and other hard things are said about him." In fairness, however, the general concluded that "This we must expect if an officer is unsuccessful."[43]

Grant viewed the growing army of Johnston with alarm. He believed that the Confederacy would make strong efforts to relieve the siege, and realized that reinforcements would be needed. He worked with General-in-Chief Henry Halleck in Washington to get reinforcements from Missouri and Kentucky, and recalled two divisions of his troops stationed in Memphis.

On May 23, the day after the failed second assault, Pemberton had 29,500 troops in Vicksburg, Loring had 10,000 at Jackson, and Johnston 12,000 at Canton. Grant had approximately 51,000 men confronting Pemberton. Confederate reinforcements were closer to Johnston than those moving to Grant. The window of opportunity to relieve the garrison of Vicksburg would last only several weeks.

Johnston began to position his forces. He faced daunting challenges; the troops arriving came without wagons, and a clear supply situation had yet to be established. There were no stores of supplies in the Jackson area despite the abundance of the surrounding countryside.

Johnston's army was split into two wings, with headquarters in Canton and Jackson. During a visit by Lieutenant Colonel Arthur A.L. Fremantle of the English Coldstream Guards on May 22, Johnston and Fremantle clearly heard the cannon fire that preceded the assault of Grant's army. From Fremantle's report, there appeared to be little in Johnston's actions to relieve Vicksburg. In spite of his orders in April to Pemberton to consolidate his army, Johnston allowed his relief force to be split in two.

In the meantime, Grant had a measure of revenge on corps commander John McClernand. Grant had wanted to relieve his troublesome subordinate after the May 22 assault, but held off doing so. McClernand placed a congrat-

---

41. Ibid., 916.
42. Quoted in Carter III, *The Final Fortress*, 241.
43. *OR*, ser. I, vol. XXIV, pt 3, pg. 920.

ulatory letter to his army corps for their part in the assault, and allowed it to be published in the newspapers. Such an action was a violation of War Department regulations, and gave Grant the opportunity to relieve McClernand. This was done on June 18, and West Pointer Edward O.C. Ord replaced McClernand.

There were two primary approaches by which Johnston could move to Vicksburg. The first would be via Jackson, and follow the Southern Mississippi Railroad. This route would pass the late battlefield of Champion Hill, and the primary point of contention along this route would be the crossing of the Big Black River. Grant had a single brigade of infantry contesting those crossing points.

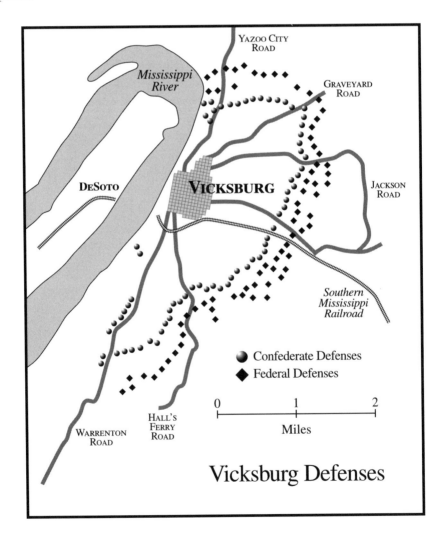

The second route to Vicksburg ran through an area known as the "Mechanicsburg Corridor." This was a strip of land bordered on the south by the Big Black River, on the north by the Yazoo River, and to the west by Vicksburg and the Mississippi River. It ran from northeast to southwest, and followed a ridge road bounded by very fertile Mississippi bottomland. Food to sustain an army could be found along the way. Most importantly, the upper crossings of the Big Black along this route were under Johnston's control.

Grant was aware of the two approaches. Reacting to reports that heavy reinforcements were moving into the area, he sent Major General Frank Blair and 12,000 troops in the direction of Mechanicsburg on May 26. This was a dangerous course of action, because Blair had no support and could possibly be destroyed in detail if Johnston reacted aggressively. Johnston had a force of equal size to Blair's at Canton, and another 10,000 men at Jackson under Loring.

Blair's force reached Mechanicsburg on May 29, and was opposed by little more than Confederate cavalry. Grant, however, began having second thoughts about the safety of Blair's force, and ordered his subordinate to return to Vicksburg that same day. The troops returned safely over the next several days, destroying crops and stores of food along the way.

It was not until the evening of May 30 before Johnston reacted to Blair's presence. That evening he asked Loring to move his troops from Jackson to Canton. He was still unsure of the validity of the information he had received, and was moving cautiously.

The next day, Johnston marched Major General W.H.T. Walker's division to Yazoo City (and away from Blair) while Loring moved to Canton. In the meantime, Blair made his way back to safety in Vicksburg.

On June 1, Major General John C. Breckinridge arrived in Jackson from Middle Tennessee with a division of 5,500 men. At this time, Johnston had 27,000 troops on the perimeter of Grant's forces.

In spite of these additions, Johnston remained pessimistic. "I am too weak to save Vicksburg. Can do no more than attempt to save you and your garrison," he wrote on May 29. Johnston asked Pemberton to communicate his plans and suggestions.[44]

It was now taking up to four days to carry a dispatch from Johnston to Pemberton. Pemberton responded to Johnston's dispatch of May 25, providing a status report and update. Promising Johnston he would hold "the place as long as possible," he looked forward to the arrival of Johnston's relief force.[45]

---

44. Ibid., 929.
45. Ibid., 929-930.

On June 3 the Department of Mississippi and East Louisiana finally received cavalry reinforcements when Brigadier General William H. Jackson's division of 3,000 men arrived in Canton. These were to prove to be the last of any significant reinforcements for Johnston, and brought his forces to slightly over 30,000. Grant's reinforcements, however, were arriving also. Three brigades arrived on June 3 from Memphis. Substantial reinforcements arrived over the next eleven days.

On Pemberton's front, Grant's siege lines grew tighter. The Union investment line ran from the Mississippi above the Hill City to just south of Vicksburg. Twelve miles of Federal works confronted Pemberton. The terrain that had blunted Grant's assaults in May was being negated by the siege efforts.

With arriving reinforcements swelling his troop strength to more than 70,000 and Pemberton squeezed in the grips of his siege, Grant turned to secure himself from Johnston. On June 22 he detailed Sherman to organize and man a defense line facing east that protected the approaches over which Johnston could approach. With the establishment of this defense line in late June, opportunity for Joseph E. Johnston to relieve the garrison had passed by.

By June 14 Pemberton reported to Johnston that Grant's siege approaches were within 25 yards of his works. Cannon fire from both the land and river battered the city on a daily basis. Federal engineers dug tunnels with the intent of setting off explosions designed to destroy the Confederate fortifications.

On June 25, a gallery containing 2,200 pounds of gunpowder was exploded just north of the Jackson Road at the Third Louisiana Redan. Although the Confederate defense line was breached and Federal troops filled the crater, the attempt did not end the siege. For more than twenty hours the battle for the redan raged, and on June 26 Federal forces were forced back. On July 1 another gallery in the same area was exploded, but again the breach could not be exploited. It had, however, become obvious that unless relief was attempted quickly, Vicksburg would fall.

Pemberton continued his attempts to move Johnston to action. Messages of June 15 and 19 reinforced his concern that Johnston's movement should be made quickly. The enemy, he reported in the second dispatch, were within 25 feet of one section of the works. "What aid am I to receive from you?" he plaintively closed his note.[46]

Johnston continued his note of pessimism. On June 14 he told Pemberton "All we can attempt is, to save you and your garrison." Two days later (both of these messages appear to have been received by Pemberton on June 20), he again

---

46. Ibid., 964, 967.

sounded the refrain "I am too weak to save Vicksburg." Pemberton was again admonished to communicate his plans and cooperate fully.[47]

By June 21, Pemberton was vacillating between hopes of raising the siege and resignation that he might have to cut his way out. A message sent that same day suggested a movement north of the Southern Mississippi Railroad by Johnston while Pemberton sought to escape to the south via the Warrenton and Hall's Ferry Roads.

Johnston received Pemberton's message of June 15 a week later. Johnston remained despondent, noting he did not have the 30,000 to 35,000 men Pemberton had estimated in late May would be needed to raise the siege. In actuality, however, he had more than 30,000 men at this time.

On June 22 despair entered Pemberton's correspondence. He suggested, for the first time, that Grant be contacted regarding the surrender of the garrison, rather than attempting to cut a way out of Vicksburg. He suggested that the communication would come best from Johnston, who held the freedom of maneuver outside Vicksburg. The explosion of the mine at the Third Louisiana Redan was but three days away.

In the meantime, Johnston continued to vacillate. He sent orders to his division commanders in mid-June indicating that the long-anticipated move on Vicksburg would soon commence. A message from Davis, ironically, informing him of Grant's reinforcements, caused Johnston to cancel the plans.

Johnston turned to the Trans-Mississippi forces of Lieutenant General Edmund Kirby Smith, stating in a message that if Smith's troops could send in cattle, and reinforce the garrison with 8,000 men, Vicksburg could be saved. On June 27, however, he informed Pemberton that Smith's command had been "mismanaged." He also told his subordinate (in response to the note of June 22) that Pemberton himself would have to propose terms, should events lead to that eventuality.[48]

As June drew to a close, the soldiers and civilians of Vicksburg were starving. A circular from his soldiers told Pemberton that their rations were "one biscuit and a small amount of bacon per day, scarcely enough to keep body and soul together. ..." Although they had "as much confidence in you as a commanding general as we perhaps ought to have," they believed he had "displayed as much generalship as any other man could have done under similar circumstances." The soldiers concluded: "If you can't feed us, you had better surrender us."[49]

---

47. Ibid, 963, 965-966.
48. Ibid., 979-980.
49. Ibid., 982-983.

Johnston finally moved, planning an attack on Sherman's exterior line on July 6. Grant, coincidentally, had concluded to attack Pemberton's lines that day. Neither intention had enough time to mature.

Pemberton recognized that his troops, and the civilians under his control, were about to break. On July 1, he queried his four division commanders whether they could break the siege lines and cut their way out. Without resupply of food and ammunition, the garrison was doomed. The majority of Pemberton's subordinates agreed the army was too weak to make the attempt.[50]

In the Mississippi heat of on July 3, Pemberton sent Bowen forward under a flag of truce. Bowen had a relationship with Grant prior to the war, and he hoped that sending Bowen would lead to better terms. Pemberton proposed an armistice, and offered the surrender of the garrison.

Grant's terms were simple. "The useless effusion of blood which you propose stopping by this course can be ended at any time you may choose, by an unconditional surrender of the city and the garrison," he wrote. Pemberton and Grant met later in the day.[51]

The site of the meeting was between the lines of the two armies. Bowen and a staff officer accompanied Pemberton; Grant brought a number of officers with him, including Ord and McPherson. One can only imagine Pemberton's emotions as a Northern-born Confederate general about to surrender a Southern army.

Pemberton began by asking about the terms Grant that was willing to offer. Those in his note—unconditional surrender—replied Grant. The meeting did not go well, and Pemberton finally said that perhaps it would be better to close discussions, and turned to leave. Someone, perhaps Bowen suggested that the subordinate officers talk about terms. While they did, Pemberton and Grant sat in stony silence beneath an oak tree. It was determined that Grant would send a letter through the lines later that night.

With the cease-fire intact, the soldiers of both sides began to fraternize. Soldiers who had been engaged in the brutal work of killing each other just the day before now engaged in banter and trade. It was, however, a one-sided trade from Union to Confederate soldier, since the Confederates had little remaining at this point of the siege.

Although Grant proposed unconditional surrender, he had a problem. The surrender would require shipping all 29,500 prisoners north to prisoner-of-war camps. Pemberton was uncomfortable with the terms, and a negotiated offer of parole to the Confederates might bring Pemberton to terms. There was a large difference between being a prisoner-of-war in a Federal prison camp and a

---

50. *OR*, ser. I, vol. XXIV, pt 2, 368.
51. *OR*, ser. I, vol. XXIV, pt 1, 60.

paroled soldier in a Southern camp of instruction. In addition, Grant did not have the logistical support to transport Pemberton's army north. Finally, it was hoped that if they were paroled many of the Southern soldiers would view themselves as "out of the war," and simply return to their homes.

Grant decided to offer terms of parole. He offered to march a detachment of two divisions into Vicksburg the next morning (July 4) to act as guard, and after paroles were signed, allow the Confederates to march out of Vicksburg. Officers would be allowed side-arms and clothing. Staff officers could take one horse each. Private soldiers could take their clothing. All would be allowed to carry such provisions as they had (for Pemberton had tried to bluff Grant into believing the Confederates still had ample supplies).

Pemberton called his senior officers together to consider the terms. The majority (17 to 2) expressed the opinion that the terms were as good as could be expected. There was some dissension, and Stephen D Lee expressed hope that Johnston might still arrive to relieve the garrison.

Pemberton countered to Grant, and requested that the Confederate soldiers be allowed to march out of their lines, stack arms, and then permit Union troops to enter. Grant assented to Pemberton's request. At 10:00 a.m. on July 4, 1863, the Confederate garrison of Vicksburg surrendered. It was not long before Yankee soldiers were sharing rations with their Confederate counterparts. In all, 29,500 soldiers and 172 cannon surrendered. More importantly, the Mississippi River, with the surrender of the Confederate garrison at Port Hudson just five days later, was opened to Northern commerce forever.

The Federal command's assumption that providing Pemberton's soldiers with paroles would effectively dissolve his army was in part prophetic. As the troops were marched towards Jackson, many simply left the ranks to return home, some never to fight again. Pemberton tried to keep them together, but had little success. Without arms to enforce his orders, his valiant army melted away.

In the meantime, Joseph Johnston had moved very slowly, towards Vicksburg. The opportunities that had been available in late May had disappeared. Worse, Grant had instructed Sherman, who was watching the Big Black River crossings from the railroad north, to move against Johnston. Grant, by this time, had more than sufficient manpower to send a large force after Johnston.

Johnston slowly approached the Big Black and probed for an opening. There were none. After remaining in place on July 3, he resolved the next day to probe south of the railroad at Edwards Depot for an opening. On July 5, still unsure as to his plan of attack, Johnston heard of the surrender of the Vicksburg garrison.

Johnston was a good enough general to realize that with Pemberton's force captured, Grant would quickly move against him. On July 6, Johnston and his army retreated to Jackson, and closed the history of the Vicksburg Campaign.

Part Three

The Controversy

Part Three — The Controversy

*"General Pemberton made not a single
movement in obedience to my orders
and regarded none of my instructions…"*

— Gen. Joseph E. Johnston[1]

Vicksburg had fallen, Pemberton's army had surrendered, and the Mississippi River was open from Minnesota to the Gulf of Mexico. The controversy and blame for the Confederate disaster, however, had just begun. The war of words, which would extend well into the post-war period, erupted shortly after the surrender of Pemberton's army. At the center of the controversy were Confederate President Jefferson F. Davis and his two ranking commanders from the campaign, Joseph E. Johnston and John C. Pemberton.

Public perception of Pemberton dropped in the immediate after-math of the surrender of the army. His failure to hold the river fortress and his Northern roots made him an easy scapegoat. Perception of Pemberton, however, had not been nearly as negative while the campaign unfolded. To be sure, there were those such as diarist Mary Chestnut whose prejudices extended to all Southern generals of Northern birth. Never one to mince words, she noted in June of 1862 that as a native-born Yankee, Pemberton seemed to have no heart for the defense of Charleston. After the fall of Vicksburg, she considered him a "stupid log of a halfhearted Yankee."[2]

Others were not as critical. John B. Jones, a clerk in the War Department in Richmond, factually reported events in his diary during May and June of 1863 with few uncomplimentary words about Pemberton. To be sure, rumors were running rampant, but Jones held out hope that Johnston would relieve the garrison.[3]

Pemberton was given a favorable impression by the press of Vicksburg in the early days of his command. He was "worthy of trust and confidence," wrote one paper. "Free from ostentation, an indefatigable and untiring worker…he has

---

1. *OR*, ser. I, vol. XXIV, pt 1, 249.
2. C. Vann Woodward, ed., *Mary Chestnut's Civil War* (New Haven: Yale University Press, 1981) 332, 469.
3. Jones, John B., *A Rebel War Clerk's Diary*, (1866; reprint, New York: Time-Life Books, 1982) vol. 1, 324-337.

traversed the whole department and overlooked all our works of defense." Wrote another paper: "It is but an act of simple justice to record what seems to be a common, universal judgment upon the merit and efficiency of Gen. Pemberton's administration, that the projection and execution of the proper defenses of the Mississippi River, and perfecting those already planned and partially completed, accomplished by the ceaseless, untiring personal efforts of this commander, justly entitle him to the confidence and gratitude of the country."[4]

As long as Grant was unable to maneuver in front of Vicksburg, Pemberton's strengths as an administrator enhanced his image. Once Grant crossed the Mississippi River, however, blame understandably shifted to him. Noted a Vicksburg resident in her diary after the army retreated into the defenses: "Poor fellows, it made my heart ache to see them, for I knew from all I saw and heard that it was want of confidence in the general commanding that was the cause of our disaster."[5]

Much was expected of Joseph E. Johnston. The officers and soldiers in his growing army near Jackson wrote home of their expectations that the relief of the Vicksburg garrison was not only possible, but expected. British observer Arthur Fremantle was quite impressed with Johnston while visiting his camps near Canton. Johnston "had undoubtedly acquired the entire confidence of all of the officers and soldiers" he noted in his diary. Pemberton, on the other hand, was "freely called a coward and traitor." On the evening of May 21, when asked when he expected to start his campaign to relieve Vicksburg, Johnston said he was too weak at present and had no idea when he could attack Grant. Fremantle concluded that in the absence of a forthcoming campaign in Mississippi he would continue his journey through the Confederacy. In a little more than a month, he would view the Battle of Gettysburg with Robert E. Lee's army.[6]

Others were not as sanguine of Johnston's success. Robert G.H. Kean of the Bureau of War in Richmond, wrote on May 17: "I have little confidence in the General who came near to losing Richmond and who thinks so much of himself. Grant is now in a position where a man of daring and energy like the lamented "Stonewall" Jackson would destroy him. He [Grant] is far inland from his base."[7]

Pemberton spent most of the remainder of July 1863 attempting to move his paroled army to Alabama and keep the soldiers from deserting en masse. Commanding an army without guns proved to be a nearly impossible task. President Davis communicated with Pemberton frequently about the logistics

---

4. Quoted in John C. Pemberton III, *Defender of Vicksburg* (1942; reprint, Wilmington: Broadfoot Publishing Co., 1987) 44-45.
5. Emma Balfour, quoted in Carter III, *The Final Fortress*, 205-206.
6. Lt. Col. Arthur J.L. Fremantle, *Three Months in the Southern States: April-June 1863* (1864; reprint, Lincoln: University of Nebraska Press, 1991) 116-118, 120-121.
7. Edward Younger ed., *Inside the Confederate Government: The Diary of Robert Garlick Hill Kean* (1957; reprint, Baton Rouge: University of Louisiana State, 1993) 62.

of his situation, but little was said about the recently concluded campaign. Davis was, however, in almost daily communication with Johnston, and it was clear it was on Johnston that Davis placed most of the blame for the loss of Vicksburg.

Johnston's inactivity at Canton had upset Davis considerably. The two spent the second half of May arguing over how many troops Johnston had from reinforcements sent by Richmond. This was the very period of time, however, that the best opportunity for the relief of Vicksburg presented itself to Johnston. As time progressed, the tone in Davis's letters displayed increasing exasperation. In an argument, both men had to have the final word. The dispute over troops quickly took an uglier turn.[8]

Johnston disputed the scope and limits of his command. He was clearly uncomfortable with and did not approve of Richmond's theater command system, and believed a single commander could not accept and fulfill responsibility for commanding both Bragg's and Pemberton's armies. Davis, however, had been very clear as to the limits and scope of responsibility of Johnston's command when he was ordered to Tennessee in November of 1862.

The controversy began on June 12 during the siege, when Johnston suggested to Richmond that his authority to transfer troops from Bragg's army to Mississippi had been restricted upon receipt of orders to report to Mississippi in early May. Davis immediately expressed puzzlement at Johnston's interpretation, and attempted clarification.

The arguments continued throughout the month. On June 30, Davis wrote Johnston with all of the care of an attorney arguing a brief: "After full examination of all the correspondence between you and myself and the War Office, including the dispatches referred to in your telegram of the 20th instant, I am still at a loss to account for your strange error in stating to the Secretary of War that your right to draw re-enforcements from Bragg's army had been restricted by the Executive or that your command over the Army of Tennessee had been withdrawn."[9]

On July 5, the same day that Johnston learned of the surrender of the garrison at Vicksburg, he responded to Davis. "I considered my assignment to the immediate command in Mississippi as giving me a new position and limiting my authority to this department..."[10]

The back and forth communications continued well into the middle of July. Mixed in with the arguments and counter-arguments was a July 7 dispatch from Johnston to Secretary of War James A. Seddon announcing the surrender of Vicksburg (it is curious that it took two days for Johnston to forward the impor-

---

8. For examples of their bickering, see *OR*, ser. I, vol. XXIV, pt 1, 192-195.
9. Ibid., 198.
10. Ibid.

tant news). The episode finally blew up when President Davis wrote a lengthy response that reflected considerable effort to assemble and write. The letter is important to the unfolding controversy, because it clearly established Davis and Pemberton on one side of the argument and Johnston on the other. Johnston thought it important enough to reproduce in its entirety in his memoirs, and Pemberton discusses it at length in the manuscript response that follows.

For clarity and ease of reading, the version of the Davis letter that appears in Johnston's memoirs, *Narrative of Military Operations*, follows:

"General:

I. "Your dispatch of the 5th instant, stating that you 'considered' your assignment to the immediate command in Mississippi' as giving you a 'new position' and as 'limiting your authority', being a repetition of a statement which you were informed was a grave error, and being persisted in after your failure to point out, when requested, the letter or dispatch justifying you in such a conclusion, rendered it necessary, as you were informed in my dispatch of 8th instant, that I should make a more extended reply than could be given in a telegram. That there may be no possible room for further mistake in the matter, I am compelled to recapitulate the substance of all orders and instructions given to you, as far as they bear on this question.

II. "On the 24th November last you were assigned, by Special Orders No. 275, to a definite geographical command. The description includes a portion of Western North Carolina, and Northern Georgia, the States of Tennessee, Alabama, and Mississippi, and that part of the State of Louisiana east of the Mississippi River. The order concluded in the following language: 'General Johnston will, for the purpose of correspondence and reports, establish his headquarters at Chattanooga, or such other place as in his judgment will best secure communication with the troops within the limits of his command, and will repair in person to any part of said command, whenever his presence may for the time be necessary or desirable.'

III. "This command by its terms embraced the armies under command of General Bragg in Tennessee, of General Pemberton at Vicksburg, as well as those at Port Hudson, Mobile, and the forces in East Tennessee.

IV. "This general order has never been changed nor modified so as to affect your command in a single particular, nor has your control over it been interfered with. I have, as commander-in-chief, given you some orders, which will be hereafter noticed, not one of them, however, indicating in any manner that the general control confided to you was restricted or impaired.

V. "You exercised this command by visiting in person the armies at Murfreesboro', Vicksburg, Mobile, and elsewhere; and on the 22d January I wrote you, directing that you should repair in person to the army at Tullahoma, on account of a reported want of harmony and confidence between General Bragg and the officers and troops. This letter closed with the following passage: 'As that army is part of your command, no order will be necessary to give you authority there, as, whether present or absent, you have a right to direct its operations, and do whatever else belongs to the general commanding.'

VI. "Language cannot be plainer than this, and, although the different armies in your geographical district were ordered to report directly to Richmond, as well as to yourself, this was done solely to avoid the evil that would result from reporting through you, when your headquarters might be, and it was expected frequently would be, so located as to create delays injurious to the public interest.

VII. "While at Tullahoma you did not hesitate to order troops from General Pemberton's army, and, learning that you had ordered the division of cavalry from North Mississippi to Tennessee, I telegraphed you that this order did not change your orders, and, although I thought them injudicious, I refrained from exercising my authority, in deference to your views.

VIII. "When I learned that prejudice and malignity had so undermined the confidence of the troops at Vicksburg as to threaten disaster, I deemed the circumstances such as to present the case foreseen in Special Orders No. 275, that you should 'repair in person to any part of said command whenever your presence might for the time be necessary or desirable.'

IX. "You were therefore ordered, on 9th May, to 'proceed at once to Mississippi and the chief command of the forces, giving to those in the field as far as practicable the encouragement and benefit of your personal direction.'

X. "Some details were added about reenforcement, but not a word affecting in the remotest degree your authority to command your geographical district.

XI. "On the 4th June you telegraphed to the Secretary of War in reference to his inquiry, saying, 'My only plan is to relieve Vicksburg; my force is far too small for the purpose; tell me if you can increase it and how much.'

XII. "To which he answered on the 5th: 'I regret inability to promise more troops, as we have drained resources even to the danger of several points. You know best concerning General Bragg's army, but I fear to withdraw more. We are too far outnumbered in Virginia to spare any, etc., etc.'

XIII. "This dispatch shows that, up to the 5th June, the war-office had no knowledge of any impression on your part that you had ceased to control Bragg's army, but, on the contrary, you were clearly informed that you were considered the proper person to withdraw troops from it, if you deemed it judicious.

XIV. "On the 8th June the Secretary was more explicit, if possible. He said: 'Do you advise more reinforcements from General Bragg? You, as commander of the department, have power so to order, if you in view of the whole case so determine.'

XV. "On the 10th June you answered that it was for the Government to determine what department could furnish the reinforcements; that you could not know how General Bragg's wants compared with yours, and that the Government could make the comparison.

XVI. "Your statement that the Government in Richmond was better able to judge of the relative necessities of the armies under your command than you were, and the further statement that you could not know how General Bragg's wants compared with yours, were considered extraordinary; but, as they were accompanied by the remark that the Secretary's dispatch had been imperfectly deciphered, no observation was made on them till the receipt of your telegram to the Secretary, of the 12th instant, stating: 'I have not considered myself commanding in Tennessee since assignment here, and should not have felt authorized to take troops from that department after having been informed by the Executive that no more could be spared.'

XVII. "My surprise at these two statements was extreme. You had never been 'assigned' to the Mississippi command, you went there under the circumstances and orders already quoted, and no justification whatever is perceived for your abandonment of your duties as commanding general of the geographical district to which you were assigned. Orders as explicit as those under which you continued to act up to the 9th May, when you were directed to repair in person to Mississippi, can only be impaired or set aside by subsequent orders equally explicit; and your announcement that you had ceased to consider yourself charged with the control of affairs in Tennessee because ordered to repair in person to Mississippi, both places being within the command to which you were assigned, was too grave to be overlooked; and, when to this was added the assertion that you should not have felt authorized to draw troops from that department (Tennessee), after being informed by the 'Executive that no more could be spared,' I was unable to account for your language, being entirely confident that I had never given you any such information.

XVIII. "I shall now proceed to separate your two statements, and begin with that which relates to your 'not considering yourself commanding in Tennessee since assignment here,' i.e., in Mississippi.

XIX. "When you received my telegram of 15th of June, informing you that 'the order to go to Mississippi did not diminish your authority in Tennessee, both being in the country placed under your command in original assignment,' accompanied by an inquiry about the information said to have been derived from me restricting your authority to transfer troops, your answer on the 16th of June was, 'I meant to tell the Secretary of War that I considered the order directing me to command here as limiting my authority to this department, especially when that order was accompanied by War Department orders transferring troops from Tennessee to Mississippi.'

XX. "This is in substance a repetition of the previous statement, without any reason being given for it. The fact of orders being sent to you to transfer some of the troops in your department from one point to another, to which you were proceeding in person, could give no possible ground for your 'considering' that Special Order No. 275 was rescinded or modified. Your command of your geographical district did not make you independent of my orders as your superior officer, and, when you were directed by me to take troops with you to Mississippi, your control over the district to which you were assigned was in no way involved. But the statement that troops were transferred from Tennessee to Mississippi by order of the War Department, when you were directed to repair to the latter State, gives but half the fact; for, although you were ordered to take with you three thousand good troops, you were told to replace them by a greater number then on their way to Mississippi, and whom you were requested to direct to Tennessee, the purpose being to hasten reenforcements to Pemberton without weakening Bragg. This was in deference to your own opinion that Bragg could not be safely weakened, nay, that he ought even to be reenforced at Pemberton's expense, for you had just ordered troops from Pemberton's command to reenforce Bragg. I differed in opinion from you, and thought Vicksburg far more exposed to danger than Bragg, and was urging forward reenforcements to that point both from Carolina and Virginia, before you were directed to assume command in person in Mississippi.

XXI. "I find nothing, then, either in your dispatch of 16th June, or in any subsequent communication from you, giving a justification for your saying that 'you have not considered yourself commanding in Tennessee since assignment here' (i.e., in Mississippi). Your dispatch of the 5th instant is again a substantial repetition of the same statement, without a word of reason to justify it. You say, 'I considered my assignment to the immediate command in Mississippi as giving me a new position and limiting my authority to this department.' I have characterized this as a grave error, and in view of all the facts cannot otherwise regard it. I must add that a review of your correspondence shows a constant desire on your part, beginning early in January, that I should change the order placing Tennessee and Mississippi in one command and under your direction, and a constant indication on my part whenever I wrote on the subject, that in my judgment the public service required that the two armies should be subject to your control.

XXII. "I now proceed to your second statement in your telegram of 12th June, that 'You should not have felt authorized to take troops from that department' (Tennessee), 'after having been informed by the Executive that no more could be spared.'

XXIII. "To my inquiry for the basis of this statement, you answered on the 16th by what was in substance a reiteration of it.

XXIV. "I again requested, on the 17th, that you should refer by dates to any such communication as that alleged by you.

XXV. "You answered on 20th June, apologized for carelessness in your first reply, and referred me to a passage from my telegram to you on 28th May, and to one from the Secretary of War of 5th June; and then informed me that you considered 'Executive' as including Secretary of War.

XXVI. "Your telegram of 12th June was addressed to the Secretary of War in the second person; it begins 'your dispatch,' and then speaks of the Executive in the third person, and, on reading it, it was not supposed that the word Executive referred to any one but myself; but, of course, in a matter like this, your explanation of your meaning is conclusive.

XXVII. "The telegram of the Secretary of War of 5th June, followed by that of 8th June, conveyed unmistakably the very reverse of the meaning you attribute to them, and your reference to them as supporting your position is unintelligible. I revert, therefore, to my telegram of 28th May. That telegram was in answer to one from you in which you stated that on the arrival of certain reenforcements, then on the way, you would have about twenty-three thousand; that Pemberton could be saved only by beating Grant; and you added: 'Unless you can promise more troops, we must try with that number. The odds against us will be very great. Can you add seven thousand?'

"My reply was: 'The reenforcements sent to you exceed, by say seven thousand, the estimates of your dispatch of the 27th instant. We have withheld nothing which it was practicable to give you. We cannot hope for numerical equality, and time will probably increase the disparity.'

XXVIII. "It is on this language that your rely to support a statement that I informed you no more troops could be spared from Tennessee, and as restricting your right to draw troops from that department. It bears no such construction. The reenforcements sent you, with an exception presently to be noticed, were from points outside of your department. You had in telegrams of the 1st, 2d, and 7th of May, and others, made repeated applications to have troops withdrawn from other departments to your aid. You were informed that we would give all the aid we possibly could. Of your right to order any change made in the distribution of troops in your own district, no doubt had ever been suggested by yourself nor could they occur to your superiors here, for they had given you the authority.

XXIX. "The reenforcements, which went with you from Tennessee, were (as already explained and as was communicated to you at the time) a mere exchange for other troops sent from Virginia.

XXX. "The troops subsequently sent to you from Bragg were forwarded by him under the following dispatch from me of the 22d of May: 'The vital issue of holding the Mississippi at Vicksburg is dependent on the success of General Johnston in an attack on the investing force. The intelligence from there is discouraging. Can you aid him? If so, and you are without orders from General Johnston, act on your judgment.'

XXXI. "The words that I now underscore suffice to show how thoroughly your right of command of the troops in Tennessee was recognized. I knew from your own orders that you thought it more advisable to draw troops from Mississippi to reenforce Bragg, than to send troops from the latter to Pemberton; and, one of the reasons which induced the instruction to you to proceed to Mississippi was, the conviction that your views on this point would be changed on arrival in Mississippi. Still, although convinced myself that troops might be spared from Bragg's army, without very great danger, and that Vicksburg was, on the contrary, in imminent peril, I was unwilling to overrule your judgment of the distribution of your troops while you were on the spot, and therefore simply left to General Bragg the power to aid you if he could, and if you had not given contrary orders.

XXXII. "The cavalry sent you from Tennessee was sent you on a similar dispatch from the Secretary of War to General Bragg, informing him of your earnest appeal for cavalry, and asking him if he could spare any. Your request was for a regiment of cavalry to be sent to you from Georgia. My dispatch of 18th May pointed out to you the delay which a compliance would involve, and suggested that cavalry could be drawn from 'another part of your department' as had been previously indicated.

XXXIII. "In no manner, by no act, by no language, either of myself or of the Secretary of War, has your authority to draw troops from one portion of your department to another been withdrawn, restricted, or modified.

XXXIV. "Now that Vicksburg has disastrously fallen, this subject would present no pressing demand for attention, and its examination would have been postponed to a future period, had not your dispatch of the 5th instant, with its persistent repetition of statements which I had informed you were erroneous, and without adducing a single fact to sustain them, induced me to terminate the matter at once by a review of all the facts. The original mistakes in your telegram of 12th of June would gladly have been overlooked as accidental, if acknowledged when pointed out. The perseverance with which they have been insisted on has not permitted me to pass them by as mere oversights, or, by refraining from an answer, to seem to admit the justice of the statements.

> Very respectfully, Your obedient servant,
> Jefferson Davis"

Johnston notes in his memoirs that the paragraphs, as numbered above, were placed by him for "precision of reference."[11]

Johnston could not allow such a clear attack to go unchallenged. Responding on August 8, he penned a four and-a-half page response. At heart to his arguments were the weak contention that because the dual command was "not in accordance with military principles," his determination not to consider himself in such a command position was not only justified, but should have been understood by his superiors in Richmond. Forgotten by Johnston was the inactivity while commanding in Mississippi, and the repetitive requests for information that had come from the War Department.[12]

The war of words between Johnston and Davis only subsided because Johnston's August 9 response was delayed until June 11, 1864 by problems of courier delivery. Although the Confederate Congress called for copies of all correspondence between Johnston and the War Department, the issue finally quieted—although the controversy remained unsettled.

President Davis and Secretary of War Seddon compiled an impressive amount of correspondence with Johnston during the period of May through July 1863. Johnston's correspondence during this time is both confusing and odd. Twice, while Seddon attempted to converse via telegraph over interpretation of command, Johnston had inexplicable difficulties with the deciphering process. It is not clear whether the problems with ciphers were real or simply convenient. A Seddon message of June 21 even offered to take full responsibility for any future action taken by Johnston to relieve the siege. When Johnston finally deciphered the message three days later, he omitted any reference to Seddon's offer.[13]

On July 22, Adjutant and Inspector General Samuel Cooper notified Johnston that "In accordance with your expressed wish, you are relieved from the further command of the Department of Tennessee." Although the problem of command was seemingly settled, Johnston still had Cooper send two separate telegrams, as well as two distinct Special Orders, better defining his command.[14]

---

11. Johnston, *Narrative of Military Operations*, 230-241; the original may be found in *OR*, ser. I, vol. XXIV, pt 1, 202-207.

12. Ibid., 209-213.

13. Ibid., 226, 229.

14. Ibid., 232, 234-235.

A staff officer under Johnston prepared a letter for publication in the newspapers, and absolved Johnston of wrong doing and placed blame on Pemberton. The letter provided the impetus for Pemberton (through the urging of Davis) to begin the preparation of his official report of the campaign.

Pemberton settled in Gainesville, Alabama and wrote his report while Johnston (from his perspective) languished in insignificant command in Mississippi. The situation was not appreciated by Johnston, his wife, or their supporters in the Confederate Congress. Johnston worried that Pemberton was afforded unfair opportunity to absolve himself of blame for the failures of the late campaign.

On August 25, Pemberton forwarded his campaign report directly to Richmond, and in doing so bypassed Johnston. It is unclear whether Pemberton at this time reported directly to Johnston, having been captured with the garrison and subsequently paroled. In any event, Johnston was upset with Pemberton's direct communication with Richmond.

The report was voluminous, running to more than 80 pages in the *Official Records*. Pemberton was surprisingly kind to Johnston, never coming directly forth and placing blame on his commander. It may be that at this time, Pemberton did not fully realize how acrimonious the relationship had become. The following summarizes Pemberton's explanation of Johnston's inactivity:

> On May 25, thirty-four days previous, he [Johnston] had informed me that on the arrival of an expected division from Bragg's army [Breckinridge's division] he would "move to me." I supposed then, with my co-operation, to raise the siege. No subsequent dispatch from him sustained my understanding of his communication; all, without exception, of later date, spoke only of the possibility of extricating the garrison. His dispatch of July 3, received by me six days after the capitulation, held out no such hope, and I am fully and entirely satisfied that no efficient aid would have been given me even to effect an evacuation. I do not mean nor desire to be understood as implying that it might have been given me. I only express my conviction, that had I been able to hold the enemy at bay for yet a month, I do not believe, anxious as I was to co-operate, that I would have been relieved by any force from the outside.[15]

Pemberton painstakingly detailed the correspondence of the period to ensure that Richmond understood the activity and circumstances that characterized the campaign. Appendices provided discussions and correspondence concerning the ammunition and supply status of the garrison.[16]

Johnston, in his report dated November 1, 1863, was much more direct and pointed at Pemberton. He positioned himself as the helpless commander facing daunting odds. In addition, he believed he had to put up with a subordinate who

---

15. Ibid., 287.
16. Pemberton's *OR* report begins at *OR*, Series I, Vol XXIV, Part 1, pg. 237.

challenged his authority and did not obey orders. For the first time, Johnston clearly alleged that Pemberton had failed to obey his orders.

Johnston's report makes it very clear he considered Pemberton doomed as long as he used Vicksburg as a base, and even more so once he retreated into a siege. "His disasters were due not merely to his entangling himself with the advancing columns of a superior and unobserved enemy, but to his evident determination to be besieged in Vicksburg, instead of maneuvering to prevent a siege," he wrote.[17]

"In this report I have been compelled to enter into many details and to make some animadversions upon the conduct of General Pemberton," he continued later. "A proper regard for the good opinion of my Government has compelled me, therefore, to throw aside that delicacy which I would gladly have observed toward a brother officer suffering much undeserved obloquy, and to show that in his short campaign General Pemberton made not a single movement in obedience to my orders and regarded none of my instructions, and, finally, did not embrace the only opportunity to save his army—that given by my order to abandon Vicksburg." Of his own efforts in the field from May through July of 1863, he says little. The failure of the campaign, Johnston concluded, was assured from the start due to the nature of his dual command and the fallacy of the strategic significance of Vicksburg.[18]

Pemberton asked for a court of inquiry to determine culpability for the loss of Vicksburg. The three members of the controversy would have welcomed such a court. The war, however, interfered and caused the action to be postponed indefinitely. It was never held.

For Pemberton, the Civil War as lieutenant general was over. Some thought was given to send him to the Army of Tennessee in the aftermath of the post-Chickamauga purge of officers by General Braxton Bragg, but Pemberton's lack of popularity and support killed the idea. Finally tired of awaiting assignment, he resigned his commission as lieutenant general, and accepted a position as lieutenant colonel of artillery in the Richmond defenses. In that assignment, he served out the remainder of the war. Such a selfless act should have put to rest any remaining questions of Pemberton's loyalty to the Confederacy.

Johnston had a more active role in the final year and-a-half of the war. The Confederate debacle at Missionary Ridge in November 1863 led to Bragg's resignation as commanding general of the Army of Tennessee. In spite of his intense dislike for Johnston, Davis named him commander of the most powerful Confederate army in the western theater shortly after Christmas, 1863.

---

17. Ibid., 248.
18. Ibid., 248-249.

Johnston led the Army of Tennessee for much of the Atlanta campaign, abandoning position after position as his Federal counterpart William T. Sherman maneuvered towards Atlanta. Frustrated by Johnston's lack of aggression and continued retreat, Davis relieved him in mid-July 1864 and replaced him with General John Bell Hood. In late February 1865, Johnston was reassigned to command the remnants of the Army of Tennessee and other units, and fought in the Battle of Bentonville. Johnston surrendered his army to Sherman on April 26, 1865.

John Pemberton and wife Pattie purchased a run-down 200-acre farm near Warrenton, Virginia shortly after the war. The Pembertons attempted to reconcile their relationships with friends both North and South in the immediate aftermath of the war.

The ghosts of the Vicksburg campaign, however, remained. In 1865 Sarah Dorsey prepared to write a biography of war-time Louisiana governor Henry Watkins Allen, and wrote both Pemberton and Johnston regarding the Vicksburg years. Pemberton wrote back a long reply, while Johnston barely responded. The subsequent book was a vindication for Pemberton. Any partial vindication of Pemberton was a direct blow against Johnston.

The ghosts returned in force in 1874 with the publication of Johnston's memoirs, *Narrative of Military Operations*. Not surprisingly, there had been no change in Johnston's opinion regarding Pemberton's performance. He was actually more severe in his criticisms of Pemberton and the placing of blame for the loss of Vicksburg and the army. The publication of Johnston's memoirs had one significant impact on the future view of both the Confederacy's performance at Vicksburg as well as history's view of Johnston—he placed his version of history in the public's eye first—and to a large extent his story has been accepted to this day.

Pemberton was not the only Southern partisan who took exception to Johnston's work. Commenting on statements made by Johnston regarding the Peninsula campaign, Charles Marshall (who served on Robert E. Lee's staff) said in a speech: "have we not read General Joseph E. Johnston's 'Contribution of materials for the use of the future historian of the war between the States,' and has any one risen from the perusal of that interesting book, without the conviction that its distinguished author is mistaken as to some of his statements, or that all contemporaneous history is in error?"[19]

The section of Johnston's *Narrative* covering Vicksburg comes to more than 100 pages of the 465 pages of main text. Little changed in Johnston's mind in the 10 years that had passed since the transmittal of his official report. The Confed-

---

19. Col. Charles Marshall, quoted in Rev. J. William Jones, , ed., *Army of Northern Virginia Volume 1* (1880; reprint, Dayton: Morningside Bookshop, 1956) 71.

eracy had lost the war, and Johnston was intent on ensuring his actions were not associated with the loss. In order to ensure such an understanding, blame for the loss of Vicksburg and the Mississippi River had to be placed directly on Davis and Pemberton.

Pemberton was not pleased, having spent the ten years following the close of the war trying to rebuild his life and his family. He intended to publish a response to Johnston, started the work, but never finished. The whereabouts of Pemberton's efforts have remained a mystery since. An account reflecting the campaign was discovered in his papers and published as an appendix by his grandson in a work released in 1942. An additional account of the circumstances surrounding the surrender of the garrison was published in *Battles and Leaders of the Civil War.* This account was partially refuted in an article published for that same publication by U.S. Grant.

Johnston himself continued to push the controversy. He contributed a piece in *Battles and Leaders* entitled "Jefferson Davis and the Mississippi Campaign," a response allegedly to the publication of Davis' two-volume *The Rise and Fall of the Confederate States,* but one in which he managed to cast aspersions on Pemberton. Johnston sounded the argument that the true opportunity for the Confederacy was the reinforcement of Pemberton by idle troops from Arkansas. A key blunder, Johnston contented, was the lack of a peremptory order by Davis.

Johnston blamed Pemberton for disobeying orders of May 13 to march on Clinton, the subsequent disasters of Champion Hill and Big Black Bridge, and for retreating into the defenses of Vicksburg and disobeying an order to evacuate the city. As to his "army of relief," Johnston excused its inaction for having arrived in Mississippi ill-equipped for the task at hand.[20]

While working on his account, Pemberton's health failed. On July 13, 1881, he passed away. Pattie Thompson Pemberton, his wife, donated many of her husband's papers to former Confederate General Marcus Wright, who was working for the War Department compiling the Confederate side of what would become the *Official Records.* Included in these papers, we can only surmise, was the uncompleted manuscript response to Johnston's *Narrative.* Unfit as it was for inclusion in the *Official Records,* it remained lost until surfacing recently in an estate sale. The manuscript that follows is Pemberton's response to Joseph E. Johnston.

---

20. Johnston's article appears in *Battles and Leaders,* vol. 3, 472-482.

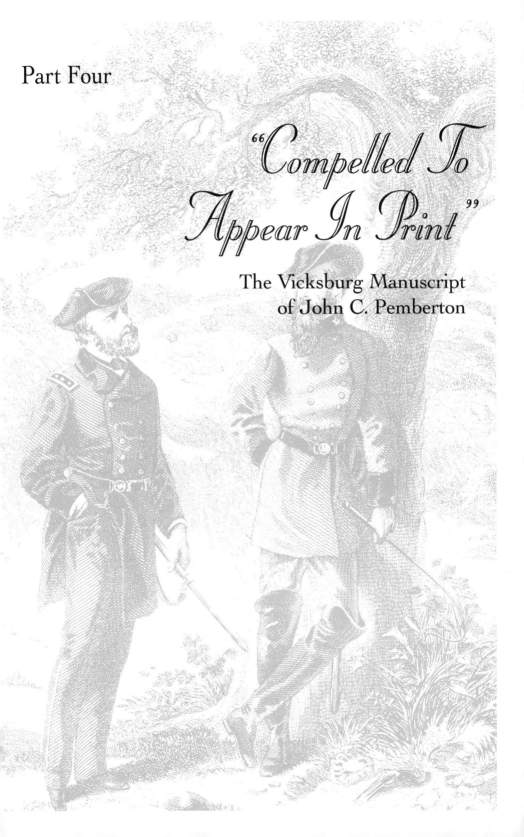

Part Four

"Compelled To Appear In Print"

The Vicksburg Manuscript
of John C. Pemberton

Part Four — The Vicksburg Manuscript of John C. Pemberton

No one who has read the book entitled "Narrative of Military Operations,"[1] recently published by General Joseph E. Johnston, will need to be informed of the reasons which compel me to appear in print, as a party to the controversy so unnecessarily thrust before the public.

I am aware that I have entered upon a task full of difficulties, which, if successfully accomplished, will be so by the force of facts, not of words. In the use of the latter, I can not pretend to compete with my opponent, nor do I altogether regret my inability to do so. Much, that he has been skillful to conceal, I shall endeavor to uncover, and shall strive to show to the future historian that a large part of the "Materials" offered for his use by General Johnston ought to be rejected, as unfit for so sacred a purpose.

He affirms that I constituted myself his adversary by my "manner of using" certain "advantages" which, he claims, I derived from having been permitted to supplement my official report twice, after I had read his. This privilege accorded to me he regards as a wrong done to himself: forgetting that, *he* was allowed to withdraw his own original report as being "misperfect" and to substitute the existing one.

> *Johnston writes, page 216 of his Narrative, of Pemberton: "Notwithstanding these advantages on his part, who, by his manner of using them, constituted himself my adversary, I should have made no comments on these publications, but should have limited my defense to the preceeding narrative; because it is distasteful, even painful to me, although in self defense, to write unfavorably of a brother officer, who, no doubt, served to the best of his ability; the more so, because that officer was, at the time, severely judged by the Southern people, who, on the contrary, have always judged me with their hearts instead of their minds. But Lieutenant General Pemberton has recently revived the question, and published, or rather procured to be published, a longer, more elaborate, and more uncandid attack upon me than those contained in his official report, and its two supplements."*

---

1. Johnston's *Narrative* was published in 1874. The alternative start to Pemberton's response, contained in Appendix B, dates the start of Pemberton's writing as 1874, upon immediate receipt of the book.

"In these publications, General Pemberton endeavors, by implication, as well as by direct assertion, to fix upon me the responsibility for the course, on his part, which led him to defeat at Bakers Creek and the Big Black River, and caused the capture of Vicksburg and the gallant army that formed its garrison."

Pursuing the subject, he says, "Notwithstanding these advantages on his part, I would have made no comments on these publications, but would have limited my defense to the preceding narrative…But Lieutenant General Pemberton has recently revived the question, and published or rather procured to be published, a larger, more elaborate, and more uncandid attack upon me than those contained in his "official report, and its two supplements."

"Thus it appears that up to a certain period, General Johnston had determined that he would be no *more* unjust to me, than he had already been in his official report, and in that "preceding Narrative." But an offense on my part, alleged to be "recent," and of a more flagrant character, wrought at the same time a change in his views, and in these historic materials.

Whatever strictures my military conduct merited should have been found in their proper place; in his official report; and in the "preceding Narrative." Or, if subsequently introduced, as a *penalty* due to the alleged offense, they should have been accomplished by *specification;* that others might have the opportunity to judge whether they sustained General Johnston's ex parte statement.

My "official report, and its two supplements" may be found in the Appendix to his book: whether or not an "uncandid" attack upon him is contained in either of them, I appeal to the reader to decide. I am disposed to believe that it was not originally intended to include those documents in his publication, and that when it was afterwards determined on, the incongruity of his charge today, and the proofs supplied by the reports themselves, escapes his observation. I have never made an uncandid attack upon General Johnston: indeed I have never made any attack upon him. Whenever called on to speak, I have affirmed openly what I know to be facts, have agreed to convince others that my deductions from those facts are correct, and have employed his dispatches to me to strengthen my arguments. He on the other hand, in the confidence that his "*I* have said it" would utterly crush the officer, who "was at the time severely judged by the Southern people" and yet, pressured to defend himself, has made aspersions unsustained by proof, and without foundation.

How wide a margin he has allowed himself in the use of the word "recently", I can not pretend to decide. During the latter part of the war, when, to be considered my friend and advocate was rather a subject of reproach, several articles appeared in my defense: but of each and *all* of them, I was in complete ignorance, until I read them in the public prints. Once only, and then, over my proper signature, I replied to certain unjust remarks made in a speech, laudatory of General Johnston, by the late Mr. Wigfall, before the Confederate Senate in the winter of 1864.[2]

A Southern lady with whom I had not the pleasure of personal acquaintance, addressed me in the summer of 1866 an earnest request, that I would furnish her with *any* version of the causes that led to the loss of Vicksburg: informing me at the same time that she was about to publish the biography of a dear friend deceased, the late Governor Allen of Louisiana, who had served under my command.[3]

This lady did me the honor to embody in her book much of the material with which I had supplied her. Subsequently, in the course of a brief but friendly correspondence, she assured me, that, although by the events of the Mississippi Campaign, she had lost her all, she had learned to do me justice. An acknowledgment more grateful to me than I can easily express.

A refined and cultivated woman, whose prejudices, if she had any, were not favorable to me, was at least as capable of deciding correctly on the *character* of my statements, and of the arguments necessary to elucidate them, as the interested individual who objects to their publication, on the alleged ground, that they contain "an uncandid attack upon him": had she been of that opinion, they would not have been admitted to her pages. I believe, however, that the true cause of General Johnston's dissatisfaction may be found in a disagreeable recognition of the validity of my defense. I have had no connection, directly or indirectly, with *any* publication, since the summer of 1866 *eight years ago:* nor have I in any manner "recently revived the question".

If I shall chance to have a reader, who can put himself in my place, he will pardon the preceding remarks as not uncalled for, when he remembers the *confessed animus* that has influenced General Johnston in his unfounded criticisms upon my military conduct. The question he has thrust before the public is: Who is responsible for the fall of Vicksburg…?

In order that this question may be answered intelligently, I propose 1st: to state fairly to what General Johnston ascribes that disaster, 2d: to examine his charges against me in that connection, and finally, in reply to those charges, to show, that, if not innocent myself, I have in him an associate, who must share the offense.

It will be observed that General Johnston exonerates himself from all responsibility for the disaster of the Vicksburg campaign on the ground that he, and the reinforcements sent from Beauregard's department, had not been ordered to Mississippi in April, in time to join my army, and had this been done, he says, "I *could* have directed the Confederate forces, and *would* have been responsible for

---

2. Louis T. Wigfall was a member of the Confederate Congress from Texas, and a very good friend of Johnston.

3. The Southern lady in question was Sara Dorsey, who was preparing a biography of her father, Henry Watkins Allen.

events; but by hesitating to transfer troops and send a new commander until too late, the Administration made itself and General Pemberton responsible for consequences." I shall briefly notice this argument at once; because *all the other causes* to which he ascribes those disasters, are in fact specific charges against me.

> *In addition to the quote above, on page 225 of the Narrative Johnston continues: "...and those consequences were the ruin of our affairs in Tennessee as well as Mississippi. They were ruined in Mississippi by the long delay of the Administration in sending reinforcements to General Pemberton's army; in Tennessee, by a draft of eight thousand men from General Bragg's army, whose going to Mississippi was useless, because it was too late, while it so weakened that army as to enable its antagonist to drive it rapidly across the Cumberland Mountain and Tennessee River."*

General Johnston was clothed by the Confederate Government with equal authority over General Bragg's department and over mine: the two constituted his command. He had therefore the same right to transfer troops from one department to the other to meet such exigencies as might arise in either, that General Bragg and I had, to remove them, for like purposes, from one point to another, within our respective limits. So also, it was his province to judge of the relative necessity or advantage of his personal presence in this department or in that; and to proceed wherever he deemed would be best subserved without sending for instructions or advice from superior authority. He was entrusted with the highest *powers* of a General commanding; these necessarily carried with them corresponding *responsibilities*; both should have been felt and both acknowledged to their fullest extent: that he failed to exercise the former, under whatever pretense he may prefer to assign, can not diminish the weight of the latter.

To the unprejudiced, the letter of President Davis can not, I think, be otherwise than conclusive on this point. The special order assigning General Johnston to this command, concluded in the following language, "General Johnston will, for the purpose of correspondence and reports, establish his headquarters at Chattanooga, or such other place as in his judgment will best secure communications with the troops within the limits of his command, and *will repair in person to any part of said command, whenever his presence may for the time be necessary or desirable.*" This General Order, says President Davis, "has never been changed nor modified as to affect your command in a single particular, nor has your control over it been interfered with." "When I learned" he continues, "that prejudice and malignity had so undermined the confidence of the troops at Vicksburg as to threaten disaster, I decried the circumstances such as to present the case foreseen in Special Order No 275, that you should 'repair in person to any part of said command whenever your presence might for the time be necessary or desirable.'"

General Johnston's geographical district included "a portion of western North Carolina and Northern Georgia, the states of Tennessee, Alabama, Mississippi and that part of Louisiana east of the Mississippi River." Mine, designated a department, included the state of Mississippi and the part of Louisiana just named. His authority over *the whole*, was at least as complete as mine was over *the part*.

My geographical department was for convenience subdivided into military districts, each under the control of a General officer, who ordinarily directed his troops within its limits.

Port Hudson, on the Louisiana shore of the Mississippi, a point second in importance only to Vicksburg, is within what was known as the "Third Military District" commanded by Major General Gardner.[4] By the nearest practicable route it is distant about 180 miles from Jackson or 225 from Vicksburg.

> *Pemberton refers to correspondence contained in the Narrative. Johnston printed a letter in its entirety dated July 15, 1863, and sent him from President Davis, in which the Confederate President argues in a legalistic fashion his perception of the Vicksburg command situation. The letter is discussed in Part Three.*
>
> *While this letter, as published in the Narrative, concerns only the relationship between President Davis and General Johnston, it serves as a valuable tool in understanding the complete lack of respect and cooperation that existed between the two men. Pemberton, of course, found himself supported by Davis, and therefore on the opposite side of Johnston. The legal bickering, and need to get the last word in on the part of these two men comes through clearly in Davis's letter.*

Let us take a supposable case and applying General Johnston's arguments to it, see to which conclusion they will bring us.

We will suppose that my Head Quarters as a department commander are in the Second Military District, in which Vicksburg is situated and that there is no particular reason to apprehend an immediate conflict with the enemy there. While engaged in the ordinary routine of my office, General Johnston learned that Vicksburg was seriously threatened by Grant's army and Porter's fleet, so his presence was manifestly "desirable" if not absolutely "necessary", in my department. What is the plain duty before one? Is it not to proceed there at once, and if found necessary to reinforce that district, to transfer troops without delay from others within one's jurisdiction not so immediately threatened; or shall he remain quietly at his Head Quarters at the Second District of his department and *thus wait* for positive orders to move, and to transfer his troops?

Suppose that having thus waited until he received positive orders from President Davis by telegraph General Johnston telegraphs me from Tullahoma, Tennessee…"Proceed to the 3d Military District and take the chief command of the forces, giving to those in the field as far as practicable the encouragement and benefit of your personal direction." If it was my manifest duty as department com-

---

4. Franklin Gardner commanded the garrison at Port Hudson and reported directly to
    Pemberton.

mander to do *without* special orders what I am now *required* to do by special orders, shall I subsequently turn upon General Johnston and say to him: "You are responsible for whatever calamities have happened, because you did not sooner give me positive orders to do what my manifest duty required I should do?"

With this order I also receive instructions to take with me a designated number of troops *from* the Second district *to* the Third, and am directed to explain those taken from the former, by a greater number sent from another department, are now, en route to the latter; the purpose being to reinforce the Third district if possible without weakening the Second.

On my arrival by rail at a point forty or fifty miles from Port Hudson, I am told that the enemy has interposed a part of his army between the place I now am, and the position occupied by General Gardner's forces, and me thirty miles distant. I immediately telegraph General Johnston "I am too late" and the next moment, without any real knowledge of the position of the main body of the enemy, or of his strength, I issue General Gardner certain peremptory orders, which utterly ambush his plans of defense, made before my arrival in the district.

The attempt to execute this order results in the loss of a battle, and the siege of Port Hudson is the consequence. To raise this siege, I apply to General Johnston for more troops, *but order none* myself from the Second district, where there is a large force unemployed, and not as yet particularly threatened. He replies from Tullahoma that he "has withheld nothing that it was practicable to give me," informs me that he can send no more troops from Tennessee or elsewhere, but says, "You know best concerning the 2d Military District. Do you advise more reinforcements *from there*? *You as Commandant of the district* have *power* so to order, if you, in view of the whole case, so determine." Is there anything unreasonable in this reminder from General Johnston, that I am the Commander of the Department of Mississippi and East Louisiana, and that as such, I have the power to transfer any or all troops (if I deem it advisable) from one point to another within its limits?

Is it not reasonable, where power has been duly delegated and *accepted*, that responsibility for its proper exercise should go with it? It seems to me that these questions admit of but one opinion. Observe however my rejoinder to General Johnston, and his conclusive reply. I say to him, "It is for *you* to determine where the troops required are to come from. I can not know *here* the wants of the Second District compared with mine. You can make such comparisons *in Tullahoma* ...I have not considered myself commanding in the Second district of my department, since assignment here, and should not have felt authorized to take troops from that district after having been informed by you that no more troops could be spared."

In answer to this extraordinary statement of mine General Johnston says, "The order to go to the Third Military district, did not diminish your authority in the *Second*, *both* being in the department placed under your command in original assignment. *You have had no information from me restricting your authority to transfer*, because no *more could be spared*."

Mean time the siege goes on, while my army, estimated by me at some 23,000, and by others as well informed at about 30,000, lies inactive for a month under the pretext of want of transportation, within forty or fifty miles of the besieged. I make no attempt to relieve the garrison, which, from my long delay, has grown so weak, and the enemy so strong, that my force *may now* be insufficient for the purpose.[5]

On the forty seventh day, his troops exhausted by long confinement in the trenches, by ceaseless vigilance, and by want of proper food, there being plainly no hope of relief, General Gardner is compelled to capitulate. Ten years after this disastrous result, I give to the world, as part of my contribution to the history of the War between the States, a remarkable announcement: in which it will be observed, that I entirely ignore the fact (and disputed by my superior) that *I had full power to go myself, and to direct my troops, to any point within the limits of my assigned command without waiting for orders or advice.*

I announce that "if I and the reinforcements sent from Bragg's department had been *ordered* to the Third Military District in East Louisiana in time to join General Gardner's army, I *could* have directed the Confederate forces and *would* have been responsible for events; but by *hesitating* to transfer troops, and *send* me from one part of my command to another until too late, General Johnston made *himself and General Gardner* responsible for consequences."

If this *supposed* case in all its particulars, as I have endeavored to present to the reader, had already occurred, what judgment upon my conduct would have been promised by the Southern people and by future historians?[6]

A case in every respect parallel to it did occur, in which General Johnston held the same relation to the Confederate executive and to me, that I held, in the supposed case, to General Johnston and to General Gardner.

I might with advantage in many respects, have confined my notice of this attempt at self exculpation by General Johnston, to a reproduction of the correspondence between him and President Davis published in the "Narrative of Military Operations". It appears to me, however, that the mode in which I have presented it might in some degree serve to exemplify the sophisticated character of General Johnston's arguments, whenever he deems the condemnation of his

---

5. Pemberton is actually fairly accurate in his estimate of Johnston's forces, which reached slightly more than 32,000 at their greatest.

6. The arguments immediately preceding this statement are a long, convoluted narrative in which Pemberton attempts to apply the logic of the command situation facing Johnston into a supposed situation within his own department. The explanation is confusing, although the argument is sound.

superior or subordinate essential to secure his own acquittal. Thus, that hesitation to "transfer troops and send a new commander to Mississippi until too late"
which General Johnston endeavors to fix upon the Government; and the disaster consequent on the hesitation, all of which he would further attribute to the
Government and to me, have been shown, I think to lay at his door since he possessed the requisite authority to transfer troops, and to send in his own person, a
new Commander, whenever he deemed it advisable or necessary.

[Manuscript skips from page 14 to page 21][7]

[Continuing on at page 21]

On the other hand, I do not ask that the charge of incapacity, to which I now
bring against General Johnson, be even considered on my base operations.

It is my part to prove by authentic evidence open to any "future historian"
that I again and again warned General Johnston, my military superior and commander, of the formidable invasion which was then threatening; and that he utterly neglected to take the slightest heed of those warnings; either by directly providing against the danger, as chief of the two departments; or by instructions or
advice to me his subordinate, beyond a mere suggestion on the 17th of April that
"if I could communicate with Lieutenant General [Edmund Kirby] Smith, he
might cut off the enemy's supplies going to New Carthage." This was a suggestion that might have been dispensed with, because I had foreseen the necessity of
General Smith's cooperation, and had addressed both him and Major General
Richard Taylor on the subject on the preceding day by special messenger in these
words: "The enemy are cutting a passage from near Young's Point, into Vidal
bayou, to reach the Mississippi River near New Carthage. Without cooperation
it is impossible to oppose him. Inform me what action you intend to take." This
message was repeated on the 18th.[8]

General Johnston was notified on the 17th that the enemy were cutting a
canal, using their dredge boats, from Milliken's Bend into Walnut Bayou; thence,
through Roundaway Bayou, into Vidal Bayou, into the Mississippi at New
Carthage, also that he was constructing batteries on the state levee; and of my
counter dispositions.

---

7. Each page of Pemberton's manuscript was numbered; in several instances (as above)
    numbered pages were skipped. In most instances, Pemberton's train of thought was
    interrupted. What happened to the missing pages is unknown.
8. Of course, nothing came of these communications, as usually happened when one department
    in the Confederacy asked for help from another. Part of Johnston's series of arguments with
    Davis was his belief that reinforcements for his department should have come from others —
    especially the Arkansas troops of Theophilus Holmes.

In another dispatch I said, "The enemy has now nine boats between Vicksburg and Port Hudson: he has land forces at New Carthage, from Grant's army: he can reinforce them to any extent: he can use his nine boats to *cross his troops to their side*." In a letter of the same date, I expressed my opinion that the "arrival of Adjutant and Inspector General Lorenzo Thomas in Memphis, had made a great change in the enemy's plan of campaign," and I again warned General Johnston that "a large force of Grant's army, had established itself at New Carthage below Warrenton on the west bank, (and) another was at Richmond, Louisiana." After enumerating the vessels that had passed our batteries, I added "this gives nine vessels available for crossing troops, or operating from above against Port Hudson."

The next day, General Johnston was informed that, I had requested General E.K. Smith "to cooperate with me on the river."[9]

Another dispatch on the 20th reported a reconnaissance of the gunboats that had passed the batteries, and their armaments; and states the fact that the enemy was "endeavoring to free a diversion of my troops (infantry) to North Mississippi." Again on the 20th, in response to his wish, that, *I should aid* Colonel Roddy *in Alabama*, "he was aware" I had but little cavalry, but that "I would certainly give Roddy all the aid I could."

On this occasion, I told him "I had virtually *no cavalry from Grand Gulf to Yazoo City. While the enemy is threatening to pass (cross) the river between Vicksburg and Grand Gulf, having twelve vessels below Vicksburg."*

To the people of Mississippi, to the Army, and to me, these dangerous raids were part and parcel of the "formidable invasion preparing" under our eyes but to General Johnston with as full a knowledge of the facts as they or I possessed they were simply "predatory incursions."[10]

On the 22d information was sent him that "Heavy raids were making from Tuscagee deep into the state": that cavalry was indispensable to meet them, and he was asked to "make a demonstration on their rear" not against "predatory incursions" be it understood, but to save from destruction our communications, Depots, and manufactories; as much the sinews of our strength, as were our muskets and the soldiers that bore them.[11]

Col. B.S. Ewell, General Johnston's chief of staff had officially informed me in the earlier part of April that cavalry was much more needed in the department

---

9. Edmund Kirby Smith was promoted to lieutenant general in October 1862 and placed in charge of the Trans-Mississippi department.

10. In the then ongoing war of words, Johnston apparently had to place Grierson's cavalry raid of less priority than given by Pemberton; conversely, Pemberton's response of using infantry to contest Grierson suggested a greater emphasis and importance on his part. Both men argued with a degree of hindsight.

11. Pemberton refers to a series of cavalry raids out of western Tennessee and northern Alabama, and in particular Grierson's Raid.

of Middle Tennessee than in mine, at that time. That I had from that department *what I most required*, by five brigades of infantry, which was more than an equivalent for Van Dorn's cavalry, and that the latter could not be sent back under existing circumstances. Those circumstances, whatever they were, continued to exist, from the middle of January until after I was forced into Vicksburg. Finally on the 27th of April I once more told General Johnston that "However necessary cavalry might be to the Army of Tennessee, it was *indispensable to me to keep my communications*"; that "I could not defend every station on the road with Infantry" and "further" that "their raids endanger my vital position." Thus it will be seen by Johnston's order I was stripped of cavalry; that I was threatened with raids and with invasion; that I informed Johnston of all this and he neither came to my help; sent me cavalry or took any step to give me aid, orders or counsel.

General Johnston may have seemed to have *written* orders enough; but unfortunately he did not cause them to be executed. Like his "proposes to attack the enemy," they all perished just as he was "on the eve of executing them."[12]

The result was, that I was compelled to employ Major General Loring's whole division of near (7,000) seven thousand veterans, to guard railroads, and machine shops, Depots and manufactories; or to see them destroyed. Mean time Grant's Army, west of the Mississippi, was gradually concentrating at a point, nearly opposite Grand Gulf, whence he threatened both that place and Warrenton; where a successful attempt to land, would have placed him *west* of the Big Black River, and within nine miles of Vicksburg.[13] It was therefore, not until after the night of the 29th of April, when the Federal fleet of gun boats and some transports, ran by the battery at Grand Gulf and when the simultaneous movement of his troops by land, gave appearance that General Grant had not designed an attack on Warrenton with the force on the west shore below Vicksburg, that I felt justified in concentrating a large portion of my Army east and south of the Big Black. Feeling confident by the 28th that Grierson would make for Banks' Army at Baton Rouge, and that two brigades of General Loring's division might be safely withdrawn from the railroads, I directed General Loring on the Mobile and Ohio railroad with all of Buford's brigade but for one regiment, to come with the least delay possible to Jackson; similar instructions were given Brig. General Tilghman, on the Mississippi Central road, but not so that troops should be collected more rapidly, than they could be transported. Brigadier General Feather-

---

12. Pemberton is likely commenting on Johnston's claims of being on the verge of attacking Sherman at Peachtree Creek during the Atlanta campaign when he was relieved of command.

13. The Big Black River runs from the northeast to southwest, emptying into the Mississippi just above the fortifications at Grand Gulf. Pemberton's concern that the enemy would have been *west* of the Big Black simply meant that they would be on the Vicksburg side of the river, with a straight approach to the city.

ston, occupying positions farther north, was not ordered to move until the 1st of May. Every possible precaution had been taken as far as means allowed to ensure the rapid transit of troops in case of urgent need. General Loring was informed that "operations on that *line* were minor to those on the Mississippi River: therefore he must not be out of reach by telegraph, nor must his troops, be so disposed as to be unable to move in this direction (towards Jackson) at a moments notice."

The following dispatch dated April 29 from General Loring will explain why he, and General Buford's brigade, did not reach General Bowen, until after the battle of the 1st of May near Port Gibson:

"Troops have been delayed here, all day for want of transportation; only sufficient transportation for portion of one regiment has reached the break up to this hour. Repairing break is very slow"; the superintendent of the road explained that "being compelled to hold trains for the troops to Big Black retarded the movement from the break," and added "many of our trains are east of the break."

Thus, it will be seen that as far as General Johnston's refusal to permit me to have cavalry would allow, I proceeded at the earliest moment to "concentrate" and prepare to resist.

That, at least four fifths of General Loring's division, were not participants in the battle of the 1st of May, is due solely to the want of cavalry, and for this General Johnston is responsible.

Referring to an extract from my official report quoted correctly in his text, General Johnston says,

> In its march from Bruinsburg by Port Gibson to Jackson, and thence to Vicksburg, the Federal army drew its supplies from the country; and did not in the least depend on its communications with the Mississippi. Consequently, cavalry placed on what General Pemberton regarded as "its communications" would have been altogether useless...At the time in question General Grant had no garrison to be surprised nor Depots to be destroyed in Mississippi, and no disposition of Confederate Cavalry would have been less inconvenient to him than that by which his opponent fancies that he would have been defeated.

The quotation from my report simply expresses a firm conviction on my part that "with a moderate cavalry force at my disposal, the Federal Army would have been unable to maintain its communications with the Mississippi..." and that he would have been foiled in an attempt to reach Jackson and Vicksburg on the occasion referred to, as he had been on a previous occasion, by the employment of cavalry. Nothing is said about "garrisons being surprised, or Depots destroyed." To pretend that General Grant had no communications to preserve, is nonsense. He had his sick and wounded to be removed to his rear; he had his supplies of ammunition and other advance stores to keep up; nor could he for any protracted period have fed his army from the country in which he was operating.

With the cavalry force that had been at my disposal, I am still firmly convinced that, the Federal Army could not have reached Jackson and Vicksburg from its base on the Mississippi below the Big Black.[14]

To have compelled it to draw its supplies from that base or to retire, I certainly should not have hesitated for an instance, to destroy to the last measure the provisions of the country; nor do I believe it would have been in the power of the enemy to prevent it. In fact I am quite satisfied that though be it remembered I do not dogmatically assert it *as a fact*, "I *could* have disposed of my cavalry, in a way that would have been less inconvenient to my opponent," General Johnston to contrary notwithstanding. I claim the right, however, to declare that such a disposition would have been fatal and I resist that. It is his custom whenever he failed as he always did to achieve a success to lay the blame upon the failure to try some plan he had counseled.

Throughout the month of March, the enemy by cooperative maneuver of his land and naval forces, was actively engaged in various attempts to open a communication from the Mississippi to the high land, with the view of establishing a base of operations above Vicksburg.

Early in March, when it seemed highly probable that the canal opposite Vicksburg would prove a success, I deemed it necessary to establish a battery at the mouth of the Big Black, for the double purpose of protecting the entrance to the river, and as a necessary defense of the Mississippi. After the passage of the batteries at Port Hudson by the *Albatross* and *Hartford* under Admiral Farragut, it was ascertained that the enemy was making forced reconnaissances, to determine the practicability of moving by land to Hard-times, and New Carthage, on the west bank of the river, above Grand Gulf, and below Vicksburg. To prevent this as far as possible, the major part of General Bowen's brigade was, early in April, crossed from Grand Gulf, and occupying favorable positions, drove back the enemy on several occasions and kept him, in part at least, from the attainment of his objective. After the passage of the Vicksburg batteries by the Federal fleet, on the night of the 16th-17th April, it was manifestly impracticable to continue my troops on the west side; they were therefore withdrawn on the following night, and thence forth it was not of my power to either to prevent the enemy's movements, or to ascertain them, with any degree of certainty.

Bowen's command was immediately strengthened by another brigade under Major General Martin E. Green (killed during the siege of Vicksburg), which

---

14. Pemberton refers to Grant's now-famous cutting loose of his supply lines and living off the Mississippi countryside during the initial aspects of the campaign. We know today that Grant indeed kept wagons rolling in large numbers; it is open conjecture whether more cavalry, and a serious effort against the trains would have seriously impacted the eventual results.

with his own hereafter constituted his [Bowen's] division. General Bowen had previously been directed "to examine Bayou Pierre as a point of approach and report"; he replied "Bayou Pierre is navigable for *gun boats* as high as Port Gibson, every means will be used to defend it." This was more than a month before the Federals landed at Bruinsburg.

On the night of the 22d April the Federal fleet below Vicksburg was increased to some twenty vessels, of all descriptions. On the following day, Major General Stevenson, commanding the 2d Military district (comprising Vicksburg and its flank defenses from the Big Black to the Yazoo), as well as his own division, was instructed as follows: "Indications now are that the attack will not be made on your front or right, so that all troops *not absolutely necessary* to hold the works there, should be held as a moveable force, either for Warrenton, or Grand Gulf...Report to me the dispositions you make under these instructions." General Stevenson replied the same day "I have my division on the Warrenton side of Vicksburg. None other here can be spared for it...They must get more transport, before they can attempt Warrenton."

On the 25th, I again said to General Stevenson "It is indispensable that you keep in your line, only such force as is absolutely needed to hold them, and (that you) organize the remainder (if there is any) of your troops, as a moveable force, available for any point it may be most required."

It will not I hope be considered inappropriate here, to introduce a telegram of same date from Brigadier General Buford, then with his brigade on the Mobile and Ohio railroad, that I may demonstrate the correctness of my statement in regard to the necessity I was under of diverting large bodies of infantry for purposes of guarding duty; and also to prove, that these raids were parts of the plan of invasion, and not, mere "predatory incursions" as reported by General Johnston. General Buford telegraphs me from Meridian: "About 12:30 today the enemy demanded the surrender of Enterprise. General Loring arrived in time with reinforcements. The enemy reported to be cavalry, from five to fifteen hundred strong, fell back from Enterprise without attacking. Nothing lost or destroyed on the Mobile road, and with *five hundred cavalry could capture the enemy.*"

I replied, "I am sorry that I can not send your five hundred cavalry, because I have none." Gun manufactories at Enterprise were perhaps more important and extensive than any others in the department.

At 7 a.m. on the 29th, the Federal gun boats opened a terrific fire on the battery of five guns at Grand Gulf, and continued it without interruption for 6 1/2 hours, when they withdrew. Transports loaded with troops were in sight above, but remained inactive. General Johnston has explained the object of the Federal General had in view in this attack, and no doubt correctly, as he probably since derived his information from official reports though he does not say so.

On page 168 of the Narrative, Johnston provides the following interpretation of Grant's objective:

General Grant's design seems to have been to take Grand Gulf by a combined military and naval attack, and operated against Vicksburg from that point. The squadron, under Admiral Porter, opened its fire upon the Confederate intrenchments at 8 a.m. on the 29th, and the Thirteenth Corps was held in readiness to land and storm them as soon as their guns should be silenced. As that object had not been accomplished at six o'clock in the afternoon, General Grant abandoned the attempt, and determined to land at Bruinsburg. For this purpose the troops debarked at Hard Times, and marched to the plain below Grand Gulf; and the gunboats and transports, passing that place in the night, as they had done at Vicksburg, were in readiness at daybreak next morning to ferry the troops to Bruinsburg, six miles. The number of vessels was sufficient to transport a division at a time.

Failing to silence our batteries, the fleet, as reported to me by General Bowen, consisting of "six gun boats with two transports lashed to them" passed between 9 and 10 p.m. At the same time he stated that, the enemy was on the Louisiana shore below, and also that reinforcements be hurried up, adding "my lines are very much extended."

His next report on the morning of the 30th represented "The camp and fleet of the enemy three miles below"; he then says, "Their troops are moving, can not tell whether they will attack our left or front. When they cross again they may move to Rodney, and not renew the attack today. Will keep you advised." His next, stated, "the disposition for the morning perfected; troops in fine spirits." He then reported "Three thousand Federals were at Bethel Church ten miles from Port Gibson at 3 p.m. advancing; they are still landing at Bruinsburg." In subsequent dispatches of the same date 30th he says: "General Tracy has arrived, his men are much broken down. I will fight them the other side of Port Gibson." The following was in cypher dated and received on the night of the 30th. "There are four gun boats in Bayou Pierre. I have no guns that can check them; they can remove obstructions, and may destroy the bridge, cutting my force in two. Shall I remove all to this side, severing all communications by telegraph, or make the best of it?" Before this could be acknowledged I received the following, "General Baldwin is coming up. Please answer my cypher dispatch." It was answered after midnight on the 30th in these words:

In case the bridge is destroyed how far up before you could form a connection? Is the river navigable to the bridge? Is not the river so narrow at the raft, that with field artillery and sharpshooters, its destruction could be prevented? It is of vast importance to drive the enemy back and save our communication with Grand Gulf, and Port Gibson: You said this evening you would fight him on the other side of Bayou Pierre; why have you changed your mind? You have now about (9000) nine thousand men, and you ought to attack before he can greatly increase his strength.[15]

General Bowen at once replied: "Grand Gulf, May 1. I have prepared for defense on both sides of Bayou Pierre. The country and the jaded condition of Tracy's and Baldwin's men forbid an advance. If it can be done today I will do it. There is no raft in Bayou Pierre." He then asked for ammunition for certain field artillery, and concluded thus, "Our advance has been engaged with theirs four miles south of Port Gibson: loss small, and position maintained. I am compelled to keep a brigade at the Gulf fearing a direct attack."

In my reply, after informing General Bowen that the ammunition he asked for had been sent, I said "I think it unnecessary, to keep a whole brigade at the Gulf. They can not land under your guns. General Loring with nearly two brigades has started from Jackson to you. You had better whip them before he reaches you." These were the brigades of Buford and Tilghman before spoke of in guarding railroads, etc.

Another brigade of Stevenson's division was ordered to move at once to Bowen, and the remaining two to follow as rapidly as possible.

Brigadier Featherston of Loring's division then at Grenada, was directed to "bring his command immediately to Vicksburg" as being the most expeditious route to Grand Gulf. Thus, including the four brigades already with General Bowen, a force of ten brigades was being concentrated. I used every exertion by hastening the movement to prevent the necessity of withdrawing those troops who were in front of the enemy, and by fighting him east of the Big Black, before he had united all his forces, to place my army more nearly on a numerical equality with his, than I could hope to do at any future time.

At 1:20 p.m. on the 1st of May General Bowen informed me that his troops had been engaged in a furious battle since day light, and his losses were heavy. At 5:15 that he still held his position, but would have to retire under cover of night to the other side of Bayou Pierre. To this I replied at 7:30 p.m. "Is it not probable that the enemy will himself retire tonight? It is very important as you know, to retain your present position if possible. Your telegraphic communication will be cut off, and [the] enemy will have the road open to [the] east. You must, however, of course, be guided by your own judgment. You and your men have done nobly." Before this dispatch could have been received, General Bowen informed me, that "he was falling back across Bayou Pierre," [and] that "he would endeavor to hold that position until reinforcements arrived.; He added "want of ammunition is one of the main causes of our retreat."

---

15. The dispatches between the capable Bowen and Pemberton highlight the problems of communication and lack of overall understanding of the military situation inherent in the Confederate command. The bridge referred to crosses Bayou Pierre at Port Gibson.

Direct telegraphic communication ceased, and I heard nothing more from General Bowen, until the 3d when he informed me, that "circumstances compelled him to fall back" and asked, "shall I move to Vicksburg or Edward's Depot?" This dispatch was dated 2d but did not designate the position. I learned however that it was near Port Gibson.

The following communication by telegraph addressed to President Davis on the 2d of May will explain my instruction both to General Bowen, and to General Loring, who had joined Bowen on the 2d:

> I think the enemy has landed nearly his whole force on this side. I am concentrating all I can. General Bowen telegraphed 5 1/2 p.m. last night, that he should fall back under cover of night to this side of Bayou Pierre, and endeavor to hold position, until arrival of reinforcements. If he holds that position, I have directed him (if his communications with Vicksburg are open) to endeavor to continue it; but if he has fallen back to Grand Gulf, which is reported, and which is a cul de sac, he must endeavor to cross the Big Black, destroying his guns and stores. The battle will probably be fought outside Vicksburg.

Before the receipt of my instructions indicated in the above dispatch to President Davis, Generals Loring and Bowen had in consultation decided, that it was necessary to withdraw the troops; and in the receipt of my dispatch it was immediately put into execution by crossing the Big Black. By the time the whole of Major General Stevenson's division, all of Bowen's, nearly two brigades of Major General Loring's, and one of Major General M.L. Smith's under Major General Baldwin, making in all nine brigades, was concentrated west of the Big Black near Hankinson's Ferry and constituted an army of over 18,000, perhaps amounting to 20,000 men. This force might, in the event of an action near Hankinson's Ferry, have been increased 2,000 by Moore's brigade of Maj. General Forney's division, then near Warrenton; though, the enemy being in possession of Grand Gulf, could have thrown a cooperative force from Sherman's division on my rear, had that brigade been withdrawn. This was more than the force which I afterwards collected at Edward's Depot and which General Johnston page 221 [of the *Narrative*] says "would have had all measurable chance of success" if I had engaged the enemy when he was divided in the passage of the Mississippi. I have shown the impossibility of engaging him at that time with such a force, and also my efforts to provide it. During the operations on the Bayou Pierre, and about Port Gibson, a strong demonstration was made from above, by gun boats and land forces against Vicksburg, in the direction of Haines' [Snyder's and Drumgould's] Bluff and the approaches of Chickasaw Bayou.

Of this demonstration General Johnston says [page 171 of the *Narrative*]: "To divert General Pemberton's attention from his real design, General Grant had left the Fifteenth Corps, and a division, at Milliken's Bend under General Sherman, to make a demonstration against Vicksburg from the side of the Yazoo. This was executed by a slight attack upon Haines' [Snyder's] Bluff on the 30th of April repeated next morning, after which General Sherman returned to Milliken's Bend, and marched from that point to rejoin the Army." All this information, General Johnston derives, from subsequent official reports: he has not the candor however to point out, what he well knows to be the fact, that if I had too much weakened my strength in that direction, the "*demonstration* from such a force, as was then at Sherman's disposal, *would have become a real attack*. If Vicksburg with its stores, munitions, etc.; the whole of the campaign achieved by a coup de main what then would have been General Johnston's judgment upon me?

This is an explanation of one of the prominent causes that prevented the concentration of a sufficient force east of the Big Black to "beat the enemy" whilst he "was divided in the passage of the Mississippi."

Concluding the section of his Narrative that ends with being ordered to Mississippi to take overall command, Johnston, on page 171 offers the following regarding Pemberton and the eventual orders to go west:

The union of the Thirteenth and Seventeenth Corps was completed on the 3d [of May], near Willow Spring, where they waited for Sherman's troops until the 8th. The army then moved forward on two parallel roads, the Thirteenth on one, the Seventeenth on the other, abreast, the Fifteenth following on both; the Thirteenth turned into the road to Edward's Depot, however, while the Seventeenth kept that to Jackson, followed at an interval of a few miles by the Thirteenth.

On the 5th, as Lieutenant-General Pemberton's dispatches subsequent to that of the 1st had contained no reference to the movement of the Federal army, nor to the result of the battle near Port Gibson, I asked him to give me information on the two points. His reply, written on the 6th or 7th, contained no allusion to General Grant's forces, but gave his own positions, in cipher, so that they were imperfectly understood. He informed me, however, that General Bowen had been driven from the field with a loss of six or seven hundred men. I was thus left uncertain whether or not any but a detachment of the Federal forces had crossed the Mississippi.

On the 9th, in the evening, I received, at Tullahoma, the following dispatch of that date from the Secretary of War: "Proceed at once to Mississippi and take chief command of the forces there, giving to those in the field, as far as practicable, the encouragement and benefit of your personal direction. Arrange to take for temporary service with you, or to be followed without delay, three thousand good troops who will be substituted in General Bragg's army by a large number of prisoners returned from the Arkansas Post capture, and reorganized, now on their way to General Pemberton. Stop them at the point most convenient to General Bragg.

You will find reenforcements from General Beauregard to General Pemberton, and more may be expected. Acknowledge receipt." I replied at once: "Your dispatch of this morning received. I shall go immediately, although unfit for field-service."

I had been prevented, by the orders of the Administration, from giving my personal attention to military affairs in Mississippi at any time since the 22d of January. On the contrary, those orders had required my presence in Tennessee during the whole of that period."

In his narrative of events that occurred during the two weeks which immediately preceded the landing of the Federal army at Bruinsburg on the day and night of the 30th of April, General Johnston has skillfully contrived to divert attention from a glaring instance of his own neglect of duty. He has on the other hand, by an outrageous abuse of words, given to the telegraphic dispatches of the 1st and 2d of May, which he addressed to me from Tullahoma, a signification they do not in reality possess, and by thus disturbing their true import, he has endeavored to fix upon me the charge of disobedience of his orders.

It is at least questionable, whether the telegrams referred to were either in fact or intending what General Johnston now claims they to have been, that is in the usual military explanation. It is certain that I did not at the time regard them in that light; they left no impression whatever on my mind.

They appeared to me, merely to advise a policy I had already acted upon which was the concentration of all my troops, not indispensable to the safety of Vicksburg and Port Hudson, for operations against the enemy in the field. I could not conceive that General Johnston really advised me to abandon without a struggle to their fate these places which in my estimation were essential to the life of the Confederacy; but if such was his intention, he should have distinctly announced it. The phrase which seems to have taken a wonderful hold on the public ear "success will give back what we abandoned to win it" was mere "sound and fury, signifying nothing."

> *Pemberton is none too pleased with Johnston's phrase "success will give back what we abandoned to win it." The complete paragraph from the Narrative from which he quotes is on page 170 and reads as follows:*
>
> *While the troops were engaged, General Pemberton telegraphed to me: "A furious battle has been going on since daylight, just below Port Gibson. General Bowen says he is outnumbered trebly. Enemy can cross all his army from Hard Times to Bruinsburg. I should have large reenforcements. Enemy's success in passing our batteries has completely changed character of defense." In the reply, dispatched immediately, he was told: "If General Grant's army lands on this side of the river, the safety of the Mississippi depends on beating it. For that object you should unite your whole force." In a telegram, dispatched to him the next day, the instruction was repeated: "If Grant's army crosses, unite all your troops to beat him; success will give you back what was abandoned to win it."*

In quoting portions of my dispatch of the 1st May, General Johnston has neglected to introduce two important passages. After the words "General Bowen says he is outnumbered trebly" there should have followed, "he has about (8,000) eight thousand" (he had in fact about 9,000 — see my dispatch of 1st of May to General Bowen). If General Bowen's estimate of the enemy's relative strength was correct he must have landed at least 24,000 men, at the very time General

Johnston was reading the dispatch from which he quotes: he was not therefore "left uncertain" as he claims he was, "whether or not, any but a detachment of the Federal forces had crossed the Mississippi."

Elsewhere he sets down the Federal Army engaged with Bowen at 40,000, for he represents that officer to have been "outnumbered five to one." On the 1st of May I stated to him distinctly "The enemy's forces here, *is double what I can bring into the field.*" I deny therefore, that he "was left uncertain whether or not any but a detachment of the Federal forces had crossed the Mississippi."

Another important passage in my dispatch of the 1st of May has been omitted: apparently its tendency was to throw his machinery somewhat out of gear; "*am hurrying all reinforcements I possibly can to Bowen*": he was therefore aware, that I had not waited for advice, or suggestions, or orders from him; but that I had in my capacity of Departmental commander anticipated all that his ex post facto dispatches, when *construed by common sense*, could possibly require.

General Johnston had been informed by me on the 1st of May that "a furious battle had *been going on since day light* just below Port Gibson." I have shown, that the same dispatch conveyed the information that General Bowen "had about 8,000" and that he reported the enemy thrice his strength, whereupon, General Johnston says: "In the reply, dispatched immediately, he (I) was told 'If General Grant's army lands on this side of the river, the safety of *the* Mississippi depends on beating it. For that object you should unite your whole force.'" There are, I may remark, here two interpolations in this dispatch: the original in my possession does not contain the work "General" which I presume was added to give more dignity to the *order*. The second is of some importance as by the insertion of the article "*the*" before the word Mississippi, "the safety" of the state, as it is in the original, is made to become the safety of the river, a very different and far more serious matter. General Johnston goes on to say: "In a telegram dispatched to him (me) the next day, the instruction was repeated: 'If Grant's army crosses, unite all your troops to beat him, success will give (you) back what was abandoned to win it.'" The pronoun "you" is here interpolated, as it in some degree lessens the extreme vagueness of the expression. This dispatch of May 2d came to me, not separately and independent, as given in General Johnston's text, but in connection with other matters, which evidently had precedence, at the time, in his mind. It was in these terms: "Enemy reported falling back. Forrest moving west. Four thousand cavalry instructed to operate in Mississippi, let General Ruggles communicate with him. If Grant crosses unite all your troops to beat him, success will give back what was abandoned to win it."

As a party interested, it is not for me to decide, neither should it be permitted to General Johnston to decide, whether or not the dispatches just given do really carry with them the *weight and force* of military *orders*.[16] I maintain that they do not; that they are simply cautionary in their nature; and necessarily, only of that nature; because, General Johnston being in Tennessee, could not possibly direct my movements on the Mississippi, as to time, place and manner, and as he did not designate particularly *what* was to be abandoned, to win the success which was to give it back; it follows necessarily that I was left to decide what was to be held, as well General Johnston says:

> *On page 221 of the Narrative:*
>
> *Our best opportunity to engage the Federal army was, manifestly while it was divided in the passage of the Mississippi. Such a force as that which Lieutenant General Pemberton afterward placed near Edward's Depot, used for this object, and directed with vigor, would have had all reasonable chance of success. As well convinced of it there as now, I directed Lieutenant General Pemberton to attack the enemy with all his force, as soon as I was informed by his dispatch of May the 1st that General Bowen had been attacked by a large body of Federal Troops. This order was repeated on the 2d only to be disregarded.*
>
> *If Lieutenant General Pemberton had obeyed either of my orders to march eastwardly from Edward's, an army of thirty-five thousand men might have been formed. Such a force, properly commanded, would have prevented the siege of Vicksburg.*

It must be evident to every reader, that to refute, or even to discuss comprehensively, the themes and statements set forth in the preceding extract, is a matter of no small difficulty.

He starts with the assumption, that it was *entirely in my power to have engaged this Federal army while it was divided in the passage up the Mississippi, with a force equal to that which I afterward placed near Edward's Depot.* This imposes upon me the necessity of proving the negative; and I shall treat of this portion of the paragraph first, and independently of what succeeds.

I think I have conclusively shown in preceding pages, that unless I chose to give up Vicksburg to the enemy I could not withdraw, on my own responsibility, and in the absence of any instructions from General Johnston (for at that time I had received none), any troops which *I deemed indispensable* to its safety. It must be remembered, that while General Grant was crossing a *division* [discussed at page 169 of the *Narrative*] at a time, of McPherson's and McClernand's corps, from the west bank of the Mississippi below Vicksburg to Bruinsburg, on the day and night of the 30th of April, General Sherman with his corps [discussed on page 171 of the *Narrative*], and a division, was demonstrating against Vicksburg at Haines' [Snyder's and Drumgould's] Bluff and Chickasaw Bayou,

---

16. Pemberton misses here an opportunity to note that Johnston, as stated in the *Narrative*, did not feel himself in command of Mississippi while physically located in Tennessee. Johnston argued extensively with President Davis over this matter, especially after the campaign had concluded.

not less than *fifty five* miles distant from Bruinsburg. That this demonstration of Sherman's did not become a serious attack, was solely due to the presence of an adequate force to repel it. It is manifest therefore that the troops thus employed, Hébert's and Vaughn's brigades could not be made available at the same time to engage the enemy while divided on the passage of the Mississippi. The only remaining troops at my disposal in the vicinity of Vicksburg was Moore's brigade of Forney's division, which held Warrenton on the river nine miles below and protected my rear towards Bruinsburg, as well as the left flank of Vicksburg.

The reasons why troops equal in number to those concentrated on 13th May could not be concentrated east of the Big Black whilst the enemy was divided in crossing the Mississippi were:

1st: The necessity of retaining a sufficient force, to hold Haines' [Snyders] Bluff, approaches by Chickasaw Bayou, Vicksburg and Warrenton against a coup de main from Sherman's force which was threatening these points until after the 1st May. Those Confederate troops could not have been available whilst the enemy was divided in crossing the Mississippi.

2d: The dispersion of Loring's Division, caused by want of cavalry for which General Johnston was responsible.

3d: That before a sufficient force could be got to General Bowen, he was compelled to retire west of the Big Black, although by the 2d May seven brigades had crossed.

4th: That in the morning of the 3d May nine brigades, a force greater than that afterward collected at Edward's Depot was concentrated near Hankinson's Ferry on the west side of the Big Black and Moore's brigade within cooperation distance at Warrenton, but that the enemy in much larger force was in possession then, of the east bank of that river.

5th: That from want of cavalry I could never ascertain with certainty the enemy's position and number east of Big Black.

6th: I could not ascertain the movements of Sherman's corps west of the Mississippi, nor of the arrival of reinforcements from Memphis, and therefore could not remove the troops I thought might be necessary to repel an attack.

Manuscript skips to marked page 50. Copies of dispatches to and from Pemberton and Johnston (see Appendix A) were inserted prior to this new section. The marked manuscript above ends at page 45.

But as General Johnston has inaugurated this system, and has hypothecated or found various failures or mine in General Grant's official reports where I ought to have attacked and defeated the Federal Army. I shall use freely the same documents to quash his indictments against me, and to sustain mine against him.

The following statement of Johnston (page 216 of the Narrative) is noted by Pemberton:

Before entering upon the immediate causes, I assert, on the contrary, that in the short campaign preceding the siege of Vicksburg, he [Pemberton] obeyed none of my orders, and regarded none of my instructions; and his disasters were due to his own misapprehension of the principles of the warfare he was directing. He would have observed those principles by assailing the Federal troops with at least three divisions, instead of two or three brigades, on the 1st of May, when they were divided in the passage of the Mississippi, or after that time, by attacking McPherson's and McClernand's corps with all his forces, near Hankinson's Ferry, where they waited for Sherman until the 8th, or having failed to seize those opportunities by falling on McClernand's corps on the 12th, when it was between 14 Mile Creek and his camp near Edward's Depot, and Sherman; and McPherson's corps were at and near Raymond. On all those occasions, the chances of success would have been decidedly in his favor, and the consequences of victory much greater, and of defeat much less, to him than to his adversary.

Before entering upon the immediate causes of the battle of Baker's Creek on the 16th of May, I shall endeavor to show the following of General Johnston's theories in regards to favorable opportunities of attacking the Federal Army prior to that date and to prove that the order of the documents he quotes from is presented to sustain his theories.

General Johnston says: 1st: "His disasters were due to his (my) own misapprehension of the principles of the warfare he was directing. He (I) would have observed those principles by assailing the Federal troops with at least three divisions, instead of two or three brigades on the 1st of May when they were divided in the passage of the Mississippi."

I have demonstrated that the great want of cavalry to protect vital interests elsewhere had compelled the diversion of Major General Loring from the vicinity of the Mississippi to distant points in the interior and that despite every effort on my part to hasten the movement of those troops, they were delayed by reason of the destruction of railroads, bridges and by the enemy's cavalry until too late to participate in the battle of the 1st of May whilst the enemy "was divided in the passage of the Mississippi." Thus General Johnston is responsible for the absence of one division & three brigades on the occasion because he compelled the diversion of the Infantry whose presence might and probably would have prevented the advance of the Federal army beyond Bayou Pierre, until I could "unite my whole force to beat it."

"Or after that time" General Johnston says, I would have "observed the principles of warfare I was directing," by attacking McPherson's and McClernand's Corps with all my forces, near Hankinson's Ferry, where they waited for Sherman until the 8th.

According to General Johnston's statement "the Fifteenth Army Corps and a division of the Federal Army under Sherman" were threatening "Vicksburg from the side of the Yazoo" on the 30th of April and the 1st of May, the day on which the enemy effected his landing at Bruinsburg and was divided in the passage of the Mississippi about 50 miles from Vicksburg, and some 63 miles from Haines' [Snyder's] Bluff on the Yazoo.

On page 171, Johnston says:

To divert General Pemberton's attention from his real design, General Grant had left the Fifteenth Corps and a division at Milliken's Bend, under General Sherman, to make a demonstration against Vicksburg from the side of the Yazoo. This was executed by a slight attack upon Hayne's [Haines'] Bluff on the 30th of April, repeated next morning; after which General Sherman returned to Milliken's Bend, and marched from that point to rejoin the army.

Now this corps and division at Sherman's disposal numbered probably about 20,000, while I had so far weakened my strength in that direction, a force sufficient to have changed a demonstration into a serious attack and if successful must not only have resulted in the immediate capture of Vicksburg, but would at the same time have cut off all from my army in the field. As it was impossible for me to learn accurately either the numbers or movements of the enemy west of the Mississippi, I could not ascertain which was in reality his main force until after he had landed the greater portion of them on this side, and as my whole army including that portion occupying Vicksburg and its flank defenses, a line of 22 miles, did not exceed 28,000 fighting men, it was manifestly impossible, in the absence of Loring's division to concentrate three divisions east of the Big Black, with which "to assail the Federal troops while they were divided in the passage of the Mississippi on the 1st of May."

There is an important misstatement of facts in this portion of General Johnston's criticism. He says McClernand's and McPherson's corps waited near Hankinson's Ferry (on the Big Black) for Sherman's until the 8th and quotes General Grant's report in confirmation. General Grant says nothing of the sort; his words are these "Whilst lying at Hankinson's Ferry waiting for wagons, supplies and Sherman's corps, *which had come forward in the meantime...demonstrations were made successfully I believe* to induce the enemy to think that route and the one by Hall's Ferry above were objects of much solicitude to me...on the 7th of May an advance was ordered." General McPherson as a corps commander is naturally more particular in his official report of the events this period than General Grant. He says

[Manuscript ends page 55]

[Manuscript picks up at page 69][17]

---

17. Pemberton has shifted from discussion of concentration to contest the crossing of the Mississippi to concentration for the battle of Champion Hill.

by me *"in conjunction with the troops at Jackson,"* he criminally failed to notify me in time that those troops *could not cooperate,* while he left the execution of my part of the movement still imperative upon me.

General Johnston says "Early next morning (i.e., the 14th) it was reported that another Federal corps, Sherman's, was on the Raymond road twelve miles from Jackson: and soon after intelligence was received that both it and McPherson's were marching toward the place (Jackson) one on each road."

> Of major contention between Johnston and Pemberton is the order by Johnston for Pemberton to march on a detached portion of Grant's forces near Clinton, meet up with Johnston, and destroy this part of the Federal army. Pemberton, by the time he moved, was too late. The battles of Champion Hill, or Baker's Creek, and of Big Black Bridge, led to Pemberton's retreat to the fortifications of Vicksburg, and the eventual siege. Pemberton contends that the move was impracticable and his lack of movement the correct one. Of this, Johnston writes, on page 176 of the Narrative:

> Under the impression given me by General Pemberton's dispatch of the 12th [of May], that the main body of General Grant's army was to the south of Edward's Depot, I inferred that McPherson's corps had been detached to Clinton to hold the Confederate line of communication, and prevent the junction of reenforcements with the army. I therefore sent a note to that officer by Captain Yerger, who happened to be in Jackson and volunteered to bear it, informing him of the position of McPherson's corps between us at Clinton; urging the importance of reestablishing his communications, that reenforcements might join his army, and ordering, "if practicable come up on his rear at once. To beat such a detachment would be of immense value. The troops here could cooperate. All the force you can quickly assemble should be brought. Time is all-important."

> Early next morning it was reported that another Federal corps, Sherman's, was on the Raymond road, twelve miles from Jackson; and, soon after, intelligence was received that both it and McPherson's were marching toward the place, one on each road. A brigade was sent forward to meet each corps, to delay the enemy's approach by skirmishing with the heads of the two columns. The resistance offered in this way so impeded the progress of the Federal troops as to give ample time for the evacuation of the place, and the removal of such military property as we had the means of transporting. Fortunately, Major Mims, the chief quartermaster of the department, was at Jackson; and, foreseeing, from the intelligence received the day before, that a movement was inevitable, had begun to prepare for it.

> Regarding the battle of Jackson, General Johnston minimizes the conflict in a footnote, "In the Federal official report, their skirmishing with Gregg's and Walker's brigades is exaggerated into a heavy engagement of two hours, in which the Confederate main body was badly beaten and pursued until night. On the contrary, the skirmishing was trifling, and there was nothing like pursuit—into Jackson even. And no body of Federal soldiers was discovered by our rear-guard and reconnoitering-party between Jackson and our camp."

It is here plainly stated that the corps, or detachment which General Johnston says "I was (on the night of the 13th) to march seventeen miles to the east, for the express object of attacking, *in conjunction with the troops at Jackson"* was ascertained "early next morning" to have left Clinton and to be marching towards Jackson, and that another corps was simultaneously moving on the same place from the direction of Raymond.

Measures were taken to retard the advance of the enemy by sending forward a brigade to skirmish with the head of his column on either road to give time for the evacuation and removal of military property. "Fortunately" says General Johnston, Major Mims the chief quartermaster of the department was in Jackson, and *foreseeing* from *the intelligence received the day before* that a *movement was inevitable* had begun at once to prepare for it.

But affirming for the present that General Johnston's statement is correct, that, "I was ordered to march seventeen miles to the east, for the expressed object of attacking a large detachment in conjunction with the troops in Jackson," was it not the manifest duty of General Johnston to use every exertion to communicate with me in time to prevent this march "seventeen miles to the east" the moment he ascertained on the morning of the 14th the movements of the enemy on Jackson, both from Clinton and Raymond, that there was no longer "a large detachment" at the former place to be attacked: but if I advanced in obedience to his order that I should encounter the whole Federal Army then in my front and on my flank, and that, without the promised cooperation of the troops at Jackson? The failure to send it was a criminal negligence. This timely information was not sent me. If General Johnston has a trusty courier dispatched to me when he saw that cooperation was impossible and when "orders were sent to Brigadier Generals Gist and Maxey for the security of the troops under their respective commands," he would have had ample time to reach my army before it moved on the afternoon of the 15th from its position or certainly before the night of that day, and thus the disastrous battle of Baker's Creek would have been avoided.

Pemberton introduces here a system of referring to orders and communications with letters. These orders and communications are used throughout the text in support of his arguments. Two dispatches are discussed below — "A" and "B", as well as a dispatch sent to Richmond by Johnston upon his reaching Jackson on the 13th of May.

Jackson, May 13, 1863.

Hon. J.A. Seddon, Richmond:

I arrived this evening, finding the enemy in force between this place and General Pemberton, cutting off the communication. I am too late.

J.E. Johnston, General.

Dispatch "A" is the order to attack Sherman's detachment as ordered below:

Jackson, May 13, 1863—8.40 p.m.
Lieutenant-General Pemberton:

I have lately arrived, and learn that Major-General Sherman is between us, with four divisions, at Clinton. It is important to reestablish communication that you may be reenforced. If practicable, come up on his rear at once. To beat such a detachment would be of immediate value; the troops here could cooperate.

All the strength you can quickly assemble should be brought. Time is all-important.

Your obedient servant,
J.E. Johnston, General.

Dispatch "B" announces the evacuation of Jackson:

Camp Seven Miles From Jackson, May 14, 1863.
Lieutenant-General PEMBERTON:

GENERAL: The body of troops mentioned in my note of last night compelled Brigadier-General Gregg and his command to evacuate Jackson about noon to-day. The necessity of taking the Canton road at right angles to that upon which the enemy approached prevented an obstinate defense. A body of troops, reported this morning to have reached Raymond last night, advanced at the same time from that direction. Prisoners say that it was McPherson's corps (four divisions), which marched from Clinton. I have no certain information of the other; both skirmished very cautiously. Telegrams were dispatched when the enemy was near, directing General Gist to assemble the approaching troops at a point 40 or 50 miles from Jackson, and General Maxey to return to his wagons, and provide for the security of his brigade, for instance, by joining General Gist. That body of troops will be able, I hope, to prevent the enemy in Jackson from drawing provisions from the east, and this one may be able to keep him from the country toward Panola. Can he supply himself from the Mississippi? Can you not cut him off from it, and, above all, should he be compelled to fall back for want of supplies, beat him? As soon as the re-enforcements are all up, they must be united to the rest of the army. I am anxious to see a force assembled that may be able to inflict a heavy blow upon the enemy. Would it not be better to place the forces to support Vicksburg between General Loring and that place, and merely observe the ferries so that you might unite, if opportunity to fight presented itself? General Gregg will move toward Canton to-morrow. If prisoners tell the truth, the forces at Jackson must be half of Grant's army. It would decide the campaign to beat it, which can be done only by concentrating, especially when the remainder of the eastern troops arrive—they are to be 12,000 or 13,000.

J. E. JOHNSTON.

But General Johnston neglected to write to me until after he reached his camp seven miles N.N.E. from Jackson, on the Canton Road, and at least ten hours after he knew that his order "A" of the 13th had become impracticable of execution, but even this late information of the events of the day was not delivered to me until 5:40 p.m. on the 16th, about 48 hours after its date and after the battle had been fought and lost;[18] the explanation of this strange delay may probably be found in a communication to me from General Frank P. Blair of Missouri, who at the time referred to commanded a division in General Grant's army. It will be introduced in place, in order that the future historian may fully comprehend, how completely General Johnston had on the morning of the 14th abandoned all idea of cooperative movement with me by my army and the troops under his direct command. I must request him to examine carefully General Johnston's dispatch to me of the 14th marked "B", already noted in full, and to compare it with that of the 13th "A" which immediately preceded it. He will find a curious contrast throughout between these papers. The first of May 13th peremptorily orders a movement of the army at Edward's Depot upon the rear of the divisions of the enemy represented to be at Clinton. It is positively stated that my *troops* [Johnston's] *in Jackson could cooperate,* and I am cautioned that "time is all important."

That of the 14th "B" makes no allusion whatever to its antecedent of the 13th; it begins (with) these opening words "The body of troops mentioned in my note of last night compelled Brigadier General Gregg and his command to evacuate Jackson about noon today."

The march of "seventeen miles to the east" which General Johnston says I was ordered to make "to take part in a combined attack upon a detachment" is utterly ignored, but I am asked whether I can cut off the enemy from supplying himself with provisions from the Mississippi. "And above all, should he be *compelled to fall back* for *want of supplies,* beat him." I am informed that telegrams were dispatched when *the enemy was near* directing General Gist to assemble the *approaching* troops (those from Smith's division) at a point *forty or fifty miles from Jackson* "and General Maxey (from Port Hudson) to provide for his safety, for instance by joining General Gist."

"That body of troops" (Gist's and Maxey's), he notes, "will be able to prevent the enemy in Jackson from drawing provisions from the east, *and this one* (that which was to cooperate with my movement) may be able to keep him from the country towards Panola, that is from the country towards the Northern part of Mississippi" and then I am told "General Gregg will move *towards Canton* (not Clinton) *tomorrow.*"

Now Canton is twenty-five miles N.N.E. from Jackson; Clinton is *ten* miles due west. Yet these troops, according to his order "A" of the night of the 13th, were to cooperate in the movement I was directed to make towards Clinton with all the troops I could quickly assemble, and thus did actually encamp on the 15th *eighteen*

---

18. The battle of Champion Hill, or Baker's Creek.

miles N.N.E. from Jackson and at least 21 miles from Clinton. I request that the reader will keep this fact in mind for a moment and note particularly the date of the 15th. In his official report to the Confederate War Department General Johnston says, "on the next day, *May 15*, Friday, the *troops under* me, marched ten and a half miles further, to Calhoun Station (on the road to Canton). On the morning of that day, I received a letter from General Pemberton, dated Edward's Depot May 14th (Thursday) five forty p.m." He then gives an extract from my letter and adds "This was the first communication received from General Pemberton, after my arrival in Jackson." *Why it* was *the first* will probably be understood from the letter of General F. P. Blair to me and from it I learned that he had not moved towards Clinton, ten hours after the receipt of my order to do so, *and that the junction* of the forces *which could have been* affected by the 15th "was deferred."

This is certainly a most extraordinary statement, (at) least it shows the reliance General Johnston makes on the influence of bold, but unproved, and unprovable assertions.

The order referred to "A" was received by me at ten minutes after 9 a.m. on the 14th when I was on the road, six miles west of my army. About this hour, probably (see his dispatch "B" of the 14th) General Johnston was in the act of ordering Brigadier General Gist and Maxey to assemble the reinforcements coming from South Carolina and from Port Hudson "at a point *forty or fifty miles from Jackson*," to the east of that place, and therefore ten miles further, or fifty or sixty miles from Clinton. He could not therefore by any possibility have expected a junction of those troops with mine on the 15th.

> *Pemberton footnotes page 179 of Johnston's Narrative for the following section. The appropriate paragraph is as follows:*
>
> *On the 15th the march of Gregg's and Walker's troops was continued ten miles, to Calhoun Station. While on the way, at ten o'clock a.m., a letter to me, from General Pemberton, was delivered by Captain Yerger. It was dated Edward's Depot, 5:40 p.m., May 14th, and contained no reference to mine of the 13th, carried to him by that gentleman, and delivered, he told me, about 7 a.m., on the 14th. In this note General Pemberton announced that he would "move as early as practicable on the 15th, with a column of seventeen thousand men, to Dillon's, on the main road from Jackson to Port Gibson, for the purpose of cutting the enemy's communications," and compelling them to attack him, as he did not think his force sufficient to justify him in attacking.*

In the same dispatch "B" dated from his camp on the *Canton Road* seven miles from Jackson, and at least thirteen from Clinton, he announced in these words, his *intention* of moving on the next day the 15th further from me, and farther from Clinton. "*General Gregg will move towards Canton tomorrow.*" This dispatch was written as late or later on the afternoon of the 14th than mine to him which was dated 5:40 p.m. on the same day and which he says was delivered by Captain Yerger "while on the way (that is on the way to *Canton not to Clinton*) at ten o'clock a.m. on the 15th."

Johnston continues, on page 179 of the Narrative, with his view of the exchange of these communications:

The fact that this letter was written almost eleven hours after my order had been delivered, and announced continued inaction for many more, when every hour was so important, was very discouraging, especially when the movement for which the preparations seemed to be made so deliberately would greatly increase the difficulty of our junction. In a reply, written and dispatched without delay, General Pemberton was told that the only mode by which we could unite was by his moving directly to Clinton and informing me, that I might meet him there with about six thousand men.

Can the future historian believe that General Johnston expected to cooperate with me in an attack upon a detachment at Clinton on the 15th or to form a junction with my troops on that day? General Johnston says "The fact that this letter (of mine) was written almost eleven hours after the receipt of my (his) order, and announced continued inaction for many more, when every hour was so very important, *was very discouraging.*"

As a superlative specimen of speculative fiction, I think this extract surpasses anything to be found in the pages of the *Narrative.*

If he can be so deluded, let him explain the significance of one more extract from General Johnston's dispatch "B" of the 14th. After asking me whether the enemy "can supply himself from the Mississippi" and whether I cannot "cut him off from it" he says "*As soon as* the reinforcements are *all up, they must be united to the rest of the army.* I am anxious to see a force assembled that may be able to inflict a heavy blow upon the enemy."

I reassert, that, when General Johnston ascertained that cooperation on his part to be impracticable, he criminally failed to give me timely notice of the fact, but left it imperative upon me to carry out unaided the part assigned to my army in the cooperative movement designated in his order.

It is now my unpleasant duty to show that by the bad faith of his agent, the Federal General was so well informed of the purpose of General Johnston's peremptory order to me "A" and of my intended obedience to that order, that "availing himself of this information," he so disposed his entire force to meet the expected movement "to come upon his rear" by whatever route I might select for that object.

At half after nine o'clock on the morning of the 14th of May, a courier from General Johnston handed me the dispatch "A". I was near Bovina west of the Big Black and en route to take the immediate command of my Army then in position, a mile, or more in advance of Edward's Depot on the line of the Jackson and Vicksburg railroad. I received this order with great regret, for I believed it to be unwise and unnecessary. I thought it unnecessary, because the reinforcements then in Jackson and expected there, could be readily united with my army if the enemy were in Clinton, by making a detour to the north of the railroad, and then turning to the west. With *timely* notice from General Johnston of his intentions to make such a movement, I might have cooperated effectively to aid it. If his health did not permit him to march with the troops, Brigadier General Gregg, the senior brigadier was quite competent to the occasion, as Walker would have been, or Gist, or Maxey, should he have deemed it advisable to send forward each brigade as soon as it arrived in Jackson. It is plain that General Johnston supposed the enemy would remain in Clinton for he expressly says "under the impression given me by General Pemberton's dispatch of the 12th...I *inferred* that McPherson's corps had been *detached* to Clinton, to *hold* the Confederate line of communications, and prevent the junction of reinforcements with the Army." [This was] a strange inference since the *destruction* of the railroad effectively prevented its use as a Confederate line of communication, while his presence at Clinton would not "prevent the junction of reinforcements with the army" which could be effected by making the detour I have mentioned, without lengthening the march more than 12 or 15 miles at the utmost.

I replied immediately to General Johnston's dispatch as follows:

This communication, marked Dispatch "C" by Pemberton, reads:

Bovina, May 14, 1863.

General JOSEPH E. JOHNSTON, Jackson:

I have the honor to acknowledge receipt of your communication. I move at once with whole available force, about 16,000, from Edwards Depot, leaving Vaughn's brigade, about 1,500, at Big Black Bridge. Tilghman's brigade, 1,500, now at Baldwin's Ferry, I have ordered to bring up the rear of my column. He will be, however, from 15 to 20 miles behind it. Baldwin's Ferry will be left necessarily unprotected. To hold Vicksburg are Smith's and Forney's divisions, extending from Snyder's Mill to Warrenton, numbering, effective, 7,500 men. To this should have been added Waul's Legion, the Mississippi State troops, and Higgins'. The men have been marching several days, are much fatigued, and, I fear, will straggle very much. In directing this move, I do not think you fully comprehend the position that Vicksburg will be left in, but I comply at once with your order.

J. C. PEMBERTON.

Referring to this letter General Johnston says "In the afternoon of that day (May 16th) a reply "C" to my first dispatch "A" to General Pemberton was received, dated Bovina, 9:10 o'clock a.m. of the 14th that is, more than *fifty hours* after I delivered it in the hands of his *own courier*, who remained on the spot while I was writing it, and who *volunteered* to carry it to General Johnston.

Another letter, "D", of the same date, is thus referred to by General Johnston: "While on the way (to *Canton* on the *15th*) at ten o'clock a.m. a letter to me from General Pemberton, was *delivered by Captain Yerger*. It was dated Edward's Depot,

5:40 p.m. May 14th, and contained no reference to mine of the 13th ("A"), *carried to him by that gentleman,* and delivered, he told me, about 7 a.m. on the 14th."

Dispatch "D" as discussed below, is as follows:

Hdqrs. Dept. Miss. and E. La., Edwards Depot, May 14, 1863.

General JOSEPH E. JOHNSTON:

GENERAL: I shall move as early to-morrow morning as practicable with a column of 17,000 men to Dillon's, situated on the main road leading from Raymond to Port Gibson, 7? miles below Raymond and 9? miles from Edwards Depot. The object is to cut enemy's communications and to force him to attack me, as I do not consider my three [divisions] sufficient to justify an attack on enemy in position or to attempt to cut my way to Jackson.

At this point your nearest communication would be through Raymond. I wish very much I could join my re-enforcements. Whether it will be most practicable for the re-enforcements to come by Raymond, leaving it to the right if the march cannot be made through Raymond, or to move them west along the line of the railroad, but leaving it to the left, south of the line of march to Bolton Depot or some point west of it; in either movement I should be advised as to time and road, so that co-operation may be had to enable the re-enforcements to come through.

I send you a map of the country, which will furnish you with a correct view of the roads and different localities.

I am, general, very respectfully, your obedient servant,

J. C. PEMBERTON.

[Indorsement.]
CANTON, May 24, 1863.

The within dispatch was sent in answer to one from Lieutenant-General Pemberton, in which he says that he would move early on the 15th instant to a place called Dillon's.

A. P. MASON.

Your dispatch just received. Our being compelled to evacuate Jackson renders your plan impracticable. Therefore, move in the direction of Clinton, and communicate with me, that I may unite with you with about 6,000 troops.

There is something nonetheless about the manipulation of this correspondence which needs explanation. It seems from General Johnston's statement that my letter "D" dated 5:40 p.m. on the 14th from Edward's Depot, was delivered to him on the Canton Road by Captain Yerger, at ten o'clock a.m. on the 15th while that dated "C" from Bovina 9:10 a.m. on the same day, eight and a half hours earlier was not delivered to him until the afternoon of the 16th at least ninety-six hours later.

My impression is that a Captain Yerger reached my headquarters after the delivery of General Johnston's dispatch "A" to me and that he carried my second letter "D" of the 14th, which was delivered to General Johnston in due time, on the morning of the 15th. I have been informed, whether correct or not, I cannot say, that Capt. Yerger, unable to find his way to my army, transferred the dispatch on the night of the 13th to another at a certain point on the route, the same person, I presume, who gave it to me, and to whom I entrusted my reply.

> *Pemberton believed the subject of the betrayal of the dispatch to be extremely sensitive. The manuscript has two cross-out attempts to write the preceding paragraph prior to his settling on what is presented immediately above.*
>
> *The first reads: "I have been informed, whether correctly or not I can not say, that the name of the person who delivered to me General Johnston's dispatch "A" of the 13th and to whom my reply "C" of the 14th was entrusted, was not Yerger, but the latter, not knowing how to reach my Army, transferred the dispatch in this way to another (I presume this was the individual who delivered it to me)."*
>
> *The second reads: "My impression is that Capt. Yerger arrived at my Head Quarters later on the 14th, and that he carried my second dispatch of that date, to General Johnston, which was received at his hands, by General Johnston, in due time on the morning of the 15th."*

General Johnston says (on page 180 of the *Narrative*): "General Grant had been told in Jackson that General Pemberton had been ordered peremptorily to march from Edward's Depot to attack him *in rear*. He determined, therefore, to concentrate his own forces, and fall upon General Pemberton." In his official report General Grant does not state where or how he received this important information; he says, however, that he availed himself of any "immediately opened orders" to meet the case. Two years since I learned from friends who were residents of Mississippi at the time that General Frank P. Blair of Missouri had in conversation with them and others stated that the correspondence between General Johnston and myself had been betrayed by General Johnston's courier, previous to the battle of Baker's Creek, to General Grant. Hearing that General Johnston intended to assail me particularly in reference to that battle in his forthcoming book, I addressed a note to General Blair to which the following is a reply (here copy General Blair's letter).[19]

Blair's letter was not in the manuscript papers, but was as follows:

ST. LOUIS,
January 24, 1874.

Dear General: I take pleasure in answer to your letter of January 19, in saying that it was generally understood in our Army that General J. Johnston's courier conveying dispatches to you previous to the battle of Baker's Creek, or Champion's Hill,

---

19. Johnston's memoirs, *Narrative of Military Operations.*

betrayed his dispatches to General Grant and also your answers to General John-ston's orders, so that in fact General Grant had the most precise information as to your movements and those of General Johnston. I do not know positively from Gen-eral Grant these facts but the matter was spoken of by the officers of our Army in such a way as to leave no doubt in my mind.

Very respectfully, your obedient servant,
FRANK P. BLAIR.

As General Blair stated, that he did not "know positively from General Grant these facts," I addressed a note of inquiry to the President, without naming Gen-eral Blair as my informant, as to their authenticity. Mr. Levi P. Luchy his secre-tary promptly replied: "The President authorizes me to say that the statement of the officer to which you refer was correct…He says the dispatches were brought in our lines and given to General McPherson, and by him, immediately brought to Head Quarters."

When General Johnston wrote his Official Report of operations in Missis-sippi and East Louisiana dated November 1, 1863, it is very possible he had not seen the report of General Grant, dated July 6, 1863. He may therefore have been as ignorant of the position and strength of the Federal Army then, as he was, when he ordered me on the 13th of May "to come up on the rear" of what he sup-posed to be a detachment composed of five divisions at Clinton, but in reality upon *all* most the entire force of that army. It is reasonable to believe, also that General Johnston was ignorant of the fact until he read General Grant's report, that the latter was fully informed of the proposed combined movement against him before it could possibly be put into operation. Under the supposed circum-stances, it was perhaps not altogether unnatural that General Johnston should struggle against his own convictions, and should succeed in persuading himself that he had not committed an inexcusable military blunder after having thor-oughly deluded himself he should use the same reasons to delude others.

But, when this state of ignorance had ceased to be [no] longer possible: when he had possessed himself of the Federal reports, and when theories had given place to ascertained facts, it is unaccountably strange that General Johnston should persist in his original statements; nay, that he should even go beyond them and apparently for the sole purpose of injuring me in public opinion "because I had constituted myself his enemy," [to] introduce new matter against me, which is positively disproved by the very evidence he addresses in the support of his operations. I have given various instances of this in the preceding pages, where I have cited *the language* of the Federal reports to which General Johnston refers in marginal notes.

After I had handed to General Johnston's courier my reply to his dispatch "A" of the preceding night, I directed Maj. General Loring, the senior Maj. Gen.

with the troops at Edward's Depot to "Have the whole army in readiness to move forward at a moment's notice." I was still delayed until near 11 o'clock by the numerous changes necessary to be made to meet the circumstances which had so unexpectedly arisen and by which all my previous arrangements had become not only useless, but were absolute impediments to an immediate movement under General Johnston's orders.

I did not, therefore, reach the position occupied by my army until after 12 p.m. There I learned, from Maj. General Loring, that the confirmation of prior report(s) as to the advance of the *main body* of the enemy's forces towards Raymond and Jackson but it was also positively ascertained through scouts and otherwise, that he had a division if not a corps on my right flank to hold his line of communication and to threaten my rear if I should directly move directly towards Jackson or Clinton both immediately in *my front*, the one 18 and the other 28 miles distant.

It was evident to my mind, that, the only practicable route by which I could come up on the rear "of the four divisions" of the enemy under Sherman at Clinton, which General Johnston's order specified, was that route, which would place me on his line of communications. This would compel me to fall back from Clinton as well as from those points in my front to the assistance of the troops he had left near Dillon's plantation at the junction of the Edward's Depot and Raymond road, with the Raymond and Port Gibson road. This movement against the detachment near Dillon's if successful would reopen direct communication with Jackson and enable reinforcements there to join my Army, which was the main purpose indicated in General Johnston's order "A" of the preceding night. I regarded it as impractical, though I considered it extremely hazardous and of very doubtful result, because from want of cavalry. I could not accurately ascertain the strength nor position of the main body of the *enemy*, which might be so disposed as to be within supporting distance of the detachment he had left in his rear, and which I hoped to encounter, while too far separated for reinforcements to reach this.

I had however been ordered peremptorily "if practicable" to come upon the rear of the four divisions under Sherman at Clinton. I did deem the movement by the route I had described practicable, but of very doubtful issue, for the reasons given. I was therefore greatly adverse to any change of position, believing that I could defend it against thrice my numbers and confident that General Grant must attack me there or withdraw (to his base on the Mississippi the major part of his army) where the heavy reinforcements of cavalry promised me, and the concentration of 12 or 13,000 infantry at or near Jackson would enable me at least partially to take the offensive. With the hope that the *all* officers would sustain me in my opposition to *any* advance I...called a council of war, the first I had ever assembled either during a six month's administration of the military affairs of the Dept. of S.C. [South Carolina] and Georgia, or during a longer period of command in that of Mississippi and East Louisiana.

My views, except perhaps by Brig. General Bowen commanding the division of Missouri and Arkansas troops, by Brig. General Featherston, and by Colonel Wirt Adams commanding the cavalry (and of their opinions I am not positive) were not sustained by the officers present, at least three fourths of them were against a forward movement. I have stated in my official report that "a majority of the officers present expressed themselves favorable to the movement indicated by General Johnston."

General Johnston has endeavored to use this admission to my prejudice; he frequently refers to it, and perverts the sense of the order, to make my admission sustain the construction he wishes to give to it: a construction which if correct and attempted to carry out, would have inevitably resulted in the destruction or capture of my entire army of the troops left to protect my rear, and of Vicksburg itself (before I could possibly have reached Clinton, with three divisions averaging 6,000 each, the enemy would have had 10 divisions against me). No one knows this fact better than General Johnston, yet he persistently ignores it, and, although he does not actually assert that a march direct upon Clinton (which he pretends his Order "A" required), would have had successful results, he strives indirectly to convey that impression, relying upon the ignorance, not upon the intelligence of the reader to accept that conclusion. But as a matter of fact, I was in error as to the views of "a majority of the officers present": the majority advised and urged that movement upon the Federal rear which I eventually though against my own judgment acceded to because I believed it to be the only practicable obedience I could give to General Johnston's orders.

I shall here introduce an extract from the report of Major Jacob Thompson, at the time a member of my staff under a commission from the Confederate Government, and formerly Secretary of the Interior in the Cabinet of President Buchanan. Few if any of the citizens of Mississippi had greater interests at stake in the success of the Confederate cause. He cannot therefore reasonably be supposed to have been biased in favor of my views by any partiality towards me. This gentleman was initially associated with me by official relations; he was well acquainted with my views on all important points connected with the defense of the Department. In common with the rest of my staff, who accompanied me from Vicksburg when I left that place to take the immediate command of the Army, Major Thompson was directed to furnish a written report, especially of the *orders* delivered on the battle field, and generally of other matters coming within his personal observation under date 21 July 1863 while the subject was yet fresh in his memory.

Major Thompson says:[20]

> I was present at that council, and heard your views, and those of the different officers expressed. You stated at great length and to my mind with great force, that the leading and great duty of your army, was to defend Vicksburg; the disproportion of numbers of the enemy and your forces; the bad effect of a defeat, and the probability of each result if you moved forward. After *canvassing* the question, there was not a voice in favor of a movement on Clinton. But in as much as the enemy had moved in force on Jackson, leaving (as was supposed) only a single division on the Big Black, it was first suggested by General Loring, and *afterward* acquiesced in by all the other officers that it would be wise and expedient to move on the next day, on the southern or Raymond road to Dillon's which was on the *main leading* road by *which the enemy carried on his communications*, give battle to the division *left in the rear* and thus effectively break up the enemy's communications.
>
> In this council it seemed to be taken for granted by all the officers, that the enemy was then engaged in an effort to reduce Jackson; and was therefore too far removed to participate in the expected fight. You gave in to the views of the officers with reluctance, and expressed yourself, ordering it *against your convictions*. But being present and hearing every thing said I did not see how you could have done other wise with any expectation of retaining your hold upon the army. It had been intimated again and again to me, that you were adverse to a fight with the enemy, and that everybody believed the time for active operations had come. Though possessed *of your views and concurring in them*, yet this feeling had so great an influence on me that I believed at the time that a fight was inevitable and so expressed myself to you.

Now the convocation of this Council resulted immediately from the receipt of General Johnston's order "A" of the preceding night. If that order had not been received, a council would not have been called. When it was handed to me on the road, some six miles west of the position where the council was held, I believed that it was practicable though very hazardous to move upon Clinton by the direct, or stated route, only diverging from that route only after I came upon the enemy's rear (at some point in the vicinity of Clinton) should he still occupy that place.

When I received General Johnston's vague order to come up with "all the force I could quickly assemble" on the rear of the four divisions of the enemy which, he represented, were at Clinton under General Sherman, I inferred, not from any instructions to that effect, for the dispatch contained none, but I imply from the general tone, that he expected me to do so by the most direct route. After reaching Edward's Depot, I found that an attempt to come up on the enemy's rear by *that route* would most certainly involve the loss of the army and Vicksburg, because in addition to the greatly superior forces in my front, my right-flank and rear...

[Manuscript skips from the conclusion of Pemberton's Page 84 to Page 89]

---

20. The full text of Thompson's report may be found at *OR*, Ser. I, vol. XXIV, pt 2, 124-127.

The section that follows is Pemberton's response to Johnston's summary of the Vicksburg campaign. Starting on page 218 of the Narrative, Johnston states:

General Pemberton received four orders from me during this campaign.

The first, dated May 1st, and repeated on the 2d, directed him to attack the Federal army with all his forces united for the purpose.

The second, dated May 13th, is that by which he professes to have been instigated to the movement which tangled him with Federal skirmishers in the morning of the 16th, and involved him in the battle which he lost. He was ordered to march seventeen miles to the east, for the expressed object of attacking a large detachment, in conjunction with the troops in Jackson, to reopen his communications and enable reenforcements to join him. His intended movement was to a point nine and a half miles almost south, for the avowed object of compelling the Federal army to attack him in a position where our cooperation would have been impossible, and where reenforcements could not have reached him. He was ordered to the east, to take part in a combined attack upon a detachment. He moved southward, to fight an army in a position where aid could not have reached him. His movement defeated my purpose, distinctly expressed to him, of uniting all the expected reenforcements with his army, a measure necessary to give a reasonable hope of success. Yet, in all his publications on the subject, General Pemberton repeats the assertion, that obedience to this order exposed him to attack and led to his defeat—when his design and objects, and mine, were founded on exactly opposite military principles.

[Johnston says:] "He was ordered to march seventeen miles to the east, for the express object of attacking a large *detachment* in conjunction with the troops in Jackson to reopen his communications and enable arriving reinforcements to join him...he moved southward to fight an army in a position where aid could not have reached him..."

All this is mere assertion. I was not ordered to march seventeen miles to the east, nor was I ordered to *attack* any detachment large or small. I was ordered to "come up, *on the rear*" of four divisions at Clinton in my front and 18 miles east. These troops had marched that day from Raymond on their main line of communication, south west of Clinton, and therefore in the rear. Front, flank and rear have a recognized meaning in military language which even General Johnston can not change. In the case in point the enemy's left flank was towards me, his right flank to General Johnston and his rear towards Raymond, the direction of my proposed march to come up on his rear.

The object was expressed plainly enough "it is important to reestablish communications that you may be reinforced" and it was added "to *beat* such a detachment *would be* of immense value...the troops here *could* cooperate." It is a curious fact that in no one of his dispatches to me has General Johnston used the word "*attack*," nor is there a single instance in which, he can, without a palpably forced construction, be made to express the idea conveyed in those dispatches. The "immense value" expected to accrue to us, was in the "beating of such a detachment"; to *attack*, and not "to beat" would have been an immense detriment. But

General Johnston says, "He moved southward to fight an army in a position where aid could not have reached him"; I have already shown, that, when I moved towards the enemy's rear, I had no reason to suppose that General Johnston was not still in Jackson. I have also shown by his own admission, [that this] prevented his cooperation and a junction of our forces. He has no authority for referring as he does assert that my movement was "for the avowed object of compelling the *Federal army* to attack me."

My expression was (see my Dispatch "D") "to compel *the enemy* to attack me." If I fought "an army" instead of a detachment it was because the correspondence between General Johnston and myself, was betrayed to the Federal general by his agent or agents; not by mine, it ill becomes him therefore to make this fact a subject of reproach against me.

The "military principle in which my design and objects were founded," has been explained. That principle which requires from the General a regard for the safety of his own army by securing its rear and flanks, and protecting the communication with its base and magazines of supplies, was at least observed, as far as any movement to the front permitted its observance. General Johnston seems to have conceived the strange idea that the design and object which he enumerates as his simply because they were his are to be considered irrespective of their absolute impracticability, and of the certain ruin which must have resulted from their literal adoption; and these may be treated as purely as if they were compatible with the military principle upon which he implies they were founded—while in fact they were applied to this, and to every other principle of warfare.

According to his own statement, General Johnston's order "A" of the night of the 13th was based on information derived from me, and on an inference drawn therefrom by himself. He says, "under the information given me by Lieut. General Pemberton's dispatch of the 12th, that the *main body* of General Grant's army was to the *south of Edward's* Depot, I *inferred* that McPherson's corps had been detached to Clinton..." I have already shown that this impression was entirely correct; the inference was equally so. "The main body of General Grant's army," to wit the corps of Sherman and McClernand, were moved on the 12th from the Port Gibson and Raymond road, in a direction nearly due north towards Edward's Depot. Both corps, crossing Fourteen Mile Creek, approaching by converging roads, to within seven or eight miles of that station. McPherson's corps was pushed forward on the same day, to Raymond, where he encountered Gregg's brigade, and forced him back towards Jackson.

Page 90 of the manuscript has a lengthy paragraph crossed out as an earlier version of the above.

The next day McPherson moved eight miles to Clinton. This was the "large detachment" I "was ordered to march *seventeen miles to the east* for the expressed object of attacking in conjunction with the troops in Jackson" because he says he "was under the impression that the main body of General Grant's army was south of Edward's Depot." He got that impression from my dispatch of the 12th: "The enemy is apparently moving his heavy force towards Edward's Depot on southern railroad. With my limited force I will do all I can to meet him; that will be the battlefield if I can carry forward sufficient forces, leaving troops enough to secure the safety of this place (Vicksburg)."

He must have known, therefore, when he ordered me to abandon the position named in my dispatch to "march seventeen miles to the east" the main body of General Grant's army to the south of Edward's Depot could interpose itself between Vicksburg and my army, come upon its rear, or flank, while on the march; or move direct to Clinton and unite with the "large detachment" there, or concentrate the entire force in my front. Whichever course General Grant might adopt, the distance to be marched by either of his corps was less than "seventeen miles to the east" assigned to my army. General Johnston has declared "his design and objects." With the preceding statement of facts, and his own admission before them, I leave to his enthusiastic admirers, the agreeable task of explaining the "military principles" in which they were founded.

Having determined, although against my own judgment and to the subversion of my matured plans, but by the urgent advice of an almost unanimous council, that I would carry out as far as practicable General Johnston's instructions, I addressed him the following letter (Dispatch "D") (here insert second letter of the 14th) delivered he says by Capt. Yerger no doubt faithfully and in due season.

Pemberton, in his notes, indicated he wished Dispatch "D" inserted here. Although placed through edits earlier in the manuscript, it is inserted here also:

HDQRS. DEPT. MISS. AND E. LA., Edwards Depot, May 14, 1863.

General JOSEPH E. JOHNSTON:

GENERAL: I shall move as early to-morrow morning as practicable with a column of 17,000 men to Dillon's, situated on the main road leading from Raymond to Port Gibson, 7? miles below Raymond and 9? miles from Edwards Depot. The object is to cut enemy's communications and to force him to attack me, as I do not consider my three sufficient to justify an attack on enemy in position or to attempt to cut my way to Jackson.

At this point your nearest communication would be through Raymond. I wish very much I could join my re-enforcements. Whether it will be most practicable for the re-enforcements to come by Raymond, leaving it to the right if the march cannot be made through Raymond, or to move them west along the line of the railroad, but leaving it to the left, south of the line of march to Bolton Depot or some point west of it; in either movement I should be advised as to time and road, so that co-operation may be had to enable the re-enforcements to come through.

I send you a map of the country, which will furnish you with a correct view of the roads and different localities.

I am, general, very respectfully, your obedient servant,

J. C. PEMBERTON.

[Indorsement.]

CANTON, May 24, 1863.

The within dispatch was sent in answer to one from Lieutenant-General Pemberton, in which he says that he would move early on the 15th instant to a place called Dillon's.

A. P. MASON.

Your dispatch just received. Our being compelled to evacuate Jackson renders your plan impracticable. Therefore, move in the direction of Clinton, and communicate with me, that I may unite with you with about 6,000 troops.

This dispatch, and that of the same date marked (Dispatch "C") heretofore given were the only communications I addressed to General Johnston previous to the battle of Baker's Creek. It will be observed that I supposed General Johnston's troops to be still in Jackson and that I had provided for their junction with my army in the movement contemplated and explained to him. By it, I avoided the danger to my rear from the force I knew to be "to the south of Edward's Depot," a force which General Johnston was under the impression was "the main body of General Grant's army" and prevented it from interposing itself between Vicksburg and my army; while the "detachment of four divisions" represented to be in Clinton, could be headed off if it attempted to move west upon Edward's Depot. Having only half the distance to march, I could retrace my steps to that point in half the time "the detachment" would require to reach it.

Of course the possible betrayal of the correspondence between General Johnston and myself did not enter as an element into consideration of the advantages or disadvantages of either movement; as it was, however, it had the most important result because the information thus acquired enabled the enemy to concentrate against my army of three divisions seven of his divisions instead of two or three at most, which I had hoped to encounter whilst they were separated beyond supporting distance from the others. But disastrous as those results were, they were fortunate compared with the consequences which must have ensued from an attempt to march seventeen miles to the east which General Johnston asserts he directed.

General Johnston's absurd pretense, that whatever then was a delay on my part in executing his order of the 13th, was "very discouraging" to him and the equally absurd assertion made in his official report, that, "the junction of the forces, which *could have been effected on the 15th,* was deferred" have been sufficiently exposed by the introduction of his letter (Dispatch "B") of the 14th and by the movements he made towards Canton on that day, *and* on the 15th. Not that there was not unreasonable delay; I think (it) will be apparent to those who remember, that, it was not a detachment from the army that the army that was to be there moved off, but the main army itself, which had for seven months had been opposing the enemy under my exclusive direction, and had been established by me in the position it occupied when the order was received, with special reference to the defense of the vital point of the department, and as I regarded it, of the Confederacy.

That a fundamental change of place had become necessary, a new disposition of troops; the division of wagons from other service to furnish transportation by dirt road, for troops that would otherwise have received supplies by the railroad between Vicksburg and the camp. And finally, that, a heavy rain which fell for hours made the roads and creeks impassable, at least for wagons and artillery before the morning of the 15th.

Continuing on in his summary of the events that led up to the battle of Champion Hill (Baker's Creek), Johnston further discusses on page 219 of the Narrative (continuing the discussion last quoted above):

But this march of Pemberton's would have involved no other commander in a battle. He moved but three or four miles on the 15th. The presence of the enemy was reported to him that night. It frustrated the intention in such slow course of execution; therefore, he must have felt himself free to return to the "chosen ground" near Edward's Depot, on which his "matured plans" were to have been executed. His army could have marched to it in about an hour.

Even if he had a right to think himself acting under my order on the 15th, he could not have thought so on the 16th; for at 6:30 a.m. he received my third order, again directing him to march to the east to meet me, that our troops might be united. Obedience was easy, for the engagement did not begin until near mid-day; and in the mean time there was but a division of the enemy before him. Instead of remaining passive four or five hours, until the Federal army was ready to attack him, he could have extricated himself in a few minutes from the skirmishers of a force so inferior to his own, and obeyed the last order. Instead of pursuing this obvious course, General Pemberton remained inactive while General Grant was assembling his forces and preparing to attack him.

In discussing this question, Lieutenant-General Pemberton assumes that the loss of the battle of Baker's Creek was inevitable. It certainly was made probable by the complete separation of Gregg's and Walker's brigades from his army, and his detaching Vaughn's and Reynold's. The presence of these four brigades would have added not less than ten thousand men to his fighting force. It is not unreasonable to think that such an addition would have given us the victory; for but three Federal divisions actually fought, while four were held in check by Loring, or rather, by two of Loring's three brigades.

But, says General Johnston, "This march of Pemberton's would have involved no other commander in a battle. He moved but three or four miles on the 15th. The presence of the enemy was reported to him that night. It frustrated the intention in such slow course of execution; therefore, he must have felt himself free to return to the "chosen ground" near Edward's Depot, on which his "matured plans" were to have been executed. His army could have marched to it in about an hour."

Here is another instance of the faculty possessed by the distinguished author (of) the faculty of condensing multum in parvo [much from little]. But as this gift, where I am concerned, is generally employed in misrepresentation of my acts and motives, the only result it has is to compel me to weary the reader who may accompany me in my endeavor to refute them. As I do not pretend to infallibility, it is as well to let pass the assertion that "This march of Pemberton's would have involved no other commander in a battle." General Johnston says it would not, and General Johnston is an infallible man. "He moved but three or four miles on the 15th...His army could have marched to it in about an hour." I moved six or seven miles on the 15th. The army was put in motion about noon and the last division did not bivouac until after midnight in consequence of the heavy and narrow road by which it was compelled to advance. Possibly the great master of retreat might have made the march back "in about an hour"; no other commander I think could have accomplished it. "The presence of the enemy was reported to him that night. It frustrated the intention in such slow course of execution, therefore, he must have felt himself free to return to the "chosen ground" near Edward's Depot at which his "matured plans" would have been executed."

[The manuscript continues on Pemberton's Page 99]

Pemberton is discussing the battle of Champion Hill, or Baker's Creek. The above passage is perhaps the most sarcasm as will be found in the manuscript. Continuing on, he is still referring to the last section of the Narrative on page 219 and quoted above.

"was easy for the engagement did not begin until near mid day; and in the meantime there was but a division of the enemy before him. Instead of remaining passive four or five hours until the Federal army was ready to attack him, he could have extricated himself in a few minutes from the skirmishers of a force inferior to his own and obeyed the last order."

I can not believe that any just man will be unwilling to weigh fairly the evidence I shall bring to refute the charges made against me in the shape of assertions without proof in the foregoing extract. General Johnston's criticism must be viewed from this standpoint. That, my army was not in position near Edward's Depot when it had bivouacked late in the preceding night with the head of the column. Brig. General Tilghman's brigade [was] thrown forward on the lower Raymond and Edward's Depot road and about six miles from the latter point. Colonel Wirt Adams' commanding our small cavalry force had just reported skirmishing between his pickets and those of the enemy in front of General Tilghman.

A retrograde movement was immediately ordered. It hardly commenced before the cavalry pickets were driven in and the enemy's artillery opened at long range on the head of the column on the Raymond Road, by the new movement, became our lead.

It will be observed in the following extract from Major General Stevenson's report that the road, by which the army had advanced to the position then occupied, and by which along it could retrace its steps to execute General Johnston's order, was not open for the passage of Infantry and Artillery until 9:30 o'clock a.m. The road being narrow, and for the most part hedged in on either side by dense woodlands rendered the movement of the wagon train, as described by General Stevenson, indispensable before a movement of the troops could be made. General Stevenson says:

> At sunrise I was summoned to appear at Headquarters, where I was informed by the Lieutenant General commanding, that he had received instructions from General Johnston to join him near Canton as soon as possible, and that he had decided to move at once, in pursuance thereto, towards Brownsville, on the north of the railroad, by the route as far as the railroad, by which we had advanced the previous night. He directed me to move the trains, as rapidly as possible to a point at least three miles beyond the Jackson road, and then halt there, arranged to the right and left of the road in such a manner as would offer an uninterrupted passage to the Infantry and Artillery. I immediately caused the trains to be turned, and in charge of my fourth brigade of Col. Reynolds to be moved rapidly to the rear, in accordance with the instructions I had received. Col. Reynolds was directed to place one regiment in front of the train, and to form the remainder of his brigade in line of battle, and, covering the Clinton and Raymond roads, there to remain until relieved by the next brigade in his rear. It was intended to *hold these roads* by the brigades as they *successively arrived* until the *passage of the entire army could be effected*. The success of this movement, depending mainly on the speedy relief of the road from the obstructions caused by the presence of the trains, I dispatched two of my staff officers Majors Webb and Anderson to superintend the operations of those in charge of the trains. About nine and a half o'clock a.m. the latter reported that the road was open, the trains having been placed as ordered, and free for the passage of the troops...About nine o'clock a.m., Lee relieved Reynolds on the Raymond and Clinton roads, and in a very short time his skirmishers were engaged by those of the enemy.

In execution of this plan as described by General Stevenson for effecting "the passage of the entire army" Reynolds brigade of his division had necessarily moved on with the trains, and was thus cut off from participation in the battle almost immediately begun. This was a direct consequence of the movement made imperative upon me by General Johnston's last order (Dispatch "E") then just received, the onus of which he, as usual, endeavors to lay on my shoulders.

Dispatch "E" read as follows:

CANTON ROAD,
Ten miles from Jackson, May 15, 1863—8.30 a.m.

Lieutenant-General PEMBERTON, Commanding, &c.:

Your dispatch of yesterday just received. Our being compelled to leave Jackson makes your plan impracticable. The only mode by which we can unite is by your moving directly to Clinton, informing me, that we may move to that point with about 6,000. I have no means of estimating the enemy's force at Jackson. The principal officers here differ very widely. I fear he will fortify if time is left him. Let me hear from you immediately. General Maxey was ordered back to Brookhaven. You probably have time to make him join you. Do so before he has time to move away.

Most respectfully,
J. E. JOHNSTON.

Brigadier General [S.D.] Lee, who, after Reynolds had moved off, commanded the third and left brigade of Stevenson's division, became the head of the column in marching order, says in his official report "About nine o'clock (i.e., before the road was open for the march), it was discovered that the enemy was massing troops on the left, evidently for the purpose of turning our left flank, and getting between our army and Edward's Depot." Instead, therefore, of following up the movement already in part executed by the trains and Reynolds brigade, it became necessary to check this purpose of the enemy for the rest of Stevenson's division of the left as needed by a series of flank marches under fire. But again, as General Lee says "As early as ten o'clock in the morning it became evident that the enemy was in heavy force, and determined on battle, as his skirmishers were bold and aggressive, and *several divisions* of his troops were visible in front of our left."

The extract from General Stevenson's report, under whose immediate direction the train of the Army was disposed shows that the road was not open for passage of the Artillery and Infantry until 9:30 a.m. and General Lee shows, that by nine o'clock the enemy was massing troops on our left with the purpose of getting between us and Edward's Depot, and that it was necessary to meet this action by counter movements on our part.

He also expressly states "the enemy was in heavy force" and that by ten o'clock a.m. (one half an hour after the road was open) several divisions of his troops were visible in front of our left that is, in front of the direction of our intended march. The "several divisions" referred to by General Lee were, those of General Logan and Crocker; the former having come up with Hovey's division of McClernand's corps shortly before four p.m. on the preceding day the 15th and encamped with it, while two brigades of Crocker's/Quinby's encamped two miles in rear. General Grant says "McPherson was ordered forward at 5:45 a.m. (on the 16th) to join McClernand…passing directly to the front I found Hovey's division of the 13th army corps at a halt with our skirmishers and the enemy's pickets near each other. Hovey *was bringing* his troops into line, ready for battle, and could have brought on an engagement at any moment."

General Grant then describes the position occupied by my army and continues "On the road, and into the wooded ravine and hillside Hovey's division was deployed for the attack. McPherson's two divisions, all of his corps with him, were thrown to the right of the road, properly speaking the enemy's rear, but I would not permit an attack to be commenced until I could hear from McClernand, who was advancing with four divisions…"

I learn from General McPherson's Official Report that he was notified by General McClernand at 6 a.m. on the 16th of my movement, and that his (McClernand's) columns were already in motion to meet it. McPherson says "orders were immediately given to General Logan to follow Hovey; and Crocker was directed to come forward as rapidly as possible with his whole division. After proceeding about *five miles*, and when *near Champion Hill*, General Hovey sent back word that he had met the enemy in force, strongly posted on the Edward's Depot road." Here General McPherson also describes the position occupied by my troops, then continues: "General Hovey's division was *immediately deployed* in line of battle to move against the hill, *supported on the* right by Leggett's (late Dennis') and Smith's brigade."

Now let me ask any candid reader to say if it is fair for General Johnston to assert that I "*could not* think I was acting under his orders on the 16th? Did I not communicate the execution of his order as far as possible (and) did I not execute them? What other object could the retrograde movement of the trains and Reynolds brigade have? Surely the extract I have given from Brig. [Major General] General Stevenson's report proved conclusively both my intention to obey and the adoptions of means to carry out my intentions again "obedience was easy"? Did not the engagement begin near mid day? and that in the mean time "there was but *a division* of the enemy before me?"

Is it not clear from both Confederate and Federal reports that (before the road opened for the passage of troops, and therefore, before the order to "march directly to Clinton" could possibly be further executed?) frequent changes of front were necessary and were made with heavy skirmishing to check the enemy's flank movements intended to cut off my army from Edward's Depot? If these statements are reliable, is General Johnston's base assertion to be credited that I "remained *passive four or five hours*" in the presence of a single division, and that I "could have extricated myself in a few minutes from the skirmishers of a force so inferior to my own, and obeyed the last order?"

But assuming for argument's sake that I "could have obeyed the last order" that my whole army might have been put on the march "directly to Clinton" (*immediately* on receipt of the order), was any advantage gained by this change of position and deferring the battle? On the contrary, many disadvantages must have arisen from any change that could then be made. The position held was naturally strong, and gave some prospect of success if a battle was forced upon me against a front attack, while neither flank could be turned, nor the rear reached by the enemy without heavy fighting. If defeated, the retreat across Baker's Creek might be effected at one of two points depending on the direction of the enemy's attack, that on my right, the greater part of the army eventually recrossed, but which would successively be abandoned to the enemy if I moved towards Clinton and generally in good order fell back to the Big Black. But for the issuance of the order to march "directly to Clinton" at 6:30 a.m. on the 16th received, Col. Reynolds Brigade of about 1,800 would have been added to the fighting force of my army, and by strengthening and holding its left flank, would have materially aided in checking, and possibly preventing the divisions of McPherson's corps under Logan from turning it and working on our rear; which as General Grant correctly says, "wonderfully weakened his front attack."

If the position occupied by our army, and the disposition of the various divisions of the Federal troops on the morning of the 16th were fully understood, I should without hesitation or further research leave it to the future historian to set a proper valuation on General Johnston's unsupported assertions, calumnies, and divined knowledge, as they are with the hope of screening himself from the responsibility he assumed when he undertook to control the operations of an army of whose position he was ignorant, as he was also of the strength and disposition of the forces of a far more numerous enemy, well informed of my intended movements, and therefore fully prepared to meet them.

The Confederate army as before stated occupied on the morning of the 16th a strong defensive position. The line of the intended retrograde march was that by which it had advanced on the preceding day and night. When it was found necessary to establish line of battle, the left of Maj. General Stevenson's division rested where the cross roads (our route) connecting the Clinton and Raymond roads from Edward's Depot intersects the former nearly at right angles, and about 3 1/2 miles to the east of the Depot. The head of the column, Tilghman's brigade, had bivouacked at a fork, one branch of which led to Raymond, the other direct to Dillon's plantation.

It had been my purpose to advance on the enemy's main line of communications when the army moved from its position in front of Edward's Depot, with the hope on encountering the detachment of Federal troops left in the rear and in this immediate neighborhood whilst separated from the main body which had advanced viz Raymond towards Jackson and Clinton. This hope was thwarted as has already been explained, by the betrayal of correspondence between General Johnston and myself, to General Grant on the evening of the 14th. In his official report, General Grant gives the disposition of his troops at this time as follows: Sherman and McPherson, each with two divisions of their respective corps near Jackson. McClernand occupied Clinton with one division, Mississippi Springs (seven miles from Clinton) with another, Raymond (eight miles from Clinton) with a third, and had his fourth division and Blair's division of Sherman's corps with a wagon train still in the rear near New Auburn (to the south on my right flank and nine or ten miles distant), while McArthur with one brigade of his division of McPherson's corps was moving towards Raymond on the Utica Road.

The railroad connecting Jackson and Vicksburg has a nearly east and west course. Clinton, Bolton and Edward's Depot located on this road, are respectively ten, twenty and thirty miles east [west] from Jackson. They are also connected with each other, and with Jackson and Vicksburg by good dirt roads, both north and south of, and nearly parallel with the railroad.

The positions occupied by General Grant's troops, as given in the preceding extract from his report, were either on this railroad, to wit at Clinton and Jackson, or on his main line of communication south of it; to wit at Mississippi Springs, Raymond and New Auburn; from each of these last named there are one or more good and almost direct roads to Clinton, Bolton and Edward's Depot.

Such was the disposition of the Federal forces when on the evening of the 14th of May, General Grant says he learned that General Johnston "had peremptorily ordered Pemberton to march out from the direction of Vicksburg and attack our rear." There was therefore at this time properly speaking in my front and within ten miles of Clinton, seven divisions of the enemy, or taking those of McPherson's corps as the standard organization of divisions, twenty one brigades, two other divisions, or six brigades were on my right flank, and by a nearly direct route nine to ten miles distant from Edward's Depot, and therefore were located to strike our right or rear on the march, as to move upon Edward's Depot and the Big Black bridge cutting our army off from its supplies and from Vicksburg.

At this time also, General Johnston had retreated with the *cooperating force* seven miles towards Canton, N.N.E. from Jackson. He had been informed by me on the day before, the 13th, that my army was in line of battle *eight brigades* strong. Tilghman's brigade the ninth did not come up until early in the morning of the 15th. It was with these eight brigades, therefore, that according to General Johnston's statement "I was ordered to march seventeen miles to the east, for the expressed object of attacking a large detachment in conjunction with the troops in Jackson, to reopen my communications, and enable coming reinforcements to join me."

The troops in Jackson had it is true marched off, under his immediate command, by the Canton road at an obtuse angle with the direction necessary to effect neither cooperating or a union. The larger detachment he is fully aware would have amounted to twenty one brigades in my front and in easy supporting distance of each other if I had possibly succeeded in completing the march of "seventeen miles to the east," he knows that I must have attacked six brigades coming up, or have been attacked by them coming up on my rear.

Nevertheless, and notwithstanding the fact that he announced his intentions to increase the distance between us by continuing his march at the obtuse angle on the following day, it was, he assures the future historian, "very discouraging" to him that I had not moved ten hours after the receipt of his order to do so, that is, about the time he had reached his first camp on the Canton road, and consequently that the junction of the forces which *could have* [been] *effected on the 15th* was deferred. Would it not be well for the future historian to inspect clearly the materials offered for his use by General Johnston, if the preceding is an average sample of their quality?

General Grant at once made use of the knowledge he had acquired. He says:

> Availing myself of this information, I immediately issued orders to McClernand and Blair, of Sherman's corps, to face their troops towards *Bolton*, with a view to reaching Edward's Station, marching on different roads converging near Bolton. These troops were admirably located for such a march. McPherson was ordered to retrace his steps early in the morning of the 15th on the Clinton road. Sherman was left in Jackson to destroy the railroads, bridges etc.

The next day, on the evening of the 15th, Hovey's division of McClernand's corps, encamped near Bolton, and two [three] brigades of Maj. General Quinby's [Logan's] division and Brig. General Crocker's two miles in rear, while the third brigade of Quinby's [Crocker's] remained in Clinton for the night. These facts I learn from General McPherson's official report. At what precise points on their respective routes, the two columns, of two divisions each under McClernand's orders, encamped on this night I have not been able to ascertain. They were, however, early in the morning of the 16th within good supporting distance of each other and of the three divisions near Bolton.[21]

For General McPherson says: "At 6 o'clock a.m. on the 16th May Maj. General McClernand notified me that the enemy under Lieut. General Pemberton had moved out in a strong force from Vicksburg to attack us, and that his (McClernand's) column was *already in motion* to meet him."

---

21. Pemberton was confused as to the command structure of the Union army, but he has the relative size of the opposing force correct.

General Grant had learned (see General Grant's report) about 5 a.m. on the 16th from two employees of the Jackson railroad the position taken up by our army during *the preceding night*, and the intention of attacking his rear. He says:

> I had determined to leave one division of Sherman's corps, one day longer in Jackson, but this information determined me to bring his entire command up at once and I accordingly dispatched him at 5:30 a.m. to move with all possible dispatch until he came up with the main force near Bolton…A dispatch was sent to Blair (of Sherman's corps, who with one division of McClernand's had been left on my right flank) at the same time to push forward to Edward's Depot with all dispatch. McClernand was directed to establish communication between Blair and Osterhaus of his corps, and keep it up, moving the former to the support of the latter. McPherson was ordered forward at 5:45 a.m. to join McClernand.

Thus at 6:30 a.m. on the 16th before the retrograde movement commencing with the reversal of the train required by General Johnston's instructions could be fairly under way, seven divisions of the enemy (less one brigade of McPherson's left in Clinton the night before, and therefore much further removed) were within six or seven miles of my front and marching by converging roads almost directly on that point of the Jackson and Vicksburg railroad at which my army would be compelled to change the direction of its march, at a right angle, in order to recross the bridge over Baker's Creek and gain the road by which it could advance on Clinton in accordance with General Johnston's instructions just received to form the junction with the 6,000 under his immediate command. These 6,000 be it understood remaining meantime, and during the entire 16th, inactive at Calhoun Station on the Jackson and *Canton* railroad, thirty five miles N.E. from Edward's Depot, and at least twenty one from Clinton.

Under the circumstances I have stated, I defy General Johnston or any of his supporters to show that I have misstated them. It must be manifest that a more unfavorable position can scarcely be imagined than that in which my army would have been placed had I persevered in the attempt to continue the flank march instead of preparing for battle already begun under General Johnston's orders on a narrow road in many parts densely wooded on either side where it became in fact a mere lane. With the train of the Army leading the march instead of following in the rear of the troops, and thereby becoming an inseparable obstacle to a rapid movement, and to such change of front or other disposition of my forces, as might be necessary at any moment to meet the assaults of an enemy certainly very far superior in numbers (it was to avoid this difficulty, that Maj. General Stevenson, who commanded the left division, now became the head of the column, was directed to place it as described in the extract from his report; this arrangement he has shown was not completed until 9:30 a.m.).

The proximity of the two armies made a battle between Confederate and Federal forces inevitable on the 16th. It had to be fought, either on the ground occupied by the former, when General Johnston's instructions were received to march directly to Clinton "obedient to which he asserts was easy," or at some point on the line of march to that place selected by the latter; and in either case, without the possibility of assistance from the troops with General Johnston. The further I might advance in the direction indicated in his order, so much would the distance be diminished between my army and the seven additional brigades, which were moving rapidly in the opposite direction from Clinton and Jackson, and the more surely would my army of three divisions or nine brigades have been *surrounded and captured*.

Such are the *disadvantages*, which, in my judgment, and I am thoroughly convinced of its correctness on this point as I am that I now exist, must have ensued had I further attempted to continue the march under General Johnston's instructions. I leave it to others to *decide* the question.

Of course, it is not pretended that the movements of the enemy as detailed in the preceding pages were as fully known to me at the time of their occurrence as they are now known. The deficiency of cavalry for which certainly I was not responsible, so often referred to made this knowledge impossible to me. But if my information on this important point was very imperfect, General Johnston's was infinitely more so. I was at least aware on the morning of the 13th and into the 14th that fully two thirds if not three fourths of the Federal Army had moved practically in my front to the east of my position near Edward's Depot and that the remainder was but a few miles to the south on my right flank. It was plain to me therefore, that an attempt to "come up in the rear" of a detachment, large or small at Clinton by moving any considerable distance directly to the east, would involve the destruction or capture of the army, and the loss of Vicksburg.

General Johnston on the contrary knows nothing of the position, or strength, of the Federal army on the 13th, the date of his first order (Dispatch "A"). He was informed of the presence of what he designates "a detachment of four divisions" under Sherman. He got an *impression* from my dispatch of the 12th he says "That the main body of General Grant's army was to the south of Edward's Depot," and on the information received in regards to the detachment at Clinton, and derived from a dispatch at least 30 hours old as to the main body of the invading Federal army. He inferred an order, which, if he had committed no other military blunder, ought to condemn him as a commander. In his Dispatch "B" of the 14th from his camp on the Canton Road, he writes: "If prisoners tell the truth the force *at Jackson* must be half of Grant's Army."

But if prisoners told the truth there was an other half of Grant's army, and to that other half, there is not the slightest reference, in any one of General Johnston's four consecutive dispatches to me dated respectively the 13th, 14th, 15th and 16th of May. In the first and third, both of which contained imperative instructions, the one to "march directly to Clinton," the other to come up on the rear of the enemy at Clinton, the very existence of any *other* Federal force than that by which he had himself been driven from Jackson, is absolutely ignored.

The fourth of these consecutive dispatches dated 7 p.m. May 16 from Calhoun Station, on the Canton road, 18 miles from Jackson, 22 from Clinton and about 35 from Edward's Depot, was written after he had received my reply to his of the 15th handed to me at 6:30 a.m. on the 16th near the battle field (Dispatch "E"), and after I had reported "heavy skirmishing going on in my front" purported to be in response to my reply and was in these words (here copy dispatch in full).

The dispatch "E" reads:

Canton Road
Ten miles from Jackson, May 15, 1863—8.30 a.m.

Lieutenant-General PEMBERTON, Commanding, &c.:

Your dispatch of yesterday just received. Our being compelled to leave Jackson makes your plan impracticable. The only mode by which we can unite is by your moving directly to Clinton, informing me, that we may move to that point with about 6,000. I have no means of estimating the enemy's force at Jackson. The principal officers here differ very widely. I fear he will fortify if time is left him. Let me hear from you immediately. General Maxey was ordered back to Brookhaven. You probably have time to make him join you. Do so before he has time to move away.

Most respectfully,

J. E. JOHNSTON.

The dispatch (F) reads:

Calhoun Station, May 16, 1863—7 p.m.
General PEMBERTON:

GENERAL: I have just received a dispatch from Captain [W. S.] Yerger, informing me that a detachment of his squadron went into Jackson this morning just as the enemy was leaving it. They (the Federals) took the Clinton road. It is a matter of great anxiety to me to add this little force to your army, but the enemy being exactly between us, and consultation by correspondence so slow, it is difficult to arrange a meeting. I will take the route you suggest, however, if I understand it. We have small means of transportation, however. Send forward a little cavalry to communicate with me, orally. Is the force between us too strong for you to fight, if it interposes itself?

J. E. JOHNSTON.

Here again the sole reference is to troops in Jackson and to the direction of their march. I had received positive instructions on the morning of the date of this dispatch to move "directly to Clinton." Those instructions were not countermanded in this, but I was informed that the enemy took *the road to Clinton*, and this extraordinary question was asked me: "Is the force between us too strong for you to fight if it interposes itself?" When General Johnston wrote this at seven o'clock on the evening of the 16th he was fully informed of the position the army had occupied at 7 a.m. He was notified that "the order of countermarch had been issued," and a minute description was given him of the route the army would take for the purpose of carrying out his instructions; with this postscript: "heavy skirmishing now going on in my front." He knew therefore that there was a body of the enemy before us, other than that which represented in his dispatch as having left Jackson by the Clinton road early that morning. Its strength neither he nor I knew.

Suppose, as really did happen, that while I was in the execution of his order to march directly to Clinton, the enemy *should* interpose himself between us in too strong force for me to fight (successfully). What then? Where should rest the responsibility for the battle thus brought about, and for the disaster that must be consequent upon an unfavorable result? Should it rest on me or on General Johnston? Either he or I am criminally guilty of the military blunder that compelled the battle of Baker's Creek.

As the approach was on my right, I at this time supposed, and still suppose it was the advance of Blair's division and that division of McClernand's corps which had been left near New Auburn or Dillon's, and which I had expected to announce their presence was entirely ignored by General Johnston in his dispatch while the order to move directly to Clinton was peremptorily reiterated.

It matters not whether this dispatch was received by me, or whether it was received at all. The dispatch itself shows, that the hallucination still existed a short lucid interval on the evening of the 14th when he wrote his letter "B" of that date, but unfortunately it reached me too late to prevent the movement and its disastrous consequences, which had seized General Johnston the moment he arrived in Jackson. He was determined to risk the capture or destruction of the principal army and loss of Vicksburg and four fifths of our supplies for the purpose of forming a junction some eighteen miles to the east with a detachment, which could have united itself to the army without molestation had the latter been permitted to maintain the position from which it had been ordered; which on the contrary, for the various reasons heretofore explained, the union could not possibly have been effected by the movement indicated in either of the orders "A" or "F".

[All of this was] Notwithstanding the accurate knowledge he now possessed of the position and strength of the enemy on the 15th and 16th of May; in spite of the convincing evidence of his own intentions and actions on those days, contained in his letters of the 14th "B" and the 16th "F" showing that cooperation on his part on either the 15th or 16th was neither possible nor contemplated.

Although he confesses that General Grant was informed of the movement he had peremptorily ordered, and that General Grant had in consequence concentrated his whole army of thrice my numbers, to meet it, yet General Johnston's reply recklessly asserts "If Lieut. General Pemberton had obeyed either of my orders to march eastwardly from Edward's, an army of 35,000 men might have been formed. Such a force properly commanded would have prevented the siege of Vicksburg."

> *The section of the Narrative quoted by Pemberton concludes Johnston's criticisms of events leading up to the siege operations. It reads as follows, with the quote provided in the paragraph above occurring at the end of this section. Johnston writes on page 221 of the Narrative:*
>
> *In looking for the causes of the Confederate reverses in this campaign, it is needless to go beyond Lieutenant-General Pemberton's startling disclosure, that his movement from Edward's Depot in violation of my orders, and in opposition to the opinion of his council of war, "was made against his judgment, in opposition to his previously-expressed intentions, and to the subversion of his matured plans." The author of such a measure might well regard defeat inevitable in a battle brought on by it.*
>
> *To be successful in that campaign, it was necessary that the Confederate general should comprehend that he must defeat the invading army in the field, and that Vicksburg must fall if besieged.*
>
> *The invading army could not be defeated without the concentration of the Confederate forces; but they were always more divided than the much more numerous army of the enemy. And the whole course of the Confederate general indicates a determination, from the beginning, to be besieged in Vicksburg.*

If I have not already convinced the reader of the fallacious character of these assertions, I could not do so by dwelling longer on them. As to the formation of "an army of 35,000 men by uniting my troops with General Johnston's, I have only this to say: that supposing a junction to have been possible, no such forces could have been formed, *unless* I had been ordered to strip Vicksburg and its dependencies of every effective soldier; such an order, at that time, General Johnston would not have dared to give, nor I to obey.

The several assertions combined in the foregoing extract mean this, or mean nothing.[22] General P[emberton] could have marched eastwardly from Edward's Depot in obedience to either of General Johnston's orders of the 13th or 15th of May. If General P[emberton] had marched eastwardly his forces and those with General Johnston would have been united and an army of 35,000 men would thus have been formed, which would have been properly commanded, i.e. by General Johnston. Ergo the siege of Vicksburg would have been prevented.

---

22. Pemberton is speaking in the third person for Johnston, suggesting a summary of Johnston's arguments.

I on the other hand assert and I claim to have demonstrated the correctness of my assertion 1st: that I did obey the order of the 15th by commencing the march on the morning of the 16th when almost immediately the enemy interposed himself and thereby prevented its continuance while General Johnston remained inactive during the entire day at Calhoun Station on the Canton Road, instead of marching in the direction I did in order to obey the order of the 13th. 2d: That if I had marched eastwardly "to come up on the rear of the detachment at Clinton" the junction of General Johnston's troops with mine would not have been made because he had put his troops in a position to prevent a junction on the 14th or 15th or 16th and therefore my Army of less than 19,000 men, without the choice of position, would have encountered the whole Federal army of at least 54,000 men, so disposed that it could have attacked simultaneously in front, flank and rear; would consequently have surrounded it, and have captured or destroyed it, while Vicksburg with a garrison too small for its defense to defend it; would necessarily have surrendered on the summons of the enemy.

Blinded by personal animosity which he does not attempt to conceal, General Johnston's reckless assertions, either entirely unsupported by proof, or else absolutely disproved by his own testimony, or by that of his cited witnesses, would make him an easy victim to a skillful adversary.

Take for example the following extract from his narrative

Pemberton copies the following from page 217 of the Narrative:

It was evident, after the 12th, that the Federal army had passed to the east of General Pemberton's position near Edward's Depot, and, consequently, that that army must defeat General Pemberton's before it could "assault" Vicksburg; so that there was no shadow of reason to keep two divisions in the town. Those two divisions, and four brigades detached, including Gregg's and Walker's, ordered to Jackson, could and should have been in the battle of Baker's Creek, and would have increased the Confederate force on that field to nearly thirty-five thousand men. Such an army, respectably commanded, must have won, for Hovey's division was unsupported till eleven o'clock, when McPherson with his two divisions arrived by the Jackson Road. It was at least an hour later when McClernand's corps appeared, coming from Raymond. The advantage of engaging the three fractions of the Federal army successively, would, inevitably, have given General Pemberton the victory; and, as the enemy had abandoned their communications, such a result would have been more disastrous to them than that of the siege of Vicksburg was subsequently to the Southern army.

In like manner, when the defense of the Big Black River was decided upon, all available troops, including those in Vicksburg, would have been concentrated for the object. The opposite principle that had been controlling Confederate operations since the 1st, governed, however, on the 17th. And, instead of strengthening and encouraging the defeated remnant of his army by bringing two fresh divisions into it, General Pemberton further discouraged that disheartened remnant, by leaving one-half in front of the river to fight, and sending the other behind it, to bivouac some two miles in rear.

It has been shown by an extract verbatim from General Grant's official report that two divisions of his army to wit: one of Sherman's under General Blair and one of McClernand's did not pass to the east of my position near Edward's Depot but remained in rear near New Auburn some nine or ten miles to the west of south of that position. This force was about 2/3 of the strength of my entire army, which was composed of but three divisions averaging three brigades each. I knew this fact at the time. General Johnston did not then, but does now, yet he ignores it. He also knows that it was the presence of this force on my right flank that prevented my march eastwardly to come up in the rear of the enemy at Clinton and he knows that it was with the expectation of meeting this *same detachment unsupported* that I moved in the direction of Dillon's near New Auburn, a movement I would not have made had I been aware that General Johnston's instructions to me had been betrayed to General Grant.

If I had been permitted to execute my own plans by remaining in position I held near Edward's Depot on the 13th and 14th and which I had previously notified General Johnston would be the battle (selected principally because it covered approaches to the Big Black River and secured my rear), I say in that event General Johnston's assertion that "the Federal army must defeat mine before it could assault Vicksburg" would have had some show of reason. But under no other circumstances is that assertion true. I could make *no* forward movement which would not expose my rear. Therefore, it was requisite where I did advance, to leave sufficient troops both to protect it and to secure Vicksburg and its flank defenses against a coup de main from the Mississippi River. I was well apprised that a considerable force of the enemy was still near Milliken's Bend on the west bank and I have shown that reliable official information of the 11th of May from Brigadier General Chalmers in North Mississippi gave me every reason to expect the immediate arrival of Lauman's division from Memphis by water.

My knowledge of this force of which General Johnston takes no account, made the retention of the brigade for the defense of Haines' [Snyder's] Bluff and Chickasaw Bayou imperative. It, the keys to Vicksburg from above, required another brigade to occupy Warrenton on the left flank nine miles below Vicksburg, and to watch the ferries on the Big Black from Hankinson's to Hall's by which a small force, if those points were left unprotected, might cut off my communications with Vicksburg, by moving upon the railroad and floating bridges across the Big Black (these two brigades comprised Brigadier General Forney's division).

If I made any advance under General Johnston's order "A" of the 13th, it was indispensable to hold the tete de pont on the east side covering those bridges because as I have already explained whichever direction I marched, the other was necessarily left open to his approach both of the two diverging roads from Edward's Depot. So [with] this he could with out encountering opposition, place himself in my rear. When therefore I resolved to abandon the entrenched position on the railroad near Edwards, Vaughan's brigade, a small one, which could and would have been added to the main army had I been allowed to maintain that position was necessarily left to hold the tete de pont. This brigade was one of three which with about 500 state troops comprised Major General Smith's division.

Baldwin's Ferry was strategically too important to be left unprotected, whatever position the Confederate Army might occupy east of the Big Black. If I had succeeded in the attempt I made to march eastwardly, after the receipt of General Johnston's order to that affect early on the 16th, the four divisions of the enemy moving from Raymond and New Auburn could have been thrown to the west bank of the Big Black, whilst I was occupied with the five divisions then advancing by the Clinton road.

Another most important point to be guarded, by which Reynolds' brigade eventually occupied, was the Big Black Ferry at Bridgeport, two miles north of the railroad bridge, and accessible to the enemy by a good road diverging from the Clinton road, east of and near to Edward's Depot. This approach to the ferry was covered, so long as the army remained in position, but ceased to be so, when it advanced. To secure the rear therefore against a movement by the enemy on either of these ferries, the one north, the other south of the Big Black bridge, a second brigade of Maj. General Smith's division, with a detachment from Col. Waul's Texas Legion was employed. The only remaining brigade of this division occupied the city of Vicksburg. General Johnston says "there was no shadow of reason to keep two divisions in the town." I have shown that instead of *two divisions* in the town, there was but one brigade.

It has been shown that Reynolds' brigade was separated from the rest of Stevenson's division during the action at Baker's Creek from the fact that it had become the head of the column when the retrograde march for the purpose of executing General Johnston's order commenced and it had moved off north of the train, and was thus cut off from participation in the battle by the movements of the enemy against my left. Gregg's and Walker's brigades were under General Johnston's immediate command, and could and would have been in the battle that must have been fought on the ground I had selected within 48 hours. Instead of ordering me to come up on the rear of "the enemy at Clinton," had he marched with those brigades to join the army near Edward's Depot, this movement was not only practicable, but easy of execution, and the failure to make it on General Johnston's part is inexcusable.

With these troops and others which I might then have safely brought forward would have increased the Confederate army to about 30,000 men, a force which with the advantage of position I honestly believe would have been sufficient to have prevented the siege of Vicksburg if not to give us a decided victory.

That the Confederate Army numbered less than 19,000 fighting men in the battle of Baker's Creek which was fought on the 16th of May instead of the 30,000 which could and should have engaged the enemy, on that day or on the 17th in the position I had chosen is due to General Johnston's hasty and ill advised order subsequent to his indecision, inactivity and strange misconception of the fundamental principle which should have governed him in the warfare he undertook to direct.

It was the *relinquishment* of my own plans of defense for the purpose of executing as far as practicable, General Johnston's instructions, that brought about the battle of Baker's Creek. In a dispatch of the 12th of May, while the army was still west of the Big Black, I distinctly designated the ground six miles east of it on which, if I could unite a sufficient force, having due regard to the safety of Vicksburg, the battle would be fought. I also explained the necessity of holding back a large force to protect the ferries and flank defenses of the City. General Johnston has ignored this important part of my dispatch in what purports to be the full copy of its page.

The following day General Johnston was notified that the Army was in position eight brigades strong near Edward's Depot. On the same night (on the 13th) he issued his order "A". The moment he did so, he annulled my plans, and substituted his own. In doing so, he assumed the whole responsibility of the change. It was within his authority to designate (I became simply his execution officer) what force, if any, should be withdrawn from the position referred to in my dispatch and which I had represented as essential to be held.

When my superior declined or failed to exercise his right to order what his judgment readily approved, is it surely unjust in him to hold me up to reprobation because I did not on my own responsibility order what my judgment disapproved? If the garrison of Vicksburg and its dependencies as well as all other troops enumerated by General Johnston were not present in the battle of Baker's Creek, he is responsible that they were not there.

The brief account General Johnston has given of the action at Baker's Creek, is erroneous in several important particulars, and the impression derived from it, is, as doubtless he designed it should be, much to my prejudice. The movement in obedience to his order of the 15th had been so far executed, before the demonstrations of the enemy became too serious to permit its continuance, that the safety of the entire train of the Army was secured, and Reynolds' brigade of Stevenson's division had moved off with it. It is stated in my official report that on the morning of the 16th at about six and a half o'clock Col. Wirt Adams reported to me that his pickets were skirmishing with the enemy on the Raymond Road, some distance in our front. *While in conversation with him*, a courier arrived and handed me dispatch "E" from General Johnston (see Dispatch "E" of 15th ante).

I immediately ordered the necessary arrangements to execute General John-ston's instructions. Just as the reverse movement commenced the enemy *drove in* Col. Adams' cavalry pickets, and opened with the artillery at long range, on the head of my column on the Raymond Road. Not knowing whether this was (to be) an attack in force, or simply an armed reconnaissance, and being anxious to obey the instructions of General Johnston, I directed the *continuance of the movement,* giving the necessary instructions for securing the safety of the wagon trains. The demonstration of the enemy soon becoming more serious, orders were sent to division commanders to form in line of battle on the cross roads (from the Clin-ton to Raymond Road).

Under the caption "Pemberton's Faulty Plans," General Johnston endeav-ored elsewhere to persuade his reader that there was no obstacle on the receipt of his order to the movement he had directed; viz., to march directly to Clinton, that "obedience was easy" had I chosen to obey and that "the Confederate troops remained inactive before a single division of the enemy some five hours."

I have maintained that I required the several members of my staff who accom-panied me in the field to make written reports of the orders delivered. Major Jacob Thompson, Inspector General says: "About the time the Army was ready to take up the line of march, firing commenced in front, and soon it was ascertained the force was too large to be long resisted by one picket force…for some time it was doubt-ful whether the main attack would be on the middle Raymond Road on, which our left, Stevenson's division rested, or on our right, held by Loring's division."

Lieutenant J. C. Taylor, who had been "sent forward to ascertain if possible on what point the enemy was moving his heaviest forces" says:

> …the skirmishing was equally severe on the right and left, and no definite con-clusion could be formed as to which was the advance of the bulk of the enemy's force. A second time I went to Colonel Adams conveying the order, for him when forced to retire to fall back with his full command in front of the strongest column of the enemy. About this time, I should think about *9 a.m.,* I found Col. Adams with all his cavalry about retiring on a by road just to the left of the Raymond Road. The infantry skirmishing on this road, and on its right were ordered to retire as their flank was exposed on the left by the withdrawal of the cavalry.

The circumstances narrated by Lieutenant Taylor be it remembered occurred on the right of the line [which] became the rear in the new line of march, and at least 1/2 an hour before General Stevenson commanding the left and now the leading division had reported to me that the road was open for the passage of troops. I had for the second time relinquished my own designs in deference to General J[ohnston]'s instructions. My original plans had been entirely subvert-ed by his first order and the purpose for which I had abandoned them, was equal-ly frustrated by the second order I had just received.

It at once became my leading object to regain the road by which the Army might "march directly to Clinton" and it continued to be so as long as there was a hope of effecting it. The arrangements made to that end, are clearly set forth in the extract from General Stevenson's report where it is also shown, that the separation of Reynolds' brigade from his division, was the direct consequence of the change of plan brought about by General Johnston's order. The extracts given in preceding pages from Generals Stevenson's, Lee's, Grant's and McPherson's reports are sufficient evidences of the little confidence that should be given to General Johnston's unsupported assertions in matters of controversy between himself and myself.

They entirely refute the statement (Page 182 of the *Narrative*) that "the Confederate troops remained passive before a single division of the enemy some five hours." General Lee, who commanded the left brigade of Stevenson's division, says:

> By eight o'clock my brigade was in line of battle, and skirmishing on both roads (the Clinton Middle Raymond Road: JCP). At about nine o'clock it was discovered that the enemy was massing troops on the left evidently for the purpose of turning our left flank, and getting between our Army and Edward's Depot. My brigade was at once marched, under fire, by the left flank, for the purpose of checking the enemy...*As early as ten o'clock* in the morning, it became evident that the enemy was in heavy force and determined on battle, as his skirmishers were bold and aggressive, and *several divisions* of his troops were visible in front of our left.

> *Pemberton refers to pages 182 and 183 of the Narrative, in which Johnston says:*

> *Early in the morning of the 16th, Lieutenant-General Pemberton received my order of the day before, and prepared to obey it by directing Major-General Stevenson to have the baggage-train turned and moved as rapidly as possible across Baker's Creek on the road by which they had advanced the day before. While the troops were waiting for the clearing of the road by this movement, that they might take the same direction, Colonel Wirt Adams's cavalry-pickets were attacked by the skirmishers of the Federal division; upon which Lieutenant-General Pemberton formed his three divisions for battle on a line extending from the Raymond to the Clinton road—Loring's division on the right, Bowen's in the centre, and Stevenson's on the left.*

> *In this position the Confederate troops remained passive before a single division of the enemy some five hours—until near noon—when they were attacked by General Grant, who had then completed the concentration of his forces, uninterrupted by this adversary.*

If General Lee's statement is correct, and I know him to be a skillful, brave and enterprising officer not likely to deceived or to exaggerate, the "several divisions visible in front of our left as early as ten o'clock" were those of Logan and Crocker of McPherson's corps. Those troops, according to General McPherson's report encamped on the preceding night in close proximity to Hovey's division of McClernand's corps and followed the advance of the latter at about 6 a.m. on the

16th. As the distance to be marched was only six or seven miles they would have been within easy supporting distance of General Hovey if, relinquishing the attempt to execute General Johnston's instructions to march directly to Clinton, I had abandoned the position occupied by my army to attack him in the dense wood which in great measure concealed both his strength and position.

I find the following (also on page 182 of the *Narrative*) as a marginal note. "General Grant says the action commenced at eleven o'clock." What General Grant does say is this:

> There had been continuous firing between Hovey's skirmishers and the rebel advance which by eleven o'clock grew into a battle. For some time this division bore the brunt of the conflict, but finding the enemy too strong for them at the instance of Hovey I directed first one, and then a second brigade from Crocker's division to reinforce him. *All this time* Logan's division was working upon the enemy's left and rear, and weakened his front attack most wonderfully.

> *Continuing on page 182 of the Narrative, Johnston further states:*

> *When McPherson, with two divisions, had come up, and McClernand with four, including Blair's of Sherman's corps, was within an hour's march of the field, the action was begun by Hovey's division, which assailed the left and centre of Stevenson's. Logan's division, moving by the right of Hovey's, passed the left of Stevenson's line as if to take it in reverse. Stevenson transferred Barton's brigade from his right to the left rear to meet this movement, while with Cumming's and Lee's he opposed Hovey's attack. This opposition was so effective that General Hovey called for aid, and McPherson's other division, Quinby's [Crocker's], was sent to his assistance. In the mean time Logan had engaged Barton, and Stevenson's three brigades were forced back by the three Federal divisions; and at two o'clock they had lost the ground on which they had just stood, many men, and much of their artillery. Lieutenant-General Pemberton restored the fight by bringing Bowen's division, unemployed till then, to the assistance of Stevenson's.*

General Johnston says, referring to the opposition of Cumming's and Lee's brigades to Hovey's attack, "This opposition was so effective that General Hovey called for aid." It was at this juncture when the aspect of affairs on our left seemed most favorable, that I determined to strengthen General Stevenson by throwing Bowen's two brigades into the fight; at once moving up at the same time most of Loring's division, close upon his right, to be employed as events should require. With this view, I sent instructions to General Stevenson, embodied in the following extract from Lieutenant J. C. Taylor's report: "My next message of importance was to General Stevenson, after the skirmishing had become very fierce in his front and when the enemy seemed to be wavering, and the fire then somewhat receding, to advance at once if the enemy faltered, and push him vigorously." This I should judge was at 12 1/2 o'clock.

The enemy, though speedily reinforced, had not pressed Stevenson back when Captain C. McR. Selph bore the following order to General Loring and

Bowen: "Tell General Bowen to move up at once to assist Stevenson, and tell Loring to move his division, leaving Col. Scott and Adams' cavalry at the ford, also to the assistance of Stevenson and crush the enemy." Capt. Selph then continues: "The order was carried to each. General Bowen rode up himself and reported that the enemy was in heavy force in his front. General Loring sent a major of his staff to report that the enemy were in his front moving in heavy columns…General Pemberton in answer to the reports from both General Bowen and Loring that the enemy were moving in their front, sent me with an order for them to "move at them at once."…and then return to the assistance of Stevenson. This brought the remark from General Loring which he had communicated to General Bowen that he would seize the proper moment to attack the enemy." The same order was conveyed by Lieutenant Taylor A.D.C. he says: "General Bowen in the center and General Loring on the right were ordered to advance together on the force in their front, and drive them from their position."

This is a sufficient reply I think to General Johnston's impression that Bowen's division remained unemployed, until the fight was restored by bringing it to the assistance of Stevenson.

This order I carried myself to General Bowen, and heard it said several times by different staff officers to General Loring. We were looking every moment for the advance, not comprehending why there was delay, until after sometime, say 3/4 of an hour since the order had been first sent, General Bowen rode up and said "he was merely waiting to see the left of General Loring's division advance to put his command in motion" (this explanation he had before sent by an officer) and seemed to feel confident of his ability to drive the enemy before him. He said further, that he understood from General Loring that the enemy seemed so strong in his front, *that he would wait*, hoping that they would advance and attack him in his position, a strong one. Meanwhile Stevenson on the left was hard pressed, and called for reinforcements. Bowen was ordered to his support, and Loring to move with two brigades to the left to take Bowen's position in the center. This important order I heard urgently and repeatedly sent, and two or three of General Loring's staff officers who rode up mean time were sent immediately back with these instructions. (There seemed to be great delay in obeying this order. For a considerable time, no movement was made from the left to the center which was very much exposed during this interval.)

By this time, the enemy were pressing Stevenson back; the order was repeated through Captain Selph and Colonel Taylor of my staff, the language of the latter I use in that officer's report to me: "General Pemberton sent me with an order to General Bowen to move one brigade to Stevenson's left, and added 'tell General Bowen to follow it up with another brigade.'"

The 2d brigade following the whole of Bowen's division came up under that gallant officer at a double quick and in conjunction with Stevenson's troops who had been driven back by vastly superior forces, but promptly rallied, not only regained all we had lost, but drove the previously successful enemy before them for fully half a mile. In my official report I thus expressed myself, and I still entertain the same opinion:

> Had the movement in support of the left been promptly made, when first ordered, it is not improbable that I might have maintained my position and it is possible the enemy might have been driven back, though his vastly superior and constantly increasing numbers would have rendered it necessary to withdraw during the night to save my communications with Vicksburg.

"The tide of battle," says General McPherson, "was turning against us when Boomer's brigade came up…checked the advance of the enemy and held him at bay, until Holmes' brigade came up; when a dashing charge was made, the enemy rolled back, and the battle won." During this critical period of the battle Loring's division remained inactive. I had hoped and expected that he could promptly follow up Bowen's movement in accordance with repeated and urgent orders; had he done so, the brigades of Buford and Featherston would have undoubtedly been in position to support the effective and almost victorious charge of Bowen's and Stevenson's divisions. What the ultimate result would have been, I do not, as General Johnston does, assume to know.

It is certain that the delay of more than an hour before obedience was attempted did not prevent defeat. As Commanding General on the field, I was responsible that the order I had given was proper for the occasion. General Loring was only responsible for their prompt execution to the best of his ability. I therefore protest against General Johnston's attempt to place me before the public in a false position in regard to my conduct of this battle, which his language in the following statement is calculated to effect. He says on page 183 of the *Narrative*:

> *In the mean time Logan had engaged Barton, and Stevenson's three brigades were forced back by the three Federal divisions, and at two o'clock, they had lost the ground on which they had just stood, many men, and much of their artillery. Lieutenant General Pemberton restored the fight by bringing Bowen's division unemployed 'till then, to the assistance of Stevenson's.*
>
> *In the meantime General McClernand with his four divisions had been confronting Loring and not venturing to attack, on account of the strength of the Confederate position, while Loring felt himself well employed in holding four divisions of the enemy in check with his single one.*
>
> *After bringing Bowen's troops into action, General Pemberton directed Loring to join in it with at least a part [The first order was for his whole division less one regiment (see Captain Selph's report ante). The second (was) for two brigades.] of his. That officer, for some time did not obey, from the consideration that his movement would be fol-*

lowed by that of the Corps that he had been keeping out of action, and our defeat thus made certain.

Johnston concludes his description of the end of the battle of Baker's Creek and the retreat of Pemberton's army on pages 183 and 184:

Stevenson's and Bowen's troops, and the reserve artillery, well placed and served under the direction of Colonel W.T. Withers, its commander, maintained the contest until four o'clock; then the battle seemed to be so completely lost that retreat was ordered. The withdrawal of the troops that had been engaged was covered by Loring with his division; Featherston's and Buford's brigades protecting Stevenson's and Bowen's divisions in their retreat; and Tilghman's resisting the advance of the enemy by the Raymond road. Tilghman himself fell in this duty, while encouraging his troops, when hardest pressed, by his brave example.

By the time that Stevenson's and Bowen's divisions had crossed Baker's Creek, the Federal troops were so near the stream as to render its passage by Loring's division impracticable; so that officer marched southward, and, after passing entirely beyond the enemy's left, turned to the east and led his division to Jackson.

I have as far as possible employed the language of the officers who bore my orders on the field, as they convey a correct idea of the several changes therein made necessary by the alternatives of the battle. It will be observed that General Johnston sustains my subordinate, who constituted himself the judge of the propriety of the order he received in the heat of the engagement, and that he excuses that officer a long delayed obedience not because immediate obedience was impracticable, but because *he* did not think it advisable. It has been also shown that Bowen's division was "unemployed until it moved to the assistance of Stevenson's" because, when his division and Loring's were directed to attack the enemy in their front simultaneously, General Loring preferred *to wait*, hoping the enemy would attack him.

It is true that after bringing Bowen's troops into action I ordered General Loring to join in. It is not less true that he received similar orders at the same time with Bowen, but delayed obedience until the favorable opportunity was lost and only in time to cover the retreat.

I shall conclude this subject with the following statement from the Honorable Jacob Thompson, then a member of my staff, and ask particular attention to the language in which the order was delivered. He says:

> ...orders were sent to Bowen to fall on the left with all his force. His division came up at double quick, and charged on the enemy in fine style, driving him back for more than half a mile. At *the same time* orders were sent to General Loring to follow up the movement of General Bowen. When there was some delay at his coming, you directed me to carry the order, which I did at the full speed of my horse. The order I delivered was "General Pemberton desires you to come *immediately* and with all dispatch to the left to the assistance of Stevenson, *whatever may be in your front.*" General Loring replied, by asking me if General Pemberton knew that the enemy

was in great force in his front. I replied I did not know whether General Pemberton knew the fact or not, but I know I repeated the order correctly, and that if he did not comply with it, the responsibility was his and not mine...

General Loring's division, three brigades strong and one of the best of the department, took no active part in the battle of Baker's Creek. It was fought on the Confederate side by less than eleven thousand men; to wit by three brigades under Maj. General Stevenson sixty five hundred, and two under Brig General Bowen forty three hundred strong, about sixty six per cent of the force that had marched from Edward's Depot, and at least 10,000 less than that which would have encountered the enemy in entrenched lines near that point, if I had been permitted to carry out my own arrangements for the defense of Vicksburg made before General Johnston entered the limits of the department, and which were announced to him before his arrival in Jackson.

After covering the retreat of Stevenson's and Bowen's divisions across Baker's Creek, General Loring failed to follow the movement with his own division, but he withdrew his entire command and marched to Jackson. This action of General Loring's was the immediate cause of the disaster at the Big Black on the following morning, and necessitated the abandonment of that line of defense, and the occupation of the entrenchments around Vicksburg as the last resort. General Loring failed to make to me a report of the operations of his division in the battle of the 16th, nor do I know his version of the causes which compelled him to pursue the course he did.

General Johnston without offering any evidence in support of his assertions, positively declares that "By the time Stevenson's and Bowen's divisions had crossed Baker's Creek, the Federal troops were so near the stream as to render its passage by Loring's division impracticable." If this assertion is correct, General Loring's action was necessary and therefore justifiable. But on the other hand, Maj. General Stevenson, who was in command of the troops on the spot and was witness of all that transpired, thus narrates the facts in his official report:

> On my arrival about sunset at the ford on Baker's Creek, I found that the enemy had crossed the bridge above, and were advancing artillery in the direction of the road on which we were moving. The battery had already taken position, and was playing on the road, but at right angles, and with *too long range to prevent the passage of the troops*. I found *on the west side* the brigades of General Green and Colonel Cockrell, of Bowen's division, who had there halted and taken up position to *hold the point until Loring's division could cross*. I found Colonel Scott, of the 12th Louisiana regiment, halted about a half mile from the ford on the east side, and directed him to cross. I then addressed a note to General Loring, informing him of what I had done, telling him of the change I had caused Colonel Scott to make in his position, stating that with the troops then there, and others I could collect, *I would hold the ford and road until his division could cross*, and urging him to hasten the movement. To this note I received no

answer but, in a short time, Colonel Scott moved off his regiment quickly in the direction of his original position, in obedience, I was informed, to orders from General Loring. Inferring from this that General Loring did not intend to cross at that ford, *he having had ample time to commence the movement*, I suggested to General Green and Colonel Cockrell to move forward to the railroad bridge.

It is probable that the battery which it is stated "was playing on the road but at right angles, and at too long range to prevent the passage of troops," would have somewhat enfiladed General Loring's columns and might perhaps have caused a slight loss, but there was little damage to be apprehended. General Loring's own division, halted at the ford to cover his crossing, would have made up a force sufficient to repel the enemy should he attempt to interpose between it and the Big Black.

That Col. Scott's regiment to the west side of the creek crossed, and after some time recrossed under General Loring's orders, and with the rest of its division made its way unmolested to Jackson is, it appears to me, sufficient evidence that there was no pressure from the enemy's advance from the east side, and therefore that General Johnston cannot be correct in his assertion that "By the time Stevenson's and Bowen's divisions had crossed the Creek, the Federal troops were so near the stream as to render its passage by Loring's division impracticable."

But, whether the passage at that point was practicable or impracticable, it was not tested. I was firmly convinced, however, that General Loring would during the night or early next morning make his way to the bridge. I could not therefore abandon the tete de pont on the east side of the river while I entertained a hope of his coming. If these works were to be held, it was necessary that they should be occupied in sufficient force throughout their whole extent, three brigades and as many field batteries were required for this purpose.

General Johnston correctly says on page 184 of the *Narrative.* "The object of this measure was to defend the bridge to enable Loring's division to cross the Big Black." I had received no message from General Loring intimating an intention to separate his division from the remainder of the army; it had not suffered in the battle of the 16th, and contributed at least 1/3 of my effective force. Without it I could not hope to hold the line of the Big Black—with it, I did hope effectively to do so—but I expected every moment to hear of its approach.

The troops assigned to hold the strong position were sufficient to have resisted assaults of the enemy in any force. I could not anticipate that the center would give way at the first approach of the enemy in any force. I know that the Missouri and Arkansas brigades that occupied respectively the right and left of the line, would as they always had done their duty in battle, and they retreated on this occasion, only because to have remained in the trenches would have induced their capture by an overwhelming force of the enemy after they were thus separated.

In the precipitous flight that followed many threw away their arms, and numbers were captured; their casualties, together with the absence of Loring's entire division, had so much reduced *[Pemberton crossed out "devastated"]* the fighting strength of the army that I had no alternative but to withdraw to the entrenched lines around Vicksburg as the last hope of saving the place. After crossing the Big Black the entire effective force over which I could exercise control was considerably less than 21,000 men. Such I assert, and can, if necessary, prove this from official documents still in my possession.

General Johnston thus comments on the situation after the disaster of Baker's Creek (previously quoted):

> ...when the defense of the Big Black was decided upon, all available troops including those in Vicksburg should have been concentrated for the object. The opposite principle that had been controlling Confederate operations since the 1st, governed however on the 17th. And instead of strengthening and encouraging the defeated remnant of his Army by bringing two fresh divisions into it, General Pemberton further discouraged that disheartened remnant by leaving one half in front of the river to fight, and sending the other behind it, to bivouac some two miles in rear.

I have explained that in my judgment the practicability of the defense of the Big Black after the defeat at Baker's Creek was contingent on the reunion of Loring's division with "the disheartened remnant of my Army," and that the hope and expectation of that reunion alone induced me to occupy in sufficient force the strong defensive position west of the river to aid the column should it approach and cover its passage to the west bank. I do not understand the force of the objection urged by General Johnston that I sent the remainder of the Army behind the river to bivouac some two miles in rear. The line of rifle pits, with a natural ditch of stagnant water from ten to twenty feet wide, and two to four feet deep immediately in front, abutted on either flank in the swampy banks of the river. The line was one mile long manned to its full capacity, and armed with seventeen pieces of field artillery. It would have served no purpose therefore to have increased the force within the tete de pont; it would have been merely a target for the enemy. As the flanks of the work rested on the swamps of the river, there could manifestly be no position for any body of troops outside of it.

It is equally plain that a proper defense of the tete de pont, such as I had the right to expect, must make the occupation of the opposite west bank a necessity. Baldwin's Brigade and Waul's Legion (portions of the two "fresh" divisions referred to by General Johnston) held the river immediately on the right and were available either to reinforce the center, or to concentrate against an attempt to cross Baldwin's Ferry, nearest the railroad bridge, the central and most important point.

Bridgeport Ferry next on the left was sufficiently guarded until a demonstration of crossing should actually be made by the enemy. Stevenson's division, or as General Johnston states it "the other half of the disheartened Army" was therefore bivouacked just where it should have been "some two miles behind" the center; whence, by convenience of roads, the center itself, or either flank could be more readily supported if necessary than from any other point. Of the "two fresh divisions" which General Johnston says "should have been brought in to my Army to encourage the defeated remnant of it," two brigades, Baldwin's and Vaughn's and Waul's Legion, were already with it. One brigade of three regiments and the heavy artillery at the water batteries constituted the entire garrison of Vicksburg. One brigade (Hébert's) held Haines' [Snyder's] Bluff on the Yazoo and the approaches north of the city, 13 miles from it, and at least 25 from my position on the Big Black. The remaining brigade (Moore's) with 500 or 600 State troops attached held Warrenton on the Mississippi south of the city and watched the lower ferries on the Big Black as far as Hall's. Let it be remembered that a Federal fleet of some 20 vessels, most of them armed, was in possession of the Mississippi south of Vicksburg, and that any force, west of the river, landed at Warrenton would have been in my rear. That Haines' [Snyder's] Bluff immediately on the left flank of Vicksburg was the key to Vicksburg on the north side and to the country watered by the Yazoo and its tributaries, the only remaining supplies for my Army.

If on the morning of the 17th of May I had withdrawn the troops from the positions just indicated, a considerable part of an army of near 21,000 men might have been concentrated by the morning of the 18th on the Big Black. But this Army could not have remained massed for any protracted period of time. The enemy, flushed with success, and nearly 60,000 strong, would have attempted to force the river at different points more or less distant from the center, and would thus have compelled a separation of my troops.

The knowledge that Vicksburg, Warrenton and Haines' [Snyder's] Bluff were evacuated and in possession of the enemy (as most surely would have been the case within a few hours after evacuation) and that, consequently, that it was exposed to attack from the rear, would I judge, have [more] *discouraged* "the disheartened remnant of my Army" than the presence of three fresh brigades would have encouraged it. Such concentration of the Confederate forces at my disposal, as General Johnston's criticism suggests would inevitably have led to its capture within forty eight hours.

I was expected by the government and people of the Confederate States to hold Vicksburg and Port Hudson at any every cost: if General Johnston had adverse opinions he has carefully kept them to himself. In his Dispatch "B" of the 14th from his camp on the Canton Road after his evacuation of Jackson, and nearly 24 hours after he had ordered me to come up with all the troops I could quickly assemble on the rear of the enemy at Clinton, he asks me "would it not be better to place the forces to *support Vickъburg* between General Loring (at Edward's Depot) and that place, and merely observe the ferries, so that you might unite if an opportunity to fight presented itself?"

This is simply a suggestion in the form of an inquiry, and refers *only to the ferries on the Big Black*. Can it be pretended that it implies or suggests propriety of withdrawing the garrisons from Warrenton and Vicksburg on the Mississippi or from Haines' [Snyder's] Bluff on the Yazoo? Thus, three fifths of "the two fresh divisions" were employed in looking to the safety of these vital positions.

General Johnston had given no intimation of the little value he attached to the possession of Vicksburg, while in my estimation, it was second in importance to no point in the Confederacy, and seeing no other chance of saving it, I determined to submit to a siege rather than abandon it. It is to be deplored that the army of 30,000, which was concentrated by the 3d of June was under the command of a general who for fully four weeks after that date, kept it in a state of absolute inactivity almost within sound of the artillery of the besieged.

Not doubting that General Johnston would seize the occasion to display that great military ability with which he was credited so largely by the people, and confident that he would take prompt and decided measures to concentrate an army if it took the entire force of both departments if necessary, which would be sufficient with the resolute cooperation of the garrison to bring the siege to a speedy and glorious termination, early in the morning of the 17th [of May], General Johnston was notified that, it would probably be necessary to withdraw the Army from the Big Black because of the many points by which it could be flanked; he was also informed that in such event, Haines' [Snyder's] Bluff would not be tenable. I expected, however, at that time, to hold the position, then occupied during the day, and to retire under cover of night. But the precipitate flight of the troops from the tete de pont, resulting from the unaccountable panic that had seized the center at the first approach of the enemy, made it apparent to me that the numerical strength of the Army was not sufficient, and the morale of at least a portion of it, too much shaken to insure a successful defense of the line of the Big Black, even for the day. Moreover, the approach of General Loring's division, which had been more than once reported, had proved unfounded, and there was now almost a certainty, that its separation from the Army was complete.

Up to this period General Johnston had given no intimation that his estimate of the value of Vicksburg to the Confederacy differed from that entertained by myself, by the government and the people. It was reasonable therefore to believe he would be zealous to prove that he really merited the high reputation for military capacity with which he was generally credited, and that from the large force under his control in the two departments and with the reinforcements already arrived and arriving from other departments, he would promptly concentrate an

Army, which, with the resolute cooperation of the garrison, would not only relieve the latter, and raise the siege, but strike the Federal Government the heaviest blow it had yet received, if it did not secure the independence of the Confederacy.

General Johnston did none of this. He had *predetermined* that Vicksburg *must* fall, but there were men in the Confederate service, who I believe would have done it all. Did I entertain exaggerated or unreasonable expectations? Not so, in the opinion of the General commanding the investing forces. In his official report, General Grant says explanatory of his reasons for making his second unsuccessful general assault upon our lines (May 22d): "It was known that Johnston was at Canton with the force taken by him from Jackson, reinforced by other troops from the east, and that more were daily reaching him. With the force I then had, a short time must have enabled him to attack me in the rear, and possibly succeed in raising the siege." If this was the opinion of the Federal General in Chief, and was sufficient reason to induce him to attempt a desperate assault, rather than risk the probable consequence of delay, I was certainly excusable for the sanguine expectations I entertained that results would be what General Grant feared they might be. But, General Johnston had *predetermined* that Vicksburg *must fall*.

He has asserted (previously cited on page 221 of the *Narrative*) that the whole course of the Confederate General (referring to myself) indicates a determination from the beginning to be besieged in Vicksburg. Whether or not *any part* of my course up to the 17th of May, the day on which my army entered the entrenchments, indicates such a determination, I appeal from General Johnston, to the unprejudiced future historian to decide. I have full faith that sooner or later a just judgment will be rendered.

While I aver, in all truth and honor, that from the beginning, I did everything in my power with the force at my disposal to prevent a siege, I also place on record this statement, that *from the beginning*, I determined to hold Vicksburg, and that nothing short of the most peremptory orders from my superior to interfere with my plans might seriously interfere with the accomplishments of that purpose.

Hence it was, that, on the receipt of General Johnston's instructions to come up on the rear of the enemy at Clinton I convened a council of war in the hope that it would sustain me in my opposition to a movement which I believed might not improbably result in the capture of both Vicksburg and the Army.

I did not, as General Johnston asserts "assume, in discussing this question, that the loss of the battle of Baker's Creek was *inevitable*"; if I had so considered it, I should not have attempted to obey his orders. "Probable" and "inevitable" are no nearer synonymous than are "to attack" and "to beat," in both instances the misuse of words, General Johnston misrepresents facts. His order to come upon the enemy's rear, and which resulted in the battle of Baker's Creek, was the only one which I thought offered a possibility of success. I have expressly stated in my official report that the movement was to be made about noon on the 18th of May, while personally engaged in the selection of the position on the lines around Vicksburg to be occupied by the artillery. I could not therefore have considered defeat as *inevitable* if my language nowhere on this is General Johnston's assertion.

> *On Page 220 of the Narrative, Johnston says:*
>
> *In discussing this question, Lieutenant-General Pemberton assumes that the loss of the battle of Baker's Creek was inevitable. It certainly was made probable by the complete separation of Gregg's and Walker's brigades from this army, and his detaching Vaughn's and Reynolds'. The presence of these four brigades on the field would have added not less than ten thousand men to his fighting force. It is not unreasonable to think that such an addition would have given us the victory; for but three Federal divisions actually fought, while four were held in check by Loring, or rather, by two of Loring's three brigades.*

I received General Johnston's dispatch in reply to my notification of the 17th, that it would probably be necessary to withdraw the Army from the Big Black. It was of the same date and in these words:

> Your dispatch of today by Captain Henderson was received. If Haines' [Snyder's] Bluff is untenable, Vicksburg is of no value and cannot be held. If therefore you are invested in Vicksburg you *must ultimately surrender*. Under such circumstances, instead of losing both troops and place, we must if possible, save the troops. *If it is not too late*, evacuate Vicksburg and its dependencies, and move to the northeast.

This order was to me a great surprise; it expressed a sentiment and expressed theories entirely at variance with my opinions, and for which I had been in no manner prepared by previous intimations. General Johnston's strategy initiated when he took into his own hands the control of the affairs of the department had only produced its natural results as I feared most probable; it had forced the entire Army into the position it then held, after the major part had escaped capture east of the Big Black, brought about by an attempt to execute his impracticable instructions, and having thus brought about the condition of affairs that compelled me to submit to a siege. He ordered it evacuated if not too late and the decision of the question of fact with me. I had no difficulty in deciding it in my own mind, but I chose, for many reasons, under the circumstances in which I was placed, to have my opinion confirmed by the expressed opinion of division and brigade commanders.

General Johnston's instructions were therefore immediately submitted to a council of war on the question of practicability alone, and he was informed that "the opinion was *unanimously* expressed, that it was impossible to withdraw the Army from this position (Vicksburg) with such morale and matériel to be of further service to the Confederacy. While the council of war was assembled, the guns of the enemy opened on the works, and it was at the same time reported that they were crossing the Yazoo River at Brandon's Ferry above Snyder's Mills." And I added "I have decided to hold Vicksburg as long as possible, with the firm hope that the government may yet be able to assist me in keeping this obstruction to the free navigation of the Mississippi River. I still conceive it to be the most important point of the Confederacy."

Although by the terms of his order, General Johnston had relieved himself from the painful responsibility of determining the question of practicability, and had therefore devolved it upon me, he now assumes in his usual dogmatic manner to pronounce judgment that the unanimous decision of the Commanding General of the Army, and division and brigade commanders, was not sustained by facts, and is entitled to no credit.

He says that his order to evacuate Vicksburg and its dependencies "was set aside by advice of a council of war; for the *extraordinary reason* that, it was impossible to withdraw the army from this position (Vicksburg) with such morale and matériel, as to be of further service to the Confederacy." Instead of expressing myself in the language quoted by General Johnston I might with perfect truth have said:

> You have left it to me to decide whether or not it is too late to execute your orders. I will explain to you the condition of affairs. The Federal Army nearly 60,000 strong has already crossed the Big Black and is now moving into position in front of our lines. The advance troops of two corps, Sherman's and McPherson's, their united force, will be in possession of Walnut Hills, and of the road leading to the north east before this army could possibly be put in motion in that direction. McClernand's corps is advancing and will be in the best possible position to strike our flank by the time the column could clear the line of entrenchment. You must be perfectly aware that to be successful, the movement you have ordered must be from the nature of the case be made simultaneously and you must also know that an army, in the circumstances in which this one is place, can not be put in motion at a moment's notice.
>
> Its reorganization, after the disasters of yesterday and the day before, is far from completed. The whole effective force does not at this moment exceed 21,000 and the morale of a considerable portion of it could not presently be relied on to cut its way through an enemy elated by past success, very far superior in numbers, and in possession of the roads and the strong positions commanding them. We should certainly lose the artillery and wagon train, and most probably the greater part of the army in an attempt to carry out your orders. It is therefore in my opinion "too late to evacuate Vicksburg" and to march to the northeast, and in this opinion I am sustained by the unanimous voice of my division and brigade commanders.

Language I use in the preceding would have been more explicit, but neither more or less truthful than that used next to convey the same ideas. But whether my judgment, and that of my general officers was right or wrong on the practicality as a question of fact, I trust it will be believed that however much I may have "apprehended that the severance of the Confederacy should be permitted if I obeyed his order, to save my army by withdrawing it to the northeast on the 18th of May" my conviction as expressed were not less honest and sincere as those of my division and brigade commanders.

Pemberton continues in the spirit of explaining his decision to Johnston:

The army can and will defend Vicksburg; it is incumbent on you to devise the means to raise a siege, which has become inevitable, by your futile attempts to direct the operations of an Army with which you have not for months past been present in person. I trust you will not, to use your favorite phrase so often applied to others, delay your movements until "it is too late."

It is true that the army did with "courage and constancy face the dangers and endure the losses and hardships of a long siege," that fact however, *does not refute* the assertion that it was impossible to withdraw from the entrenchments around Vicksburg with such morale and materiel as to be of further service to the Confederacy *as an army*; and it is in this sense, that General Johnston ought to have construed my response to his dispatch.

Pemberton refers to discussions on page 188 and 189 of the Narrative, in which Johnston describes his reactions to the dispatches of May 18:

Early on the 19th, when near Vernon, I received Lieutenant-General Pemberton's reply to my note, conveying to him the order to evacuate Vicksburg. It was dated May 18th. After acknowledging the receipt of that order, General Pemberton said: On the receipt of your communication, I immediately assembled a council of war of the general officers of this command, and having laid your instructions before them, asked the free expression of their opinions as to the practicability of carrying them out. The opinion was unanimously expressed that it was impossible to withdraw the army from this position with such morale and material as be of further use to the Confederacy. While the council of war was assembled the guns of the enemy opened on the works…I have decided to hold Vicksburg as long as possible, with the firm hope that the Government may yet be able to assist me in keeping this obstruction to the enemy's free navigation of the Mississippi River. I still conceive it to be the most important point in the Confederacy.

Such an estimate of the military value of Vicksburg, expressed five or six weeks earlier, might not have seemed unreasonable; for then the commanders of the United States squadrons believed, apparently, that its batteries were too formidable to be passed by their vessels-of-war. But, when Lieutenant-General Pemberton wrote the letter quoted from, those batteries had been proved to be ineffective, for Admiral Porter's squadron had passed them, and in that way had made "the severance of the Confederacy," before the end of April, that General Pemberton apprehended would be permitted, if he obeyed my order, to save his army by withdrawing it to the northeast, on the 18th of May.

In my reply to this letter, dispatched promptly, I said: "I am trying to gather a force which may attempt to relieve you. Hold out."

Few military critics will deny that, a very inferior force, when aided by respectable fortifications, may successfully defend itself for a protracted period, against the assaults of an enemy numerically far superior; while, on the other hand, its chances of success in a contact with the same enemy in the open field, would [be] comparatively very small, particularly when encumbered with a train; when its flanks and rear are exposed to attack, and when all the advantages of position are with the enemy.

What I have said of the disposition of the several Federal corps late in the evening of the 18th, is in strict accordance with General Grant's official report. The Confederate Army would then have found itself exactly in the situation I have described, and having all the disadvantages I have mentioned to contend against, it would either have been forced back into Vicksburg disheartened, and diminished in numbers, or would then and there, have met the fate that unhappily awaited it at the expiration of the siege; some few, perhaps, escaping to return to their homes, or to join General Johnston at Canton.

An immediate evacuation of the city presupposes an anticipated order to that effect, and arrangements already made to execute it. This, however, was the reverse of the facts. I had not expected the order, and therefore no preparations had been made to meet it. Consequently the troops could not have been put in motion in less then four or five hours after General Johnston's dispatch was received.

"By the morning of the 19th, the investment of Vicksburg was made as complete as could be," according to General Grant, "by the forces at his command," and on the afternoon of that day he ordered his first general assault. In reply to my letter of the 18th, General Johnston says he promptly dispatched the following: "I am trying to gather a force which may attempt to relieve you. Hold out." This note did not reach me, nor did I receive a line or a verbal message from him between the 18th and 29th of May.

On the latter day [May 29], the following dated May 25 was delivered to me by a courier: "Lieut. General Pemberton. My last note was returned by the bearer. 200,000 caps have been sent. It will be continued as they arrive. Bragg is sending a division; when it comes I will move to you. Which do you think the best route? How and where is the enemy encamped? What is your force?" I replied at once, and I ask attention to the fact, that every inquiry of General Johnston's in this dispatch is distinctly answered, and that it contains all the information I could give or that was necessary, to enable General Johnston to arrange a plan of attack, and to instruct me as to my cooperation.

It is also to be observed that this note is dated on the 13th day of the occupation of the trenches, although the morale of the Army was now splendid, its numerical strength was being constantly diminished by casualties and by disease, which had already begun to tell seriously upon the physique of the men confined to man the trenches, day and night, and exposed without shelter of any kind, to the vicissitudes of the weather, it follows consequently that the longer General Johnston delayed his approach, the less would be the cooperative strength of the garrison. The enemy's power of resistance, meantime, would be increasing, not only by the acquisition of reinforcements, but also by lines of circumvallation at first, and subsequently, of counterallation also.

Hence it is manifest that the longer inaction continued the greater must be the relieving force eventually. It was for these reasons, far more than for any apprehension, that Vicksburg might fall by assault, that in almost every dispatch either directly or by implication, I urged upon General Johnston the necessity of hastening his movement.

Well might General Grant feel uneasy in his position, when he says he knew that "Johnston was at Canton with the force taken by him from Jackson, reinforced by other troops from the east, and that more were daily reaching him. With the force I had a short time must have enabled him (Johnston) to *attack* me in the rear, and possibly succeed in raising the siege," if it is to be believed when he "determined to make another effort to carry Vicksburg by assault. It was a wise resolve (on Johnston's part), although the effort failed of success."

But, it will naturally be asked, is this not a mere subterfuge of Grant's to excuse a rash and unnecessary slaughter of his troops? Johnston had even then sufficient force to give General Grant even then a reasonable cause for apprehension. I answer that on the 21st of May, the day before the assault referred to, he had at Canton and Jackson well located at points of departure (as there was no enemy east of the Big Black when a union might be made), a force as large, or larger, than that at Edward's Depot when he ordered me on the 13th to come upon the rear of the enemy at Clinton, as large or larger as that on the field of Baker's Creek and nearly or quite *twice* as large as the Confederate force actually engaged in the battle. He had on the 21st, according to his own statement, eight brigades. I had precisely the same number, on the field, five of which took an active part, in the battle.

On the 23d, the day following the Federal assault on Vicksburg, another brigade (Maxey's), joined General Johnston. He had thus nine brigades available and I shall endeavor to show that they comprised a fighting force of 20,000 men.

In his dispatch to me of the 15th of May, General Johnston states the troops with him (Walker's and Gregg's brigades) to be "about 6,000." On the 10th of May Major General Loring reported the effective strength of this division (three brigades) "a fraction over 6,500." He was not actively engaged at Baker's Creek; he carried with him from the field all but 300 men (these, made up of employees with the wagon train, and some stragglers) who reentered Vicksburg and were present during the siege. With this deduction he had about 6,200. General Maxey's brigade constituted a portion of the command which under Major General Gardner, was ordered by me from Port Hudson to Jackson. General Gardner was positively instructed to bring with him *a specified number of men* "5,000"; he was subsequently directed to return to Port Hudson himself with "2,000" (and to hold that place to the last, which was most gallantly done), Maxey to proceed to Jackson with the remaining 3,000. I have good reason to believe these instructions were literally executed.

There remain to be accounted for the three brigades of Gist's, Ector's, and McNair's. Of their strength I know nothing personally, but placing them at the very low average of 1,700, we still have a total of 5,100, and a grand aggregate of 20,300, and these were fighting men, since they were able to move with their respective commands for active service.

Now although the investment of Vicksburg was complete on the 19th, it was not until "after the failure of the 22d," as General Grant expressly states, that he "determined on a regular siege." On the 23d as I have shown, General Johnston had at his disposal 20,000 men. I had a cooperative force of 21,000, which in view of the vital importance of the object, might possibly have been increased to 23,000 by reducing to the minimum all extra duty details, river guards, etc. Indeed I am confident that, to save Vicksburg, every man who was able to carry his musket would have taken part in the defense, for all would have felt that it must be saved then or not at all.[23]

Here in my opinion was a more favorable opportunity than would be likely to occur again to beat the investment in the direction the most desirable that it should be where, i.e., towards the enemy's new base above Vicksburg, which had been established since our evacuation of Haines' [Snyder's] Bluff. A force of over 40,000 men ought to have been effected thus and thereby have compelled the Federal Army to depend upon its original base at Grand Gulf for supplies, and would thus have prevented "a regular siege."

It does not seem to have struck General Johnston then that "time was all important." That what might be done with 40,000 Confederate troops, our combined strength on the 26th or 27th of May would probably require at least 50,000 to accomplish on the 6th or 7th of June and with even less success.

In his note of the 25th of May, he says, "Bragg is sending a division," and adds *"when it comes I will move to you."* This positive assurance of assistance reached me on the 29th of May. I presumed that my reply would be received about the 3d June, that the division from Bragg's Army would be with him at least by that time, and that by the 7th he would be moving, in fulfillment of his

---

23. Pemberton is engaged in a certain amount of over and underestimating the various forces available on May 23 — but he is close enough to make his point. At that date, best estimates are that Pemberton himself had 29,500 inside the defenses, Johnston a total of 22,000 (10,000 at Jackson, and 12,000 near Canton), while Grant had approximately 51,000.

promise. There would, however, have been an interval of a fortnight between that date, the 7th of June, and the 22d of May, when the Federals made their last assault, and "a regular siege" was determined on. I knew that in the interim they were receiving reinforcements, and were strengthening their lines; the effective force of the garrison would on the contrary be constantly diminishing. Therefore it was that, in my dispatch of the 29th, I volunteered this suggestion to General Johnston: "I do not think you should move with less than 30,000, or 35,000 men, and then, if possible, towards Snyder's Mills, giving me notice of the time of your approach..." In making the suggestion, I had good reason to believe that the smaller numbers, at least, would be within his means by the time my dispatch could reach him; nor was my estimate much, if at all, out of the way. For, on the 3d of June, Breckinridge's division and Evans' of Infantry, as well as Jackson's cavalry (2,000) were added to his previous force of nine brigades estimated at 20,000. He had, beside these, Wirt Adams' regiment of cavalry and some 300 infantry, that had been mounted by impressment or purchase of horses during Grierson's raid. These animals were no longer necessary for the purpose for which they had been obtained and could therefore have been transferred to the field.

After General Johnston's unqualified assurance to me, in his note of the 25th received on the 29th of May, that, "as soon as the division from Bragg arrived, he would move to me," I had certainly the right to expect within seven or eight days thereafter, to hear that he was approaching, and to received his instructions as to or at least to be notified of any change of intention as to his movement. But although several of my messages, returned to me from General Johnston's Head Quarters, between the 29th of May and the 16th of June, I neither received through them nor through any other source, a written or verbal message, of any description, from General Johnston. My dispatches to him, in the mean time, were numerous. And from the 3d of June, they all urged directly or indirectly, to the extent that our relative positions permitted, the importance of an immediate movement on his part.

On that date [June 3] I said "Have not heard form you since the 29th (the day in which his dispatch of the 25th was received)...I can get no information from outside as to your position and strength, and very little in regard to the enemy...In what direction will you move and when? I hope north of the Jackson Road." General Johnston represents (on page 193 of the *Narrative*) that he replied to the note on the 7th as follows "cooperation is absolutely necessary. Tell us how to affect it, and by what routes to approach." I never received it. I had, however, in the dispatch to which it purports to be a reply, distinctly advised him of the direction I thought he ought to take, with the purpose I presumed he had, of raising the siege, with my cooperation.

On the 7th I told him "I am still without information from you later than your dispatch of the 25th. The enemy continues to entrench his position around Vicksburg…The same men are constantly in the trenches, but are still in good spirits expecting your approach…When may I expect you to move, and in what direction? My subsistence may be put down at twenty days."

Again on the 10th: "… we are losing many officers and men. I am waiting most anxiously to know your intentions. Have heard nothing of you, or from you since 25 May. Can you not send me a verbal message by a courier, crossing the river above or below Vicksburg, and swimming across again opposite Vicksburg?"

And on the 12th: "courier Walker arrived this morning with caps. *No message from you…*" On the 14th: "Last night Captain Sanders arrived with 200,000 caps, *but brought no information as to your position or movement.* The enemy is landing troops in large numbers on the Louisiana shore above Vicksburg…I am anxiously expecting to hear from you, to *arrange for cooperation.*"

On the 15th "…our men have no relief, are becoming much fatigued, but are still in pretty good spirits…*I think your movement should be made as soon as possible.* The enemy is receiving reinforcements…" And on the 19th: "…on the Grave Yard Road, the enemy's works are within twenty five feet of our redan…*I hope you will advance with the least possible delay.* My men have been thirty four days and nights in trenches without relief, and the enemy within conversation distance. *What aid am I to expect from you?* The bearer, Captain Wise, can be confided in."

At length, on the 21st June, twenty six days after General Johnston's assurance that, he would move to me, when the expected division from Bragg's Army arrived, I received two communications from him, and about the same time, a third, nearly three weeks old if its date of May the 29th was correct: all were of the same tune, and emphatically declared, that the siege could not be raised: that all that could be attempted was to save the garrison: that for this exact cooperation was indispensable. In the dispatches of the 14th and 16th (but, 15th as stated by General Johnston) I was informed that "his communications with the rear could best be preserved by his operating north of the railroad," and I was desired to inform him "what point would suit me best" (it was also stated that General [Richard] Taylor would endeavor to open communications in the trans-Mississippi department). This was the nearest approach to a suggestion of instructions as to our exact cooperation which was received from General Johnston from the first day of the siege to its termination.

I have already had occasion more than once to correct inaccuracies, and to supply what I have regarded as important omissions, in what purports to be copies of official documents, presented by General Johnston to his readers. I object strenuously to the assertion that I replied on the 3d of June to his dispatch of the 29th of May. I object, however, it is not true that my note of the 3d June expressly states "Have not heard from you since the 29th" which was the date of receipt of his of the 25th. None of his dispatches reached me in less than four days. It would have been absurd, therefore, for me to say, on the very day of its receipt, "I have not heard from you since this morning." But my letters of the 7th and 10th are explicit on their part. In the former the language is "I am still without information from you *later than your dispatch of the 25th.*"

> *The Official Records contain no record of a dispatch from Pemberton to Johnston dated June 3, 1863. In the Narrative, the paragraph that Pemberton refers to is on page 193 and reads as follows:*
>
> *Lieutenant-General Pemberton replied on the 3d of June: "Have not heard from you since the 29th; enemy continues to work on his intrenchments, and very close to our lines; is very vigilant. I can get no information from outside as to your position and strength, and very little in regard to the enemy. I have heard that ten messengers with caps have been captured. In what direction will you move, and when? I hope north of the Jackson road."*

But my more serious objection is that this statement conveys the impression that I was *fully aware* as early as the 3d of June, that General Johnston had *no intention to attempt to raise the siege*, and that all my subsequent dispatches up to the 21st urging upon him the vital importance of hastening his movement, had reference only to the relief of the garrison, which is absolutely and unqualifiedly the reverse of the truth. These remarks would be unnecessary if General Johnston had not suppressed the opening paragraph of the reply to his dispatches of the 14th and 16th of June, and thereby confirmed the erroneous impression which the previous statement is calculated to produce. After giving a correct synopsis of his dispatches of the 14th and 16th General Johnston continues "He (General Pemberton) replied on the 21st…I suggest that, giving me full information in time to act, you move…" The missive referred to supplies proof that, up to this period, I had not relinquished the hope of saving Vicksburg, and that my suggestions were conditional and dependent upon his final decision.

> *Pemberton is attempting to ensure that the reader understand that he fully intend-*
> *ed to hold Vicksburg, and that Johnston should have fully understood his intentions. The*
> *complete paragraphs referred to in the Narrative are on pages 194 and 195:*
>
> *He [Pemberton] replied on the 21st: "…I suggest that, giving me full information in time to act, you move by the north of the railroad, drive in the enemy's pickets at night, and at daylight next morning engage him heavily with skirmishers, occupying him during the entire day; and that on that night I move by the Warrenton Road by Hankinson's Ferry; to which point you should previously send a brigade of cavalry, with two field-batteries, to build a bridge there and hold that ferry; also Hall's and Baldwin's, to cover my crossing at Hankinston's. I shall not be able to move with my artillery and wagons.*
>
> *"I suggest this as the best plan, because all the other roads are too strongly intrenched, and the enemy in too heavy force for reasonable prospect of success, unless you move in sufficient force to compel him to abandon his communication with Snyder's Mill,*

which I still hope we may be able to do..." Captain Saunders, who brought the dispatch, told me that he was directed to say, from Lieutenant-General Pemberton, that I ought to attempt nothing with less than forty thousand men.

Pemberton continues, supplying the portions of the June 21 dispatch not quoted by Johnston.

The suppressed passage reads thus: "Your dispatches of the 14th and 16th received. If it is absolutely impossible, in your opinion, to raise the siege with our combined forces, and that nothing more can be done than to extricate the garrison, I suggest, that giving me full information in time to act..." And General Johnston was informed, that in my judgment, the plans suggested best, unless it was added "you move in sufficient force to compel him (the enemy) to abandon his communications with Snyder's, which I still hope we may be able to do. I await your order. Captain Couper understands all my views, and will explain further."

General Johnston's copyist has also suppressed the last two very brief sentences in my dispatch, an unfortunate omission, since the General has apparently been led thereby into another inaccuracy. He says (on page 195 of the *Narrative*), "Captain Saunders, *who brought the dispatch*, told me, that he was directed to say, from Lieutenant General Pemberton, that I ought to attempt nothing with less than forty thousand men." The dispatch itself bears intrinsic evidence that it was carried by Capt. Couper, who stated "understands all my views, and will explain further."

I have no recollection that any person was authorized to deliver such a message; I certainly did not express the opinion that "General Johnston ought to *attempt nothing* with less than 40,000 men" (if the attempt was to be merely confined to extricating the garrison). But if that or a similar message was in fact sent, it must have been as will be presently shown prior to the receipt by me on the 21st of June of General Johnston's dispatches of the 14th and 16th; that is, at a period when we were confidently expecting his cooperation not merely to save the garrison but to raise it. One inaccuracy he followed up with another when he asserts that (on page 195 of the *Narrative*): "This dispatch was *answered* on the 22d"; a communication cannot be answered *before it* has been received (no courier attempted to pass from the entrenchments until after dark, and hardly then to make his way on foot with the utmost caution, and by most circuitous routes) and it is therefore a physical impossibility that my dispatch of the 21st June from Vicksburg could have been received in Jackson on the 22d; consequently it could not have been answered on that day.

General Johnston did however address a note to me dated the 22d in which he says that General Taylor had been directed "to cooperate with me from the west bank of the river, to throw in supplies, and to cross with his forces if expedient and practicable." He says "I will have the means of moving towards the enemy in a day or two, and will try to make a diversion in your favor; and if possible communicate with you, though I fear my force is too small to effect the latter." And here he adds "I have only two thirds of the force you told Captain Saunders to tell me is the least with which I ought to make an attempt…" In his text he states 40,000, as the force mentioned by Capt. Saunders.

It is of course possible that this, or some similar suggestion, may have been sent, and have escaped my memory. I have never hitherto referred to the subject, because it did not strike me that it was a point in the game until a careful perusal of General Johnston's book revealed the attempt to connect this message with his dispatch of the 22d of June.

Now knowing I positively assert that if any person was authorized to say to General Johnston on my part that "He ought to attempt nothing with less than forty thousand men," that message was sent before I had any intimation from him, that, "our joint forces could not raise the siege of Vicksburg," and that any suggestion or advise urged to his numbers had reference to our expected attempt to raise the siege by our combined efforts and not at all to the extrication of the garrison, except so far as that was incidental to the main object. The same reasons, that induced me to volunteer the advice on the 29th of May, twelve days after the investment had begun, that a movement to raise the siege should not *then* be attempted with less than 30,000 or 35,000 men, may have influenced me some *seventeen or eighteen days later*, when the garrison was *considerably weaker, and the enemy much stronger*, suggest that the delay of a month had made a still further increase of his force necessary. As such delay augmented the relative disproportion of the besieged and besieging armies; because the relieving force should be correspondingly increased.

By the 4th of July an army of 50,000, with that purpose in view, would not have been relatively so strong, all things considered, as 40,000 on the 20th of June, or 30,000 on the 7th, or 20,000 on the 28th or 29th of May. At no time did General Johnston send me an intimation of his actual strength. His dispatch of the 22d June did not convey to me real information. I had therefore no data whatever on which to base my own conjecture beyond the obvious, and no doubt exaggerated estimates gathered by courier from common report or at best, from unofficial sources near head quarters.

It will be remembered that from the 29th of May, the date of General Johnston's last dispatch of the 25th until sometime after the middle of June, I did not receive either a written or verbal message from him. But as soon as I learned of his decision that "our forces could not raise the siege of Vicksburg," I at once explained in detail, a plan for combined operations, by which, it seemed to me the garrison might be extricated, provided, it could be attempted within a few days. But, to make this possible, it was necessary, that General Johnston's Army should be already on the march. If he was still inactive at Jackson awaiting my reply to his dispatches received on the 21st, there could be no hope of cooperation from his before the 30th of June or the 1st of July (he did not move from Jackson until the 29th June; see Page 202 of the *Narrative*). By that time hardly one half of the men then in the trenches would be physically able to undertake the difficult task of cutting a way through the strongly entrenched lines of the enemy. With this consideration on the 22d June, I addressed a note to General Johnston, of which I regret I have not a copy; I find a short extract purporting to be from that note, followed by another in language identical with that used by me from a previous dispatch dated the 19th. The two so combined seem to have composed a single communication under date of the 22d June, while in fact they are distinct compositions, and written with diametrically opposite purposes in view. Diametrically opposite, because, that of the 19th was an endeavor to hasten General Johnston's movements which I hoped would result in raising the siege and saving Vicksburg, while that of the 22d looked to securing for the garrison the most favorable terms possible by the surrender of Vicksburg to the enemy.

The two dispatches Pemberton refers to are contained in the Official Records, and read as follows:

VICKSBURG, June 19, 1863.

General JOSEPH E. JOHNSTON:

The enemy opened all his batteries on our lines about 3.30 this morning, and continued the heaviest fire we have yet sustained, until 8 o'clock, but he did not assault our works. Artillery is reported to have been distinctly heard about 2 a.m. toward east of Snyder's Mill, supposed to have been an engagement with your troops. On the Graveyard road the enemy's works are within 25 feet of our redan; also very close on Jackson and Baldwin's Ferry road. I hope you will advance with the least possible delay. My men have been thirty-four days and nights in trenches without relief, and the enemy is within conversation distance. We are living on very reduced rations, and, as you know, are entirely isolated. What aid am I to expect from you? The bearer, Captain [George D.] Wise, can be confided in.

J. C. PEMBERTON.

VICKSBURG, June 22, 1863.

General JOSEPH E. JOHNSTON, Jackson:

If I cut my way out, this important position is lost, and many of my men, too. Can we afford that? If I cannot cut my way out, both position and all my men are lost. This we cannot afford. Should suggest the probability of Grant's being open to terms that can result more to our advantage than either of the above actions. Not knowing your force or plans, he may accede to your proposition to pass this army out with all its arms and equipage. This proposal would come with greater prospects of success and better grace from you, while it necessarily could not come at all from me. You could make the showing of my ability and strength to still hold out for several weeks longer, which, together with his impression regarding your strength, might operate upon him to comply with your terms. While I make this suggestion, I still renew my hope of your being, by force of arms, enabled to act with me in saving this vital point. I will strain every nerve to hold out, if there is hope of our ultimate relief, for fifteen days longer. It is reported that some of the enemy's forces are moving up toward the Yazoo. It is also reported that some of his forces have moved along the Hall's Ferry road to Big Bayou, near Warrenton, where they are temporarily massing. These movements indicate the lengthening of the enemy's lines, and the increase of the area of his operations.

J. C. PEMBERTON.

In his Official report of Operations in Mississippi and E. Louisiana made to the Confederate government November 1, 1863 General Johnston says: "A day or two after this, a dispatch was brought to me from General Pemberton, dated June 22d, suggesting that I should make to Grant *"propositions to pass this Army out with all its arms and equipage"* removing his hope of my being able by force of arms to act with him, and expressing the opinion that he could hold for fifteen days longer."

In the *Narrative* (page 196) the same subject is thus referred to: "In a dispatch dated 22d Lieutenant General Pemberton suggested that I should propose terms to General Grant, the surrender of the place but not of the troops," adding however: "I still renew my hope of you being by force of arms, enabled to act with me to hold out, *if there is hope of our ultimate relief* for fifteen days longer…Federals opened all their batteries on our lines about half after three this morning, and continued the heaviest fire we have yet sustained, until eight o'clock; but did not assault our works." The following passage in brackets forms part of my dispatch of the 19th but is omitted by General Johnston ["Artillery is reported to have been distinctly heard about two o'clock a.m. towards and east of Snyder's Mills, supposed to have been an engagement with your troops on the Grave Yard Road."…"The enemy's works are within twenty five feet of our redan, and also very close on the Jackson and Baldwin Ferry's Roads. I hope you will advance with the least possible delay. My men have been thirty four days and nights in the trenches without relief, and the enemy is within conversation distance. We are living on very reduced rations…"]

The remainder of the dispatch is omitted by General Johnston; it was continued in these words "and, as you know, are entirely isolated. What aid am I to expect from you? The bearer, Captain Wise, can be confided in." After the word "Federals," which is substituted as a synonym for "Enemy," to the word *"rations,"* the whole of this dispatch which purports to bear date June 22d, is a copy of one sent by me on the 19th (that of the 21st intervening), and it is to this earliest date that the incidents mentioned are to be referred. I cannot readily believe that such incongruities could have escaped my notice; nor can I be convinced that by any evidence, short of the original document, I am responsible for them. Both of the dispatches, which have been amalgamated into one, were undoubtedly sent by me, but separately, under *different dates*, and under *very different circumstances*.

The last communication received from General Johnston during the siege was that of the 22d June, which has been already discussed (see ante). At my request, however, in the month of August, 1863, he furnished me with a copy of another dated 27th June, a synopsis of which is found in his *Narrative*: it was as follows:

> Your dispatch of 22d received. General E.K. Smith's troops have been mismanaged and have fallen back to Delhi. I have sent a special message urging him to assume direct command. The determined spirit you manifest, and his expected cooperation, *encourage me to hope something may yet be done to save Vicksburg, and to postpone both the methods suggested of merely extricating the garrison*. Negotiations with Grant for the relief of the garrison should they become necessary, must be made by you. It would be a confession of weakness, on my part, which I ought not to make, to propose them. When it becomes necessary to make terms, they may be considered as made under my authority.

The troops under my command had entered the trenches around Vicksburg, on the 17th of May; the preceding dispatch was dated the 27th of June; that is, on the forty first day of the occupation. General Johnston was well aware that the effective force of the garrison, had in the interim from various causes been *very* materially diminished, and that the enemy on the contrary had greatly strengthened his position, and increased his numbers. Surely then this was not a time for trifling and for idle words; it must be presumed that, General Johnston was fully in earnest when he says that "the *determined spirit manifested by the garrison* and the expected cooperation of General E.K. Smith encourage me to *hope something may yet be done to save Vicksburg* and to postpone both the methods suggested of *merely extricating the garrison.*"

If, after he had repeatedly announced that our joint forces could not raise the siege, General Johnston was encouraged on the fortieth day of its duration, "to hope that something might still be done to save Vicksburg," on what principle can he condemn me on the 17th of May for hoping and believing, when the day in which my army entered Vicksburg, when the condition of affairs was infinitely more promising than that later period, not only that something might be done, but that everything that might be necessary would be done, to save it? That absolutely nothing was even attempted by him is obvious to all who have read his book. His prediction that "Vicksburg must fall if besieged" conclusively proved that he made no true and earnest effort to avert the calamity he prophesized.

General Johnston asserts (on page 223 of the *Narrative*) that in its march from Bruinsburg to Vicksburg "the Federal Army drew its supplies from the country, and did not in the least depend on its communications with the Mississippi." Yet that army, then some 50,000 strong, marched one hundred and twenty miles, or there about, into the interior of an enemy's country, fought several battles, and finally set down to besiege Vicksburg with the Big Black River in its rear, with little other transportation or supplies than could be collected in the country adjacent to its line of march. General Johnston has not shown that there were insuperable obstacles that prevented him from pursuing a similar course. He was not impeded in his operations as I have always been, by the necessity of providing for the defense of Vicksburg, and protecting the rear by approaches from the Mississippi River.

His position at Jackson, or Canton, was in several aspects not unlike Grant's had been for some days after his landing at Bruinsburg. Both had small means of transportation; General Grant supplied his deficiencies by seizure, from a small district south of the Jackson and Vicksburg Railroad. The whole country north of this railroad, and east of the Jackson and New Orleans, and of the Mississippi Central was open to General Johnston and could have supplied his indispensable wants by impressment, if necessary, within a week after our Army had entered Vicksburg.

Three or four field batteries would have been sufficient for the demands of the service he was required to perform (he had at least that number); his principle reliance as should have been on the muskets and bayonets of his Infantry. He had on the 23d of May, 20,000 of those troops, as well equipped as the Confederate soldier was accustomed to be. I could have cooperated with more than one equal force of infantry, and with as much field artillery as he could desire. The enemy was not then entrenched, and numbered not over 60,000 occupying a line ten miles in length. Had he then advanced resolutely and rapidly, his very approach would probably have been so far weakened the investment, at least the effective force of the garrison might have been extricated if our joint forces should have proved too weak to raise the siege.

It is my belief that might have been accomplished in the last week of May, though I do not put forth a dogmatic assertion to that effect, ignoring all appropriate opinions. My suggestion to General Johnston, that if there was no prospect of raising the siege, it might be advisable for him to "propose terms to General Grant for the surrender of the place but not of the troops" was declined, on the grounds that "it would be an impolitic confession of weakness," and that therefore if it should become necessary to make propositions, they must be made by me: but that the terms might then "be considered as made under his authority."

There had been a public, and daily confession of weakness on his part for nearly six weeks prior to the receipt of my note of the 22d June, for there could be no other apology for his inaction during that period: to have acceded to my suggestion would not have made that confession more complete, while on the other hand there was a possibility that a proposition to surrender Vicksburg from him would be regarded by General Grant as an exercise of his superior authority to which I would yield obedience as a military duty, although I might not personally be disposed to capitulate.

It was this consideration, and the hope of avoiding thereby a useless loss of life, that induced me to propose to General Johnston that negotiations for the surrender of the place but not of the troops, should be made through him after he had thrice informed me under different dates, that it was impossible to do more than extricate the garrison and after I had replied to those notifications, by explaining in full what I deemed to be the best plan to effect that object by force of arms. I heard nothing from him subsequent to the receipt of his dispatch of the 22d June during the remainder of the siege, nor was I aware that he had moved from Jackson until some days after the surrender.

On the 10th of July, a Confederate soldier, who had probably been captured in attempting to make his way through the Federal lines, sent me from the city jail the following dispatch from General Johnston, dated camp near Birdsong's Ferry July 3d:

> Your dispatch of 28th was destroyed by messenger. He states that General Smith's troops were driven back to Monroe. This statement, and his account of your condition make me think it necessary to create a diversion, and thus enable you to cut your way out, if the time has arrived for you to do this. Of that time I can not judge; you must, as it depends upon your condition. I hope to attack the enemy in your front the 7th, and your cooperation will be necessary. The manner and the proper point for you to bring the garrison out must be determined by you, from your superior knowledge of the ground, and distribution of the enemy's forces. Our firing will show you where we are engaged. *If Vicksburg can not be saved, the garrison must.*

Consequently I should have known nothing of the attack General Johnston "hoped" to make on the 7th of July until his troops were actually engaged with the enemy, and must have remained uncertain for a considerable time, whether the firing was the result of a battle, or of a simple reconnaissance. Timely, and profitable cooperation on the part of the garrison, would probably have failed, and an attempt to cut its way out, have been unsuccessful. To have ensured the delivery of a dispatch of such vital importance, it should not have been entrusted to a single messenger, but copies should have been sent by several reliable hands, and at least five or six days earlier. Had I been aware of General Johnston's presence near the Big Black on the 3d of July (although I do not believe he would have crossed it, or have rendered me any assistance), I would not have capitulated on the 4th, even on far better terms than obtained. But, as I have already stated, not the slightest rumor reached me that he had moved from Jackson.

The condition of the garrison was perfectly well known to him. He had been informed by my dispatch (see my dispatch, ante) on the 19th June, that the enemy on one road, was "within twenty five feet" of our works and "very close on the other roads," and the enemy "within conversation distance," which was literally true, the ordinary colloquial voice being distinctly audible at those points. Hand grenades were thrown from either line into the trenches of the other and, when by tacit consent, a quasi truce existed as it occasionally did, for a brief period, an interchange of tobacco and coffee in small parcels was often effected in the same manner.

Pemberton's manuscript response ends here. While incomplete, and obviously missing some continued thoughts he intended to further develop, he did cover the eight allegations made against his generalship by Johnston.

Part Five

Conclusions

Part 5 — Conclusions

More than 115 years have passed since John C. Pemberton's death in 1881. Yet the bitterness and rancor that developed between Pemberton and Johnston after the end of the Vicksburg campaign survives in their writings today. Although debate over Civil War military history continues undiminished, discussion regarding the Vicksburg campaign generally revolves around U. S. Grant, and the campaign he led.

When John Pemberton is discussed at all, it is usually to place him in the lower tier of Confederate senior generals. One modern historian has referred to him as a "bumbler" who, along with Bragg and Hood, lost the western Confederacy. Another historian, Allan Nevins, describes Pemberton as "the leader most censurable" for the loss of Vicksburg.[1]

Noticeably absent from this list of "bumblers" is the name of Joseph E. Johnston, who has survived with his reputation for the most part intact. Although some revision of his military capabilities has appeared recently, he has traditionally been described as the frustrated commander of the army of relief who was given too little too late. Thomas Connelly presents a sympathetic view in his two-volume work on the Army of Tennessee. Johnston's major biographers have painted him in an equally sympathetic light. Much leeway is given to Johnston because history has tended to view him as a commander whose effectiveness was undercut by inept subordinates, most notably Pemberton. "[T]he two men who led the principal armies in the West—Braxton Bragg and John C. Pemberton—were arguably the two worst Confederate field commanders of the war," suggested one.[2]

Much of the view of Pemberton that survives today comes from Johnston's writings (both during and after the war) and the voluminous writings on Grant. Grant's good fortune, his ability to maneuver seemingly at will and feed an army while in hostile country, and his eventual capture of a 29,500-man army (while

---

1. James McPherson, *Battle Cry of Freedom* (New York: Oxford University Press, 1988) 857, Allan Nevins, *The War for the Union: Volume 3, The Organized War* (New York: Charles Scribner & Sons, 1971) 58.
2. Symonds, *Joseph E. Johnston: A Civil War Biography*, pg. 188.

another 32,000 viewed the situation in frustrated impotence) clearly point to the need for a Confederate scapegoat. Armed with an ego that could not admit to any culpability, Johnston set out to ensure that all blame pointed towards Davis and Pemberton—but most especially Pemberton.

What conclusions can be reached regarding the military abilities of John C. Pemberton and Joseph E. Johnston? Was Johnston blameless for the loss of Vicksburg? Did justifiable blame fall on Pemberton? Or was Pemberton successful in refuting the eight charges he believed Johnston had levied against him in his *Narrative of Military Operations*?

The answer must be sought in a mix of various arguments, both pro and con. Part of the difficulty in answering such a question rests in the fact that neither Davis nor Johnston was capable of shouldering a sharing of blame. Neither would, moreover, consider publicly admitting to any culpability. This unwillingness to accept blame led, both during the war and afterwards to an immediate polarization of allegations—and Pemberton found himself caught in the middle. In his writings, however, Pemberton was willing to take a certain amount of blame, as long as Johnston received his due share.

"If not innocent myself, I have in him [Johnston] an associate, who must share the offense," wrote Pemberton. Pemberton argued throughout his manuscript the reasonableness of his decisions, as based on the information available to him at the time. He was, however, not averse to using hindsight to justify those decisions. He believed, moreover, that Johnston had had the means to lift the siege of Vicksburg—but simply did not act. His task was to defend his record against Johnston's allegations, not to argue whether or not Grant's capture of Vicksburg was inevitable.

Johnston was extremely displeased with his assignment to departmental command in November 1862. Within the first two months of command, he twice asked Davis to relieve him of his duties. It is not clear, however, what specific command would have pleased him—other than command of his old army, which was already gaining fame under Robert E. Lee as the Army of Northern Virginia. Given Lee's string of successes in 1862, that command was clearly unavailable. Johnston wanted Davis to give him an army command outright; he was unwilling to use his authority as theater commander to replace another general and thereby achieve his goal. Davis, for his part, was apparently willing to allow Johnston such departmental latitude—but (at least in November 1862) was unwilling to replace either Bragg or Pemberton with Johnston. Each man, proud and obstinate, refused to give in to the other. Although Davis tried, on two occasions, to have Johnston relieve Bragg, Johnston used available situations to indefinitely postpone the order.

As has been noted, Johnston wrote frequently to Richmond, complaining about, questioning, and even denying the character and scope of his command.

The distance between the commands of Bragg and Pemberton was too great to allow for precise coordination of events, he argued. Moreover, Johnston found it impossible to coordinate and control events in the department in which he was located. Simply put, Johnston's heart was not in his assignment.

Interestingly, the very reasons Jefferson Davis found it imperative to create Johnston's departmental command were the reasons Johnston rebelled against them. The failures in coordination and cooperation that plagued Braxton Bragg's Kentucky invasion the previous summer and fall were the very problems that Davis expected to solve with Johnston's appointment. Commanding and coordinating a theater command, however, were not responsibilities that Johnston wished or desired.

Johnston's physical ability to command also remained an issue. At times throughout his tenure in command, Johnston found himself physically restricted by his health. One such instance occurred when Pemberton was coping with Grant's crossing of the Mississippi, and Davis peremptorily ordered Johnston to Mississippi. Although Johnston left immediately, in obedience to his order, he felt it necessary to inform Davis that he was unfit for field duty. Upon reaching Jackson, Johnston expected Pemberton (but hesitated to directly order him) to evacuate Vicksburg and move his army to Johnston, as opposed to Johnston's moving to Pemberton. An oddity of the Vicksburg campaign is that these two men, separated as late as the battle of Champion Hill by less than 40 miles, never met face-to-face.

When he was with Bragg in Tennessee, Johnston expressed indifference regarding events in Mississippi. He opposed the transfer of Stevenson's reinforced division to Mississippi and had to be pointedly asked by Davis to accompany him to Mississippi for a site visit in mid-December 1862. Returning to Tennessee, Johnston did not go west again until ordered there the following May. He repeatedly argued impending disaster in Tennessee while Pemberton was left to deal with Grant alone. Once in Mississippi, however, he argued with Richmond that he was unable to effectively coordinate with Bragg and urged that all available reinforcements be rushed to him immediately. In disgust, the War Department issued orders taking Tennessee away from Johnston's control in July 1863.[3]

Johnston's military conduct during the Vicksburg campaign—and his time in command of the relief army—has escaped significant historical scrutiny. Historians (including Johnston biographers) have been willing to accept Johnston's insistence on the inevitable futility of his situation. The tenuous grip Grant held outside the besieged forces of Pemberton and the obvious need for quick action belied the

---

3. The relationship between Davis, the War Department, and Johnston became so bitter that the Confederate Congress called for copies of all correspondence between the parties. The legalistic wrangling between Johnston, Davis and Seddon is at *OR*, ser. I, vol. XXIV, pt 1, 189-239.

seeming indifference Johnston exhibited towards a movement on Vicksburg. Hindsight is historically valueless, but it is difficult to envision Robert E. Lee, Stonewall Jackson, John Bell Hood, or James Longstreet arriving at Jackson, and sitting idly by while Pemberton was forced to surrender his 29,500-man army.[4]

Accounts of the Vicksburg campaign often represent Pemberton as having been totally befuddled by Grant's maneuvering. Until Johnston arrived at Jackson on May 13, however, Pemberton did a more than acceptable job of maneuvering his forces along the Big Black River, denying Grant access to Vicksburg. Grant could not gain the control he needed until he managed to cross the river at some point, and establish critical supply lines. Pemberton's forces were concentrated to prevent such a crossing and remained so. It was only upon Johnston's arrival that the tactical situation began to slip away from Pemberton; torn between Davis's demand that he hold Vicksburg and Johnston's conflicting demand that he move to Jackson, Pemberton could no longer keep the task at hand uppermost in his mind.[5]

What would have happened had Pemberton been left to finish the campaign without Johnston's help will always remain open to conjecture. It is no stretch however, to suggest that, without Johnston's arrival, the movement on Dillon's Plantation would not have taken place, and the battles of Champion Hill and Big Black Bridge would not have been fought. Without the losses incurred during those battles, Pemberton would have retained the equivalent of another division of men and 45 cannon as well as Loring's division to await Grant behind the Big Black River. More equal Confederate numbers would have confronted Grant behind defensible positions.

With the arrival of Johnston, however, the "irresistible force" met "the immovable object." Something had to give. What gave was Confederate military planning, thinking and strategy. Of the two choices available to the Confederates—to concentrate at Jackson or to concentrate behind the Big Black—the latter appears to be the wiser. How long Grant could have maneuvered in front of the river crossings, probing for a chance to cross, is unknown, but there certainly would have come a time when he would have been compelled to fall back on Grand Gulf for supplies and munitions. When Johnston arrived on the scene, Pemberton's flank on Snyder's Bluff (referred to by Pemberton as Haines' Bluff) remained secure, and the Yazoo River was unavailable to Grant as a supply line.[6]

---

4. It is not to argue inevitable success were any of these men sent west, but to simply suggest that something would have been tried to relieve the garrison, that this point is made.

5. A reading of the *Official Records* during early May reveals a calm Pemberton clearly dealing in a competent manner with Grant's maneuverings along the Big Black River.

6. It was the opening of the Yazoo River and the capture of Snyder's Bluff that was of critical importance to Grant. As long as Grant was kept to the east of the Big Black River, the Yazoo remained closed to the Federals.

Perhaps, when all is said and done, Jefferson Davis himself deserves the blame for Confederate failure. Although his motives and reasons were sound, in the final analysis it was he who ordered Johnston to Mississippi to take charge of the command situation.

The eight charges that Johnston made against Pemberton's military conduct can be put into three major categories: (1) mishandling the actions associated with Grant's crossing of the Mississippi, including the battle of Port Gibson; (2) mishandling events that began with Johnston's arrival at Jackson, and ended with the retreat into Vicksburg; and (3) incorrectly interpreting the strategic value of Vicksburg, willingly entering into a siege, and being uncooperative once the siege had begun.

Of those eight charges, three included the phrase "disobedience of orders"; another contained "refusing the order of my superior." It is not a stretch to suggest that these charges even today fairly summarize public opinion regarding John Pemberton's military conduct at Vicksburg.

But are they a fair assessment of Pemberton? First, Pemberton lost the only critical field campaign he commanded. The administrative competence and organizational ability he showed at Charleston and at Vicksburg prior to Grant's crossing were quickly forgotten in the aftermath of the stunning surrender of his army and the loss of the Mississippi River. His northern birth only reinforced these negative opinions.

The departmental command held by Pemberton involved much more, however, than merely confronting Grant's forces across the Mississippi River, and attempting to thwart the Federal commander's efforts to get at Vicksburg. Pemberton also commanded the Department of Mississippi and East Louisiana, which included not only a substantial stretch of the Mississippi River, but the entire state of Mississippi as well. Large sections of northern Mississippi were a brutal no-man's land populated by raiding cavalry and disaffected Confederate loyalists. The latter demanded protection from Federal cavalry raids, which Pemberton was unable to effectively deliver. In addition, he had to cope with meddlesome politicians, although he seems to have forged a reasonable working relationship with Governor John Pettus of Mississippi.

One of Pemberton's most often repeated complaints (both during and after the war) involved Johnston's transfer of Van Dorn's cavalry to Tennessee, which left only a small contingent of cavalry in his department. Johnston's claim that Pemberton's cavalry was in a state of idleness in late December 1862 implied that the department did not need it. The claim not only ignored the recent Holly Springs raid, but it also demonstrated shortsighted strategic thinking on Johnston's part. Johnston's willingness to strip a department of the majority of its mobility, especially a department that included an entire state and part of another, indicated that he was not thinking of departmental objectives but only of Pemberton's local army.

Lack of cavalry became a significant issue prior to Grant's crossing of the Mississippi when Grierson's cavalry raid into the heart of Mississippi went relatively unopposed. As departmental commander, Pemberton had been ordered by the War Department in Richmond to protect the interior industry and railroads from such raids. This policy, however, ran contrary to the one advocated by Johnston (although Johnston himself was still in Tennessee at this time and only expressed such advocacy in later writings).

Pemberton was thus forced to use his only available resource—the infantry—to protect his department's interior assets. An incorrect interpretation of reported troop movements to Memphis led Pemberton to believe that Grant was not contemplating a crossing to the eastern side of the Mississippi, and he thus committed a substantial portion of the infantry to the interior. It should be noted that Johnston made no complaint regarding the disposition of Pemberton's forces until those dispositions made it impossible for Pemberton to effectively block Grant near Port Gibson.

When Grant finally did cross the river, too large a portion of Pemberton's available infantry was stranded in the interior of the state. Loring managed to maroon his division on the wrong side of a railroad break. Although Bowen put up a spirited defense near Port Gibson, he could not stop Grant.

Although Pemberton argued that he did all that was possible to concentrate after Grant's crossing, those arguments ring hollow. Pemberton's decisions to commit infantry to the interior did leave an inadequate force available to contest Grant at Port Gibson. There was nothing either Johnston or Pemberton could have done once that decision had been made. Johnston's contention that Pemberton ignored his orders to concentrate, however, is simply not true.

Johnston maintained that all available forces should have been sent to Port Gibson, including the divisions holding the defensive line at Vicksburg. Those divisions, however, were confronting Sherman's corps on the Snyder's Bluff line. Although we know today that Sherman did not intend to storm Vicksburg, Pemberton could not ignore the possibility that he might, and correctly held two divisions in the city to check Sherman. Pemberton argued this point more than it deserved in his manuscript especially since Sherman's report indicating no real intent to storm the defenses was available to him when he was writing his response.

Pemberton concentrated his forces quickly enough to keep Grant south and east of the Big Black River and to guard the available crossings. At this early stage of the campaign, given Grant's perceived supply problems, Pemberton should have felt satisfied with his position. Grant, it was expected, would have to attack Pemberton's Vicksburg defensive line quickly, or not attack at all. As Grant maneuvered in-land, all evidence pointed to a Federal attack at the Big Black Bridge, not a movement on Jackson. Indeed, Pemberton's orders during this time reflect a calm competence that is at odds with much historical interpretation.

If Johnston's charges that Pemberton did not concentrate his forces as ordered point to any single fact, it may be the difficulties inherent in Johnston's multi-departmental command. Based as he was in Tennessee, Johnston simply could not know the status of events in Mississippi no matter how well Pemberton attempted to keep him informed. Johnston's advice, gratuitous as it was, was sound, but his after-the-fact blame and finger pointing at Pemberton was simply self-serving.

If Pemberton had had 3,000 to 4,000 cavalry in his department to confront Grierson, would the battle of Port Gibson have ended differently? The answer is open to speculation, but, given the stiff resistance Bowen's brigades put forth in the steep, tangled ravines south of Bayou Pierre and west of Port Gibson, it is not difficult to envision an improved scenario for Pemberton. If Grant's coveted foothold on dry ground east of the Mississippi could have been bought at a greater cost of both time and casualties, Confederate prospects would have been enhanced. Grant's freedom of movement (which allowed him to draw supplies off the country) and his ability to move independently on Jackson might have been restricted. In any event, it is unlikely Pemberton could have concentrated enough troops to inflict a crushing defeat on Grant. How a partial success could have been parlayed into greater success is open to conjecture.

Johnston's contention that Pemberton failed to concentrate his forces in spite of his order to do so needs to be examined carefully. At the time Johnston's telegrams were written, he had no knowledge of where Pemberton's forces were; thus, his blind assumption that Pemberton's failures to follow his orders allowed Grant to obtain his foothold is fallacious. On the other hand, one can question the wisdom of Pemberton's dispersion of infantry, even given Grierson's cavalry raid. In addition, Pemberton should have moved forward and directed the engagement personally at the decisive point. Instead, he maintained his behind-the-scenes style of command in Jackson and was not present at the battle of Port Gibson.

The events that led to the defeats at Champion Hill and Big Black Bridge are confusing, even after 135 years. Communications between Pemberton and Johnston were so roundabout and the situation in the field so fluid that events and orders as reported in dispatches were often untenable by the time they were received. Johnston's actions with his army at Jackson even suggest this.

A reading of Johnston's *Narrative* suggests that there was nothing he could do upon reaching Jackson, that Pemberton failed to obey orders, and that everything that followed resulted from Pemberton's incorrect decisions. He struck a note when he informed Richmond, upon arrival in Jackson on May 13, that he "was too late" and that communications were cut off from Pemberton. Pemberton noted that although the direct route to Jackson was indeed closed, more roundabout means were available.

Messages were sent back and forth; Johnston could have skirted Grant to the north and reached Pemberton via Brownsville, Mechanicsburg, or Yazoo City. Even so, he wrote Pemberton on May 13 to come to Clinton and attack a detachment of Grant's army. Johnston's intelligence, however, was faulty; he had no understanding of the whereabouts of the rest of Grant's forces. In addition, the wording of the order included the directive "if practicable." By the time Pemberton received the message, on May 14, the situation was rapidly changing, and the order had been rendered not "practicable."

Worse, Johnston's subsequent actions were in direct conflict with his own order. Uniting at Clinton with Pemberton would have necessitated a movement by Johnston westward from Jackson. Instead, he moved away from Grant and Pemberton, retreating to the northeast towards Canton. Moving to Clinton would have required one to two days' march for Pemberton; without cavalry to reconnoiter in his front, his 23,000-man army would have been at Grant's mercy. Although Pemberton correctly noted this dilemma in his manuscript, he again over-emphasized the point.

That same day Pemberton responded that he was complying with Johnston's order. In the meantime, Johnston had written Pemberton again, ignoring his orders of the previous night; the message did not arrive until two days later. It showed, however, how little emphasis Johnston placed at the time on his order of May 13, in spite of later assertions to the contrary.

By this time, communications difficulties, Grant's aggressive response, and his own misreading of the tactical situation drove Pemberton into a series of tactical blunders. Rather than remain behind the Big Black River and simply let the situation develop, he looked for an alternative to Johnston's May 13 order. The decision to move on Dillon's Plantation was a grave mistake, given that Pemberton was admittedly in the dark regarding the location of Grant's army.

As Pemberton was slowly moving, Johnston unintentionally added further confusion to the mix. Although his information on May 15 was no better than it was two days before, he again ordered Pemberton to move to Clinton to join him. Evidently, he did not consider the notion of moving the smaller force (his) to the larger force (Pemberton's). The order reached Pemberton at the absolute worst moment possible. His army was south and southeast of Champion Hill. Although his skirmishers were already in contact with Grant's army, Pemberton tried to turn his army around to comply with Johnston's order. The blunder was clearly his, even though he would later argue that he was merely following Johnston's order. If any order received during the campaign could and should have been ignored, this was the one.

Pemberton's manuscript attempts to show that he did, indeed, follow his superior's order and that Johnston's assertion that Pemberton's army remained inert too long on May 16 was unfounded. These arguments pale beside the mistake Pemberton made in turning his army around—a mistake to which Pemberton would not admit.

Johnston had little idea of what was happening to his west with the armies of Grant and Pemberton, and his ill-advised order to Pemberton only made a bad situation worse. To further complicate matters, his order to Pemberton to again march to Clinton (regardless of the enemy in his front) came at a very inopportune time. For Johnston to suggest that Pemberton's hesitancy to obey his order (which was written in ignorance of the facts) was a primary cause of Confederate disaster cannot be interpreted as anything other than a continued effort on Johnston's part to shift all the blame for failure onto Pemberton.

Although it had no impact on future events, Johnston did not begin to move towards Pemberton until several critical days had passed. Although Pemberton's decision to move on Dillon's and turn his army around in the face of the enemy must be questioned, his confusion regarding the intent of his superior is understandable. Johnston's orders, vague as they were, suggested the abandonment of Vicksburg. This strategy was one that Pemberton could not support. "I still conceive it [Vicksburg] to be the most important point in the Confederacy," Pemberton wrote Johnston.

Once disaster befell the Confederates at Champion Hill and Big Black Bridge, Johnston made one more effort to pry Pemberton away from Vicksburg. On May 18, Pemberton received a message from Johnston ordering him to abandon Vicksburg "if not too late." It was the only order Johnston wrote during the campaign that directly ordered Pemberton to evacuate Vicksburg; like the others, however, it allowed Pemberton's discretion in its execution. Pemberton was already inside the defensive perimeter. After consultation with his senior officers, he concluded it was indeed too late.

Did Pemberton disobey Johnston's orders? It must be concluded that he disobeyed discretionary "if practicable" and "if not too late" orders no more so than other generals—most notably Richard Ewell, who disobeyed Robert E. Lee's "if practicable" order to take Cemetery Hill at Gettysburg on July 1, 1863. One may well question the military wisdom of Pemberton's decisions but not his strict adherence to orders. Culpability, it seems, is much easier to assign when orders are allegedly disobeyed.

Once the siege began, Pemberton's troops fought valiantly. Both the men and their commander expected Johnston to make a relief effort, and the men in

Johnston's army fully expected it as well. "It was therefore reasonable to believe he [Johnston] would be zealous to prove that he really merited the high reputation for military capacity with which he was generally credited, and…that he would promptly concentrate an Army, which…would raise the siege," wrote Pemberton.

Not only did Pemberton expect the relief effort to be made, but his Federal counterpart, Grant, did as well. So concerned was Grant in late June, that he dispatched Sherman to protect the Big Black River crossings against a move by Johnston.

Of all the allegations Johnston levied against Pemberton in his writing, the most insupportable concerned his failure to raise the siege once it had commenced. Johnston believed that if Vicksburg were subjected to a siege, surrender was inevitable. Having convinced himself of this, he made little effort to raise it. Johnston's attitude and actions must be contrasted with those of Robert E. Lee, who despaired of Confederate success if his army (the Army of Northern Virginia) were to be forced into a siege at Richmond. Once the siege had begun, however, Lee worked tirelessly and acted aggressively to find a way out. Johnston either had no intention of acting or was incapable of mustering the courage and energy to face the situation.

Johnston did not believe Pemberton cooperated adequately with him in lifting the siege, and used a dispatch from Pemberton suggesting that 40,000 troops were needed to lift the siege as proof of any action on his part. In discussing this later, Pemberton expressed disbelief that Johnston would resort to such a poor excuse. The correspondence between the two in the *Official Records* supports Pemberton's incredulity.

In addition, Pemberton argued at great length (and documentation in the *Official Records* supports his claim) that he kept Johnston fully apprised, to the extent that communications allowed, of events and expected a relief effort from his superior throughout most of the siege. "I ask attention to the fact, that every inquiry of General Johnston's…is distinctly answered, and that it contains all the information I could give or that was necessary, to enable General Johnston to arrange a plan of attack, and to instruct me as to my cooperation," Pemberton wrote.

Pemberton argued further, "It does not seem to have struck General Johnston that time was all important." Once the siege was in place, Johnston planned and executed next to nothing. With a 32,000-man army located on the perimeter of Grant's forces by early June, and with freedom of movement, he nonetheless asked Pemberton where and when the movement should be made. Although Pemberton promptly replied with suggestions and bombarded Johnston throughout the siege with requests for news of his movements, nothing was forthcoming from his superior. Time and again, Johnston chose to ignore pointed questions directed to him by both Pemberton and the War Office in Richmond if he was uncomfortable with the question or if an answer might imply a commitment on his part. "That absolutely nothing was even attempted by him is obvious to all who have read his book," concluded Pemberton. "His prediction that 'Vicksburg must fall if besieged' conclusively proved that he made no true and earnest effort to avert the calamity he prophesized."

What went through Johnston's mind in late May and June of 1863? Most likely he was longing for a military command somewhere other than central Mississippi. Did fear of failure and its consequences leave him afraid to he attack Grant? Was it simply easier to sit at Jackson, painting a story of futility even while a crisis unfolded 40 miles away? One is reminded of Mary Chestnut's tale of the time when Johnston (an expert marksman) went bird hunting and never fired his gun, because he never had "the perfect shot," and was afraid to miss?

Pemberton made many mistakes during the Vicksburg campaign. But the initial mistake was not his. Jefferson Davis erred in assigning to departmental command a general who had never led troops at the brigade, division or corps level. Champion Hill was Pemberton's first taste of battle as a field commander. To face an army led by U.S. Grant was a tall task for any general, much less someone unused to the position. Pemberton was better suited to an administrative job, not to a field command. Although he made substantial improvements in his department after taking over from Van Dorn, those improvements were rendered moot once Grant crossed the Mississippi. In addition, Pemberton did not seem to understand that once Grant crossed the river, his role was that of army commander first and department head second. Jefferson Davis was hoping to compensate for Pemberton's lack of combat experience when he sent Johnston to Mississippi.

St. John Richardson Liddell, a brigadier general who served with the Army of Tennessee but not under either Pemberton or Johnston, had a unique opportunity to visit and talk with both men after the close of the Vicksburg campaign but before the end of the war. Liddell wrote his memoirs immediately after the cessation of hostilities, prior to the publication of Johnston's (Liddell himself was murdered in a family feud in Louisiana in 1870). His recollections of both Pemberton and Johnston are therefore perhaps the most unbiased accounts that exist.

Liddell met Pemberton shortly after Chickamauga, while Pemberton was traveling with President Davis. Liddell recalled the comments Pemberton made regarding the loss of Vicksburg:

I had provisions to hold Vicksburg two weeks longer — but I could not see the utility since General Johnston either could not or would not relieve me. *My* regret was that the surrender was on the 4th of July, but this was of no consequence except with the masses.[7]

Liddell concluded: "I saw in this conversation but too clearly that there was some misunderstanding between Pemberton and Johnston which could only result in mutual recrimination." Liddell further noted that Davis obviously intended to support Pemberton regardless of the facts and therefore did not do justice to Johnston.[8]

Upon leaving the Army of Tennessee for assignment in the trans-Mississippi region, Liddell happened to meet Johnston in Meridian, Mississippi (just before Johnston was named commander of the Army of Tennessee). Johnston, noted Liddell, was "exceedingly bitter about the President in reference to the turn of affairs between himself and General John C. Pemberton." Johnston felt Pemberton had willfully disobeyed orders, and Liddell inferred from the conversation that Johnston felt the disobedience was intentional.[9]

Liddell commented further that Johnston appeared to be "fortifying" his interpretation of the historical record to combat what he perceived as a possible threat to his good name at some point in the future. "I thought General Johnston showed a good deal of adroitness in putting the best construction upon his own views, stretching them naturally to suit results," he wrote. From Liddell's perspective, Pemberton was simply caught in the middle of an ugly feud between Johnston and Davis.[10]

There are probably many reasons why Pemberton's manuscript never made it to press in the late 1870s. He was engaged in that most important of duties as head of a family—providing for his wife and children. His status as Northerner who fought for the South, rendering his position precarious on both sides of the Mason-Dixon line, was one of many obstacles that must have stood in his way. He was not a gifted writer, as most readers of his manuscript will readily admit. But his words and arguments, as plagued as they were by poor sentence structure, do reveal an aspect of Confederate strategy at Vicksburg not often discussed. They pave the way, moreover, for a much-needed reassessment of the validity of Joseph E. Johnston's *Narrative of Military Operations*.

The Vicksburg campaign was the Confederate corollary to the Union's Second Manassas campaign. At Second Manassas, Abraham Lincoln made the

---

7. Nathaniel Cheairs Hughes, Jr., ed., *Liddell's Record* (1985; reprint, Baton Rouge: University of Louisiana State, 1997) 153.
8. Ibid.
9. Ibid., 169.
10. Ibid.

unfortunate choice of bringing together George B. McClellan and John Pope to face Robert E. Lee, Stonewall Jackson, and James Longstreet. At Vicksburg, Jefferson Davis brought together Joseph E. Johnston and John C. Pemberton to combat U.S. Grant and William T. Sherman of the Army and David Dixon Porter of the Navy. As was the case with Pope and McClellan, Johnston and Pemberton were found lacking in ability, and their pairing spelled disaster for the Confederacy.

Instead of defeating Grant and driving him back to the Mississippi River (a very real possibility at several points in the campaign), Pemberton surrendered on July 4, 1863, and the Confederacy was effectively cut in two. The slow, inevitable march from west to east began in earnest, culminating in Appomattox on April 9, 1865, when the western Federal army was within a couple of day's march of its eastern counterpart. If the Confederacy failed to stop Grant at Vicksburg, it was not the fault of any single general, as Joseph Johnston would have it, but of the entire Confederate high command, which included both Johnston and Pemberton. Neither was equal to the challenge at hand.

Appendix A

Correspondence

Appendix A

Correspondence

Pemberton included a number of pieces of correspondence with his manuscript intended for use with his published response.

April 9, 1863

Gen. S. Cooper:

I am confident that no important reinforcements, if any, have been sent to Rosecrans from Grant. No troops whatever are reported to have gone alone the mouth of Yazoo Pass. I endeavor to keep Gen. Johnston advised of my movements which may affect his army. The enemy is constantly in motion in all directions. He appears now to be particularly engaged with Deer Creek, by land from Greenville. I have forces there to meet him.

It is reported, but not yet confirmed, that a movement under McClernand in large force by land is in progress, west of the River and southward. I doubt it. My operations west of the Mississippi must greatly depend on the movements of the enemy's gun boats. I have several regiments now, near New Carthage. Will inform you promptly of anything important and if I ascertain that part of Grant's army is reinforcing Rosecrans. Will dispatch troops to Gen. Johnston as rapidly as possible.

(signed) **J.C. Pemberton**
Lt. Gen. Comdg

May 13th, 1863

Gen. J.E. Johnston:

Gen. Forney reports from Vicksburg this morning "four transport boats landed with troops arrived at Young's Point this morning. Five regiments and a battery passed down by Brown and Johnston's. Wagon trains continue to pass back and forth." My reinforcements will be very small, and arrive slowly. If possible, Port Hudson should also be reenforced. I have been forced to draw largely from there. I have no Maj. Gen. to command brigades arriving in Jackson. I am in position with eight brigades near Edward's Depot.

signed / **J.C. Pemberton**
Lt. Gen. Comdg

Vicksburg May 20, 1863

Gen. Jos. E. Johnston:

The enemy assaulted our entrenched lines yesterday at two points, center and left, and was repulsed with heavy loss. Our loss small. I cannot estimate the enemy's force now engaged around Vicksburg at less than 60,000; it is probably more. At this time 8 1/2 a.m. he is briskly cannonading with long range guns. That we may save ammunition, the fire is rarely returned. At present our main necessity is musket caps. Can you send them to me by hands of couriers or citizens? An army will be necessary to relieve Vicksburg, and that quickly. Will it not be sent? Please let me hear from you if possible.

(signed) **J.C. Pemberton**
Lt. Gen. Comdg

Vicksburg May 21, 1863

Gen. J.E. Johnston:

The enemy has continued a spirited fire all day, also his shelling from mortar boats; our men have replied rarely. Two large transports came down loaded with troops, they are evidently reinforcing their present large force. Am I to expect reinforcements, from what direction, and how soon? Have you heard anything from Gen. Loring? Can you sent me musket caps by courier?

(signed) **J.C. Pemberton** Lt G C

also

May 21st/63

Gen. J.E. Johnston:

The enemy kept up an incessant sharpshooting all yesterday on the left and center, and picked off our officers and men whenever they showed themselves. Their artillery was very heavy, ploughed up our works considerably and dismounted two guns on the center. The works were repaired and the guns replaced las night. The great question is ammunition. The men credit, and are encouraged by a report that you are near with a large force. They are fighting in good spirits, and the reorganization is complete.

(signed) **J.C. Pemberton**
Lt Gen Comdg

Vicksburg May 29, 1863

Gen. J.E. Johnston:

Your dispatch of the 25th received this evening with 20,000 caps. Fontaine yesterday with 18,000. No other messenger from you since the 18th. I have dispatched about 8 messengers. I have 18,000 men to man the lines and river front, no reserves. I do not think you should move with less than 30,000 or 35,000, and then, if possible, towards Snyder's Mill, giving me notice of the time of your approach. The enemy encompassed my lines from right to left flank occupying all roads. He has three corps, Sherman on my left, McPherson center, McClernand on my right, and Hurlbut's division, from Memphis, and Ellett's Marine Brigade (the last afloat). Enemy has made several assaults. My men are in good spirits, awaiting your arrival. Since investment we have lost about 1,000 men, many officers. You may depend on my holding the place as long as possible. On the 27th, we sank one of their best iron clad gunboats.

(signed) **J.C. Pemberton**
Lt. Gen. Comdg

May 29, 1863

Lt. Gen. Pemberton:

I am too weak to save Vicksburg; can do no more than attempt to save you and your garrison. It will be impossible to extricate you, unless you cooperate and we make mutually supporting movements. Communicate your plans and suggestions if possible.

(signed) **J.E. Johnston**, General

On May 30th dispatched as follows:

Gen. J.E. Johnston. Scouts report the enemy to have with drawn most of his forces from our right yesterday, leaving Hall's Ferry Road open, I apprehend for a movement against you.

(signed) **J.C. Pemberton**
Lt. Gen. Comdg

Vicksburg June 7, 1863

Gen. J.E. Johnston:

I am still without information from you later than your dispatch of the 25th May. The enemy continues to entrench his position around Vicksburg. I have sent out couriers to you almost daily. The same men are constantly in the trenches, but are still in good spirits expecting your approach. The enemy is so vigilant that it is impossible to obtain reliable information. When may I expect you to move and in what direction? My subsistence may be put down for about twenty days.

(signed) **J.C. Pemberton** Lt. Gen.

Vicksburg June 10th, 1863

Gen. J.E. Johnston:

The enemy bombard day and night from seven mortars on opposite side of Peninsula. He also keeps up constant fire on our lines with artillery and sharpshooters. We are losing many officers and men. I am waiting most anxiously to know your intentions. Have heard nothing from you since 25th May. I shall endeavor to hold out as long as we have anything to eat. Can you not send me a verbal message by courier, crossing the river above or below Vicksburg, and swimming again across, opposite Vicksburg?

(signed) **J.C. Pemberton**
Lt. Gen. Comdg

Vicksburg June 12, 1863

Gen. J.E. Johnston:

Courier Walker arrived this morning with caps. No message from you: very heavy firing yesterday from mortars and on lines.

signed / **J.C. Pemberton**
Lt. Gen. Comdg

Vicksburg June 14, 1863

Gen. J.E. Johnston:

Last night Captain Sanders arrived with 200,000 caps, but brought no information as to your position or movements. The enemy is landing troops in large numbers on Louisiana shore above Vicksburg. They are probably from Memphis, but it many be from Yazoo. I cannot ascertain positively. On the Graveyard road the enemy has run his saps to within 25 yards of our works. He will probably attempt to sink a mine. I shall try to thwart him. I am anxiously expecting to hear from you, to arrange for cooperation.

(signed) **J.C. Pemberton**
Lt. Gen. Comdg

June 14th, 1863

Gen. Pemberton:

All we can attempt is, to save you and your garrison. To do this exact cooperation is indispensable. By fighting the enemy simultaneously at the same point of his line, you may be extricated. Our joint forces cannot raise the seige of Vicksburg. My communication with the rear can best be preserved by operating north of the railroad. Inform me as soon as possible what point will suit you best. Your dispatches of 8th and 10th have been received.

(signed) **J.E. Johnston**

Vicksburg June 15th, 1863

Gen. J.E. Johnston:

The enemy has placed several very heavy guns in position against our works and is approaching them very nearly by sap. His fire is almost continuous. Our men have no relief; are becoming much fatigued, but are still in pretty good spirits. I think your movement should be made as soon as possible. The enemy is receiving reinforcement. We are living on greatly reduced rations, but I think sufficient for 20 days yet.

(signed) **J.C. Pemberton**
Lt. Gen. Comdg

Vicksburg June 21st, 1863

Gen. J.E. Johnston:

Your dispatches of 14th and 16th recd. If it is absolutely impossible, in your opinion, to raise the seige, with our combined forces and that nothing more can be done than to extricate the garrison, I suggest that giving me full information in time to act, you move by the north of the railroad, drive in the enemy's pickets at night, and at daylight next morning engage him heavily with skirmishers, occupying him during the entire day, and that on that night I move to the Warrenton road, by Hankinson's Ferry, to which point you should previously send a brigade of cavalry, with two field batteries, to build a bridge there, and hold that ferry; also Hall's and Baldwin's to cover my crossing at Hankinson's. I shall not be able to move with my artillery or wagons. I suggest this as the best plan, because all the other roads are too strongly entrenched and the enemy in too heavy force, for a reasonable prospect of success, unless you move in sufficient force to compel him to abandon his communications with Snyder's, which I still hope we may be able to do. I await your orders. Capt Cooper understands all my views and will explain further.

(signed) **J.C. Pemberton**
Lt. Gen. Comdg

Camp near Birdsong's Ferry
July 3, 1863

Lt. Gen. Pemberton:

Your dispatches of 28th were destroyed by messenger. He states that Gen. Smith's troops were driven back to Monroe. This statement and his account of your condition make me think it necessary to create a diversion, and thus enable you to cut your way out if the time has come for you to do this. Of that time I cannot judge; you must, as it depends upon your condition. I hope to attack the enemy in your front on the seventh, and your cooperation will be necessary. The manner and proper point for you to bring the garrison out must be determined by you from your superior knowledge of the ground and distribution of the enemy's forces. Our firing will show you when we are engaged. If Vicksburg cannot be saved, the garrison must.

(signed) **J.E. Johnston**

Appendix B

Another Opening

Appendix B

Among the miscellaneous papers associated with Pemberton's manuscript were sets of odd pages that do not fit with the main manuscript. Some were rehashes, or previous drafts, of sections of discussions already in the main manuscript. Others (there are several) are copies of the opening pages, written as Pemberton evidently struggled through how to start his response.

The following represents an opening section of sixteen pages. As opposed to the main manuscript, it dates the time of this portion of the writing at shortly after Johnston's autobiography came out, is more frank and open than later versions, and includes comments and discussions not in the final manuscript.

Of particular note are the two military blunders Johnston committed that are not elaborated on (written at the end of this section).

In a work purporting to be a contribution to the history of the Confederate war, but in reality a record of the personal quarrels and <illegible> of Joseph E. Johnston, has recently issued from the press, in which I am singled out for special vengeance and dragged and offered up as a sacrifice to his disappointed ambition. The silence and obscurity in which I have been living for the last 9 years is the best evidence I can offer of how distasteful controversy is to me. But justice to myself will not permit me to pass the unfounded and unjust assault to pass unnoticed.

I propose to show that much of the material offered for the use of the future historian by Gen. Joseph E. Johnston is worthless.

Aware how little public interest is likely to be excited by a controversy between Gen. Johnston and myself, as to relative responsibility for Confederate disaster in Mississippi in 1863, I approach the subject with great reluctance. More than a decade has passed since the events transpired, which for a period officially connected us. While I could not forget the wrongs I have suffered as a soldier at his hands, I have waited patiently, believing that time would uncover the truth, and that impartial history would, for good or ill, give to each his due.

But General Johnston has devoted so many pages of his recent work to angry denunciations of myself, and unfair criticism of my military conduct that a decent, self-respect forbids longer silence.

Some apology was certainly due to the "future historian" that so large a space was allotted to the shortcomings of an individual, of whose ability the author expresses so contemptuous an opinion. A space, which doubtless would otherwise have been filled with select "materials" for his use. I find no such apology, however, yet there is a sort of *excuse* attempted, for his persistent efforts to injure me. He says that "I constituted myself his adversary" by manner of using "certain advantages" which, he claims I derived, from having been permitted to supplement my report twice, after I had read his.

"Notwithstanding these advantages on his part," he proceeds to say, "I would have made no comment on these publications, but would have limited my defense to the preceding narrative . . . But Lieutenant General Pemberton has recently revived the question, or rather procured to be published, a longer, more elaborate, and more uncandid attack upon me than those contained in his official report, and its two supplements."

Now "my official report and its two supplements" are in the Appendix to the "Narrative"; how far they sustain General Johnston's assertion that "I constituted myself his adversary" or whether they contain "an uncandid attack upon him," whoever may choose to read, can determine for himself. I am disposed to believe that this paragraph was written before it was determined to admit the report, and that the incongruity between the charge today and the proof supplied by the report afterwards escaped his notice.

I have never made "an uncandid attack" upon General Johnston; indeed, I have never made any attack upon him at all. Whenever called on to speak I have affirmed openly what I know to be fact, have argued to convince others that my deductions from those facts are correct, and have employed his dispatches to me to strengthen my argument. He, on the contrary has made bold and unqualified assertions, not sustained by proof, but in the confidence that his "I have said it" would utterly crush the officer who "was at the time severely judged by the Southern people," but who nevertheless presumed to defend himself. Let the reader of the "Narrative of Military Operations" say whether my judgment is harsh or uncandid.

How wide a margin General Johnston has allowed himself in the use of the word "recently" I cannot pretend to decide.

During the war, when to be considered my friend and advocate was rather a subject of reproach, several articles appeared in my defense, but of each and all I was in complete ignorance, until I read them in the public press. One only was over my own signature, and was in reply to a laudation to General Johnston at my expense by the late Senator Wigfall in a speech delivered before the body of which he was a member in the fall of 1864.

In the summer of 1866, a Southern lady with whom I had not the pleasure of personal acquaintance, addressed me an earnest request, that I would furnish her with my version of the causes which led to the loss of Vicksburg; informing me at the same time, that she was about to publish the biography of a dear friend deceased (the late Governor Allen of Louisiana) who had served under my command.

This lady did me the honor to embody in her book much of the material with which I had supplied her. Subsequently, during a brief but friendly correspondence, she assured me that, although by the events of the Mississippi campaign, she had lost her all, she had learned to do me justice, an acknowledgment more grateful to me then I can easily express. I have good reason to believe, that she did not regard my version of the causes of our disasters, including such comments as I deemed necessary to the elucidation of the subject, as "an uncandid attack upon General Johnston."

This correspondence 8 years ago is the first, last, and only occasion, when I have attempted not to attack General Johnston, for that, I have never done, but, to defend myself. If the publication just referred to, is not that, in which I am represented to have "recently revived the question," I have not the slightest idea to what publication he alludes.

When two peoples or two parties are at war, whatever is recognized by both, as of vital importance to one, becomes ipso facto of equal importance to the other. Independent therefore of the immense value of Vicksburg to the Confederacy as a connecting link, more or less perfect, between her and the trans-Mississippi States, the fact that it could, and did, close to the North the navigation of the great river, gave to it an importance not surpassed by any other point within her limits.

The passage of the Federal gun-boats, and even of a few transports under their shelter, did not reopen navigation; neither did it sever the Confederacy, as General Johnston asserts. It was still united by the batteries of Vicksburg. Had the siege been prevented, or raised, the Federal fleet, could not have restored to the people of the North and West, that navigation which they had lost by the war, and which above all things they desired to regain. If in addition, Port Hudson had been held, that fleet must have eventually withdrawn, and the control of the river between those strongholds, have returned to the Confederacy. With great diffidence of my own judgment and deference to that of wiser men, I submit that a successful defense of Vicksburg in the spring and summer of 1863 would have brought peace, or a separation of the north west, from the then existing Federal Union.

Such at least was my conviction at the time; nor do I now believe it to have been without reasonable foundation. It can not be denied, that much dissatisfaction existed in the Army of the Tennessee, during and after, the several failures to establish a base of operations north of Vicksburg; not only by a movement from west Tennessee by land, but by any of the numerous navigable approaches from the Mississippi. Throughout the period occupied in those attempts, desertions from that Army were enormous; and included not only the rank and file, but commissioned officers. Reports from my general officers in the field of operations, and from scouts in all directions, indicated a widespread disorganization. After the passage of the gun-boats, and the practicability of a route west of the Mississippi for his land forces to a point below Vicksburg, was ascertained by General Grant, it is probable a reaction took place, but it not easy to calculate the consequences to the Federal cause, had a failure to take Vicksburg been the result of this, General Grant's last resort.

This description will, to many, appear inappropriate, and will seem an exaggerated estimate of the value of Vicksburg, as well as an erroneous view of the actual condition of the Army of the Tennessee at the period referred to: and these adverse judgments may, perhaps, be correct; nevertheless, the digression itself will explain better than I could in any other way, the guiding principle of all my actions as Commander of the Department of Mississippi and East Louisiana.

On the night of the 4th December I was notified by telegraph of the assignment of General Johnston to the command of General Bragg's department, of Lieut. General E. K. Smith's, and of mine. I communicated immediately, but briefly, by telegraph from Grenada, the position of my Army, and on the next day despatched a special message to Chattanooga with the following letter:

> GENERAL: Your telegram of the 4th instant reached me at a late hour last night, and a brief message was forwarded in reply, indicating my present position.
>
> The large reenforcements received by the enemy in West Tennessee within the last few weeks, and his concentration of forces to the amount, I believe, of not less than 60,000 at La Grange, Grand Junction, and other points between my position on Tallahatchie and his base, rendered it more than doubtful whether I should be able to hold so long a line with the very small force at my disposal. I was aware also that a considerable force (not much less than my own)had been landed on the east bank of the Mississippi River, at Friar's Point and Delta. About the 27th November the enemy commenced a simultaneous movement of his armies in my front and from the Mississippi River, threatening my rear. Gunboats and transports loaded with troops were also reported descending the river toward Vicksburg, and a demonstration from below was made at the same time against Port Hudson, on the successful holding of which point, together with Vicksburg's defenses, depends the navigation of the Mississippi River.
>
> Port Hudson is an isolated position, not naturally strong by its land approaches and at any time open to attack from below. It is by this time strongly intrenched and garrisoned by about 5,500 effectives. Port Hudson is distant 58 miles from the railroad depot at Tangipahoa. These troops are not available on a sudden emergency for any other point nor can it be readily re-enforced. Vicksburg is strongly intrenched, and about 6,000 of all arms are held in immediate vicinity for its defense. My army on the Tallahatchie, including artillery and cavalry, numbered about 22,000 effectives, most of the cavalry being in advance and covering both flanks.
>
> Under the circumstances narrated above, I determined to withdraw from the Tallahatchie and to establish my line behind the Yalabusha River. The movement was commenced on the morning of the 1st of December, the advance guard as a reconnoitering party of the enemy consisting of five regiments of infantry, two of cavalry, and two field batteries having advanced to skirmishing distance from our advanced works.

The following paragraph was deleted by Pemberton with the following comment: "One paragraph of this letter is omitted as unnecessary having relation only to certain rail-road matters connected with the movement from the Tallahatchie."

By the gross misconduct of the authorities of the Mississippi Central Railroad, and the positive disobedience by them of my orders, a small amount of public property, say 300 rounds field ammunition, a few tents, &c., were burned before leaving.

The enemy's cavalry and some mounted infantry have followed up our movement, occasionally skirmishing with our rear guard, without, however, delaying our march, which has progressed without the loss of a wagon or any description of property.

General Price's corps is now being established between this point and the Tuscahoma Ferry. Van Dorn will occupy the ground on his right.

The heavy rains which have fallen will, I believe, enable me to hold this position with my small force unless a movement is made by the enemy to turn my right by the Mobile and Ohio Railroad.

The above letter is given in full, because it seems to me to show with sufficient distinctness, the actual condition of affairs in my department at the moment General Johnston assumed the command.

The Federal army continued to advance slowly; the condition of the country from recent heavy rains, not admitting of rapid movement. On the 11th Dec. Major General Loring reported for duty at Granada; this enabled me to transfer General Van Dorn to the command of the cavalry and to organize in concert with him, a force of about 3,500, to operate on Grant's rear. Great latitude was given Van Dorn, but his general instructions were, to move cautiously and by circuitous route, upon Holly Springs, if found practicable; otherwise upon Davis' Mills, or at his entire discretion upon Memphis; to break up the enemy's communications, and to destroy his depots. The complete success of that gallant officer at Holly Springs, and the effectual stoppage of the Federal advance as its result, are too well known to need further mention.

A brief note of the 20th, written immediately after the capture, informed me of his intention "to move at once upon Davis' Mills", why this design was not executed, I have never learned.

The expedition had hardly returned to Grenada which it reached on the 28th December, I then being in Vicksburg, when Van Dorn and all the cavalry attached to my army except about 800 or 1,000, were withdrawn from my command by General Johnston, and ordered into Middle Tennessee; whence no portion of it ever again entered my department, until subsequent to the 13th of May 1863, when General Johnston arrived at Jackson from Tullahoma, assumed the immediate direction of affairs, and became responsible for the results. In regard to the expedition under Van Dorn, be it understood, that General

Johnston had no part in it: the object for which it was arranged had been fully attained, before he was even aware that it was in contemplation.

As far as the "large body of cavalry to operate in General Grant's rear, and cut his communications" (where the strength named is 4,000) which he says, immediately upon his arrival at Chattanooga, he "requested General Bragg to detach," I aver that if any such operation occurred, at or about this time, it did not come to my knowledge; it was probably of the sort, which, initiated in behalf of my department on paper, after circumstances prevented; of such, I shall have occasion to mention at least one more.

The quote above comes from page 150 of the N.M.O., and the pertinent paragraphs are as follows:

> *Several railroad accidents delayed me my journey to Chattanooga—the location for my headquarters chosen by the War Department—so that I did not reach that place until the morning of the 4th of December.*
>
> *A telegram from General Cooper, found there, informed me that Lieutenant-General Pemberton was falling back before superior forces, and that Lieutenant-General Holmes had been "peremptorily ordered" to reinforce him; but that, as Lieutenant-General Holmes's troops might be too late, the President urged upon me the importance of sending a sufficient force from General Bragg's command to Lieutenant General Pemberton's aid.*
>
> *I replied immediately, by telegraph as well as by mail, that the troops near Little Rock could join General Pemberton sooner than those in Middle Tennessee; and requested General Bragg, by telegraph, to detach a large body of cavalry to operate in General Grant's rear and cut his communications. On the following day, the 5th, at Murfreesboro', I again wrote to General Cooper by mail and by telegraph, giving him General Bragg's estimates of his own force and that of General Rosecrans, and endeavoring to show that he could not give adequate aid to General Pemberton without giving up Tennessee, adding, that troops from Arkansas could reach the scene of action in Mississippi much sooner than General Bragg's - and saying, besides, that I would not weaken the Army of Tennessee without express orders to do so. He was also informed that two thousand cavalry would be detached to break the Louisville and Nashville Railroad, and four thousand to operate on Grant's communications.*

However successful General Forrest may have been in "breaking rail-roads in West Tennessee," it did not seriously interfere with Grant's advance into Mississippi: how that advance was brought to a sudden and unexpected end, has been already seen.

> *Pemberton quotes from the following paragraph on page 155 of the N.M.O.:*
>
> *Brigadier-General Forrest, who was detached by General Bragg to operate on Major-General Grant's rear, was very successful in breaking railroads in West Tennessee. After destroying large quantities of military stores also, and paroling twelve hundred prisoners, he was pressed back into Middle Tennessee by weight of numbers. At the same time, a body of Federal cavalry under Brigadier-General Carter, supposed to be fifteen hundred, burned the Holston and Watauga railroad bridges near Bristol.*

No *occasional* movements of our cavalry in whatever strength, from Middle to West Tennessee, or into Northern Alabama, could afford adequate protection to the State of Mississippi. The enemy could fight, or not, as he felt disposed; could readily separate, and reunite at pleasure, to renew his destructive raids as soon as the danger was over.

General Johnston referring to the period just subsequent to General Sherman's failure to capture Vicksburg by a coup de main, in the winter of 1862-3, says in his usual sententious and inaccurate way: "At this time Lieutenant General Pemberton had some six thousand cavalry near Grenada unemployed, and almost unorganized. Under the circumstances described, Major General Van Dorn was directed to form a division of two thirds of these troops, and to move into Tennessee, after preparing it for the field."

This has the plausible appearance of a plain statement of fact with no other object in view than to supply the future historian with useful materials; nevertheless, it is a misrepresentation throughout.

First: I had not "some six thousand cavalry near Grenada." I had barely five thousand: of this I allowed General Van Dorn to take with him, all but about eight hundred (800). To Van Dorn (on the 13th): "Leave about 800 effectives, for picket duty." Again, Van Dorn was not directed by General Johnston "to form a division of two thirds of those troops" which would have left me according to his statement 2,000 in place of 800. The instructions were given to me, and not to Van Dorn, and were in these words: "Jackson, Jan. 11th, 1863. I wish to combine a cavalry expedition in the two Departments. Please assign Van Dorn to the same cavalry with orders to receive instructions from me." (the same that had composed the Holly Springs expedition)

Secondly: Those troops were not "almost unorganized," on the contrary: they were so well organised, that they had just executed one of the most useful and brilliant exploits of the war.

Thirdly: They were not "unemployed." They had returned to Grenada from the Holly Springs expedition on the 28th of December: two days after, on the 30th, I telegraphed General Van Dorn thus, "Organise all cavalry companies into a division, prepare your command for a movement towards Coldwater. I heartily congratulate you." He replied the next day, "General Johnston thinks I may go home for a few days. Will give directions for the expedition at once."

Not wishing to lose time, and General Van Dorn not having returned on the 2d January, I telegraphed Brigadier General W.H. Jackson, second in command as follows:

> The enemy is represented on Yazoo Pass opposite to Colonel Alcorn's: his strength is supposed to be about three thousand with artillery. I wish you to take all

the cavalry, leaving only a sufficiency to do picket and scouting duty in front of Grenada. Move to the rear of the enemy, drive him from his position, capture his artillery, and do him all the damage otherwise in your power. You had better move by the edge of the bottom, until you can pass Coldwater, north of the pass; but the route I leave to your discretion. You can extend your operations as circumstances in your judgment admit.

Just as this expedition was about moving, the enemy whether from information of the fact, or from other causes, withdrew. The interim, between this and the receipt of General Johnston's orders, was diligently employed in shooing the horses, much needed after the long journey from which they had so recently returned, and in other preparations for similar active service.

Again, on the 16th and 18th, after General Johnston had notified me of his wish to "combine a cavalry expedition" (intended to operate outside my department) but before the force under Van Dorn had moved, I was compelled to throw forward a brigade of his cavalry into La Fayette County, and towards Panola, to meet another threatened inception of the enemy; it was, however, directed that the brigade should be "held in readiness to join Van Dorn when he moved."

I regret to have been compelled to occupy so much time in explaining but one of the many misrepresentations of facts, which General Johnston's book exhibits, when he thinks it necessary to forestall public judgment on points where he and I are at issue.

Historic truth and justice to myself imperatively demand that I should distinctly charge upon General Johnston *two* great military blunders, the consequences of which, since he continues to defend the blunders themselves, he must be held accountable for.

General Johnston has always acutely felt the force of these charges, and to preserve a reputation not fairly earned, he has relied upon the strength of that reputation to carry conviction against all evidence to the contrary. An assumption of superiority on his part in all matters of controversy between us, is perhaps the most powerful weapon he employs. He rarely condescends to argue, but with a sneering depreciation of his adversary and a few tersely expressed generalities, which serve to perplex the reader, he disrupts the case in his own favor. Observe the effect of the following paragraph, which I select only because it has some connexion with the subject about to be considered.

Appendix C

Opposing Forces—
Vicksburg Campaign

Appendix C

Opposing Forces—Vicksburg Campaign

May 13 to July 4, 1863

In reading about the Vicksburg Campaign, the size of the competing armies at the different stages of the campaign is quite confusing. The issue is further compounded by having three armies (Grant's, Johnston's, and Pemberton's) in the field as opposed to the usual two.

Confederate commanders had reason to minimize the size of their forces and to over-state the size of the enemy, which both Pemberton and Johnston did in their writing. Johnston understated his forces as well as those of Pemberton; Pemberton understated his as well, but was closer in his estimates of both Johnston and Grant.

The careful reader of Pemberton's manuscript will note that Pemberton himself used conflicting numbers in various discussions, but this is most likely due to difficulties in obtaining good information, as well as the incomplete nature of the manuscript itself.

The important aspect of interpreting the conflicting claims and counter-claims of Pemberton and Johnston is realizing that by June 3, the Confederates held a collective edge in total manpower over Grant's forces.

May, 1863

13 Joseph E. Johnston arrives in Jackson, Mississippi.

14 Johnston has approximately 7,500 men (W.H.T. Walker's division). S.R. Gist with 1,500 troops arrives at Forest, Mississippi from South Carolina.

16 **Battle of Champion Hill (Baker's Creek).**
    W.W. Loring does not retreat with Pemberton to Big Black Bridge.

17 **Battle of Big Black Bridge.**
    Evander McNair and Matthew Ector (3,000 in total) reach Meridian, Mississippi.
    Gist reaches Brandon, Mississippi.

18 Gist reaches Jackson.
    Pemberton is in the defenses of Vicksburg.

19 **Grant's first Vicksburg assault fails.**

Gist with 5,500 troops (his plus McNair/Ector/others) reaches Livingston, Mississippi.

20 Johnston has with him 13,000 men.

Loring's division's vanguard (5,000) reaches Jackson less artillery.

22 Loring, still at Jackson under Johnston's command, adds Shanks Evans brigade to his division of 2,000.

Grant's second assault of Vicksburg fails.

23 Samuel B. Maxey, who had come to Jackson from Port Hudson and retreated after the fall of Jackson, returns and joins Loring with another 3,000 men.

Loring has 10,000 troops at Jackson, Johnston 12,000 at Canton, Mississippi, and Pemberton 29,500 in Vicksburg.

Grant has approximately 51,000 men total.

26 Grant sends 12,000 troops up the Mechanicsburg Corridor under Frank Blair.

28 Grant calls for massive reinforcements. He has known that reinforcements have been reaching Johnston.

Stephen Hurlbut will send 12 regiments from Memphis, and John Schofield 6 regiments from Missouri.

29 Blair approaches Mechanicsburg, only Wirt Adams's cavalry opposes him.

30 Johnston receives word of Blair's move.

Blair retreats back towards Snyder's Bluff, destroying foodstuffs in the Yazoo River valley.

31 Loring moves from Jackson to Canton to join Johnston.

Walker moves from Canton towards Yazoo City (away from Vicksburg).

June, 1863

1 Walker reaches Yazoo City.

John C. Breckinridge's division of 5,500 (from Bragg's army in Tennessee) reaches Jackson.

Johnston has 22,000 at Canton/Yazoo City, Pemberton 29,500 at Vicksburg, Breckinridge 5,500 at Jackson. Grant has 51,000.

3   William H. Jackson's cavalry division of 3,000 reaches Johnston at Canton.

Ambrose Burnside agrees to send 8,000 men to Grant from the IX Corps.

Kimball's division (from Hurlbut) arrives for Grant with three brigades.

8   Francis J. Herron's division (from Schofield) arrives for Grant.

11   William S. Smith (from Hurlbut) arrives for Grant.

14   John Parke (from Burnside) arrives to Grant

Grant now has over 70,000 troops, and is able to work to deny Johnston access to the investment lines.

July, 1863

4   **Pemberton surrenders to Grant.**

Bibliographical Sources

Bibliographical Sources

As noted in the opening chapter, this book is not a definitive discussion of the Vicksburg campaign. The second and third chapters are written from some primary sources as well as most of the available secondary ones.

A requirement of any serious study of the Civil War is the *Official Records of the War of the Rebellion* (known primarily as the *Official Records*). The Vicksburg campaign is covered in three volumes, and contains most of the correspondence that forms the basis of the controversies between Pemberton, Johnston and Davis.

The 1874 publication of Johnston's *Narrative of Military Operations* revived the controversy, and is necessary read for understanding the Vicksburg campaign. Several good biographies of Johnston are in print; Craig Symonds' *Joseph E. Johnston: A Civil War Biography* (1992) is the most recent biography, but is noticeably silent about Johnston's efforts outside Vicksburg. The 1956 publication of Gilbert Govan and James Livingood's *A Different Valor: The Story of General Joseph E. Johnston, C.S.A.* remains a good, if not overly sympathetic, biography.

Written works on John C. Pemberton are more scarce than those written about Johnston. The definitive work remains Michael Ballard's *Pemberton: A Biography*, published in 1991. A cross between a biography and a justification for Pemberton's military record was produced in 1942 by Pemberton's grandson, John C. Pemberton III, in his *Pemberton: Defender of Vicksburg*.

The primary and best work on the Vicksburg campaign itself is still Edwin C. Bearss' massive three volume work, *Vicksburg is the Key* (1985), *Grant Strikes a Fatal Blow*, and *Unvexed to the Sea* (both 1986). Samuel Carter III's *The Final Fortress: The Campaign for Vicksburg* (1982) is perhaps the best single volume account of the campaign. Steven E. Woodworth's 1990 *Jefferson Davis and His Generals* pulls together the issues surrounding Davis and much of the western command and provides good insights into the relationship between Pemberton, Johnston and Davis. Other accounts that provide contributions to the understanding of the campaign include Jerry Korn's *War on the Mississippi* (part of the Time-Life series) as well as Jim Miles' *A River Unvexed* (1994).

Much has been written on U.S. Grant's participation in the capture of Vicksburg. Until the Union Navy ran the batteries of the city and Grant crossed to the eastern side of the Mississippi River, initiative for action remained primarily with Grant, with the Confederacy in a reaction mode for the most part. Bruce Catton's *Grant Moves South* (196X) and Kenneth P. Williams' *Grant Rises in the West* (198X) are very good chronicles of the campaign from a Federal perspective.

Of the other principal players, Grant's *Personal Memoirs of U.S. Grant* and the laboriously written *The Rise and Fall of the Confederate Government* by Jefferson Davis provide some insight into the strategic thinking of the two men. Their conclusions, however, are clouded at times by selective memory and the hindsight that comes with historical knowledge of the past. Finally, biographical studies of Grant, Davis, Sherman and many of the other principle players in the campaign help understand the interlocking relationships that led to the eventual surrender of Vicksburg.

Index